Deconstructing the Mind

PHILOSOPHY OF MIND SERIES

SERIES EDITOR: *Owen Flanagan, Duke University*

Self Expressions
Mind, Morals, and the Meaning of Life
Owen Flanagan

The Conscious Mind
In Search of a Fundamental Theory
David J. Chalmers

Deconstructing the Mind
Stephen P. Stich

Deconstructing the Mind

Stephen P. Stich

New York   Oxford
OXFORD UNIVERSITY PRESS
1996

Oxford University Press

Oxford   New York
Athens   Auckland   Bangkok   Bombay
Calcutta   Cape Town   Dar es Salaam   Delhi
Florence   Hong Kong   Istanbul   Karachi
Kuala Lumpur   Madras   Madrid   Melbourne
Mexico City   Nairobi   Paris   Singapore
Taipei   Tokyo   Toronto

and associated companies in
Berlin   Ibadan

Library of Congress Cataloging-in-Publication Data
Stich, Stephen P.
Deconstructing the mind / Stephen P. Stich.
    p.   cm.—(The philosophy of mind series)
Includes bibliographical references.
ISBN 0-19-510081-6
1. Philosophy of mind.   2. Mental representation.   3. Cognitive science.
4. Connectionism.   5. Psychology and philosophy.
I. Title.   II. Series.
BD418.3.S75   1996
128'.2—dc20   95-42096

Chapter 2 "Connectionism, Eliminativism, and the Future of Folk Psychology"
by William Ramsey, Stephen Stich, and Joseph Garon appeared in
Philosophical Perspectives, 4, *Action Theory and Philosophy of Mind*, 1990, edited by
James E. Tomberlin (copyright by Ridgeview Publishing Co., Atascadero, CA).
Reprinted by permission of Ridgeview Publishing Company.

Chapter 3 is reprinted with permission from Cognition, Vol. 50 (1994), pp.
447–468, Stephen P. Stich, Ian Ravenscroft, *What is Folk Psychology?*, © 1994,
Elsevier Science B. V., Amsterdam, The Netherlands.

Chapter 5 is from *Midwest Studies in Philosophy, volume XIX: Philosophical
Naturalism*, French, Uehling, & Wettstein, eds., © 1994 by the University of
Notre Dame Press. Reprinted by permission.

1 3 5 7 9 8 6 4 2
Printed in the United States of America
on acid-free paper

For Jude
for everything

Acknowledgments

Chapter 2, which is the oldest essay in this volume, was conceived during a trip that Bill Ramsey and I took to Baja California in 1987 and discussed at length a year later as we traveled together down the Sepik River in Papua New Guinea. Chapter 1, the newest essay in the volume, was completed a few hours ago. During this eight-year period, I've gotten lots of help from lots of people. My deepest intellectual debts are to Hartry Field and Stephen Schiffer, who attended the seminar I gave on this material at CUNY Graduate Center earlier this year. Week after week, Stephen helped me see the problems lurking in my arguments, and Hartry helped me figure out how to repair them. Some of the other people who have helped me improve these essays are:

John Bennett
Michael Bishop
Earl Conee
Robert Cummins
Michael Devitt
Richard Feldman
Jerry Fodor
Carl Gillett
Peter Godfrey-Smith
Alvin Goldman
Robert Gordon
George Graham
Terry Horgan
Frank Jackson
Todd Jones
Harold Kincaid
Philip Kitcher
Stephen Laurence

Keith Lehrer
Alan Leslie
William Lycan
Brian McLaughlin
Aaron Meskin
Shaun Nichols
David Papineau
John Pollock
Yorck Rabenstein
James Rachels
William Ramsey
Ian Ravenscroft
David Rosenthal
Edward Stein
Lynn Stephens
Scott Sturgeon
Kenneth Taylor
Paul Thagard
Joseph Tolliver
and
Ted Warfield

My thanks to all of them. I am sure there are other people whose names should be on the list and would be if my memory were better. I hope they will accept my thanks anonymously.

While I was at work on these essays, two admirable institutions—the Zentrum für Interdisziplinäre Forschung in Bielefeld, Germany, and the Research School of Social Sciences at the Australian National University in Canberra—provided stimulating environments and quiet places to work. I am grateful to both of them. I'm also grateful to Rutgers University for a sabbatical term in 1994 that enabled me to complete a draft of Chapter 1.

I can think of no words that could begin to capture how important the love and support of my family—Jude, Jonah, and Becca—have been and continue to be. Fortunately, no words are needed. They know.

Princeton, N.J.   S.P.S.
August 1995

Contents

Chapter 1
Deconstructing the Mind   3

Chapter 2
Connectionism, Eliminativism, and the Future of Folk
Psychology (with William Ramsey and Joseph Garon)   91

Chapter 3
What *Is* Folk Psychology? (with Ian Ravenscroft)   115

Chapter 4
How Do Minds Understand Minds? Mental Simulation
versus Tacit Theory (with Shaun Nichols)   136

Chapter 5
Intentionality and Naturalism (with Stephen Laurence)   168

Chapter 6
Naturalism, Positivism, and Pluralism   192

References   201

Index   215

Deconstructing the Mind

CHAPTER 1

Deconstructing the Mind

1 Deconstructing a Deconstruction: A Preview of Coming Attractions

Developing and defending a philosophical position is a bit like weaving an intricate piece of fabric. When things go well, each strand of the argument adds strength and support to the others, and gradually interesting patterns begin to emerge. But when things go poorly—when one of the strands breaks—it sometimes happens that the entire fabric begins to unravel. A little gap becomes a big gap, and soon there is nothing left at all.

This book is about the unraveling of a philosophical position. In some of the chapters, including this one, I'll tell the tale in the first person, since the position that came unraveled was *my* position, or at least one that I was seriously tempted to endorse. Though it was not mine alone, of course. Several very distinguished philosophers, including Quine, Rorty, and Feyerabend, had advanced versions of the view while I was still wearing philosophical knee pants, and a number of well-known philosophers continue to advocate the position with considerable passion. The doctrine in question is sometimes called *eliminative materialism*, though more often it's just called *eliminativism*. And whatever one thinks of the merits of the view, there can be little doubt that its central thesis is provocative and flamboyant. In its strongest form, eliminativism claims that beliefs, desires, and many of the other mental states that we allude to in predicting, explaining, and describing each other *do not exist*. Like witches, phlogiston, and caloric fluid, or perhaps like the gods of ancient religions, these mental states are the fictional posits of a badly mistaken theory.[1]

3

Though a wide variety of arguments have been offered for this rather startling conclusion, all of them share much the same structure. They begin with the Premise* that beliefs, desires, and various other mental states, whose existence the argument will challenge, can be viewed as "posits" of a widely shared commonsense psychological theory—"folk psychology" as it is often called. Folk psychology, the First Premise maintains, underlies our everyday discourse about mental states and processes, and terms like "belief" and "desire" can be viewed as theoretical terms in this folk theory. The Second Premise is that folk psychology is a seriously mistaken theory because some of the central claims it makes about the states and processes that give rise to behavior, or some of the crucial presuppositions of those claims, are false or incoherent. This step in the argument has been defended in many different ways, with different writers focusing on different putative defects. After defending these two Premises, an eliminativist's argument can take one of two routes. The simplest route goes directly from the Premises to the conclusion that beliefs, desires, and other posits of folk psychology do not exist. And, of course, if that's right, it follows that no mature science which succeeds in explaining human behavior will invoke the posits of folk psychology. Beliefs, desires, and the rest will not be part of the ontology of the science that ultimately gives us a correct account of the workings of the human mind/brain. The second route that an eliminativist's argument can follow reverses the order of these two conclusions. From the Premises, it initially concludes that folk psychological posits will not be part of the ontology of any mature science. This, in turn, is taken to support the stronger conclusion that these folk psychological states do not exist.

The Premises of the argument that I've just sketched can be unpacked in many different ways, just about all of which generate controversy. In subsequent chapters, I'll take a careful look at several of those controversies, but in this chapter, I propose to put these disputes to one side. For even when the Premises are unpacked in a way that is most favorable to the eliminativists' arguments, and even if we assume, for argument's sake, that these Premises are true, neither of the two conclusions that eliminativists wish to draw follows directly. Some additional premises are necessary. And it is my contention that none of the premises that will do the trick are defensible. If that's right, then obviously eliminativists are in trouble. For even if we grant that their Premises about folk psychology are correct, their ontological conclusions simply do not follow. To support this claim, I'll begin in section 2 by elaborating on what I take to be the best version of the First Premise, from the eliminativists' point of view; then I will assemble in section 3 a catalog of the complaints that eliminativists have leveled against folk

---

*In this chapter, I will capitalize "Premises," "First Premise," and "Second Premise" when referring to the premises of the elimativists' argument.

psychology. The remainder of the chapter will be devoted to setting out my argument that there is no way to get from the eliminativists' Premises to their conclusions and exploring the options that are available if my argument is correct.

It is a bit odd that, despite its fundamental importance in eliminativists' arguments, the step linking the Premises to the conclusions has not been the focus of much attention in the literature. In my own writing, at least until recently, it was a step I took quite unself-consciously. Along with most of the other participants on both sides of the debate, I assumed that the battle would be lost or won by deciding who was right about the virtues and shortcomings of folk psychology. Once it becomes clear how much of folk psychology is denied or abandoned in the mature sciences of the mind/brain, it would be obvious what to say about the extent to which the ontology of folk psychology and of the successful sciences overlap. But gradually over the last several years I have come to realize that this crucial step in eliminativists' arguments is anything but obvious.

My first serious inkling that perhaps all was not well came while I was polishing a paper that I had written with Bill Ramsey and Joey Garon in which we set out one particularly trendy argument for eliminativism. That argument begins with some speculations about the future success of connectionist models of human memory and notes that the interactions among the states posited by those models are quite different from the interactions among beliefs, as they are construed by commonsense psychology. The argument goes on to conclude that if those connectionist speculations prove to be correct, then the ontology of scientific psychology will not include beliefs. The paper that Ramsey, Garon, and I wrote is reprinted as the second chapter in this volume. Though nothing much in this first chapter turns on the details, you might want to give chapter 2 a quick read before going on, if you haven't done so already. It will give you a feel for what the eliminativist fabric looks like before it begins to unravel.

Just as we were finishing that paper, I had occasion to reread a characteristically acute essay by William Lycan in which he notes that the conclusion in arguments like ours doesn't follow unless some additional premise is added, and goes on to suggest that the additional premise that is (often tacitly) assumed by most eliminativists is some version of the description theory of reference for theoretical terms. I suspect that Lycan is quite right about what other authors had been assuming, and he is certainly right about me. In section 4, I'll explain in some detail where the additional premise comes from and how it works. Lycan has never been much tempted by eliminativism, and in the essay that woke me from my dogmatic slumbers, he explains why. Description theories of reference have come in for a great deal of criticism in recent years, and he favors a very different account of reference. Moreover, if that account is correct, then premises detailing untenable features of folk psychology, conjoined with suitable premises about the reference of theoretical terms, will not support the sort of eliminativist conclusions that Ramsey, Garon, and I were proposing. Section 5 is devoted to setting out Lycan's argument and exploring some of its implications. In a footnote to our paper, Ramsey, Garon, and I offered a hasty rebuttal designed to show that the theory of reference Lycan favors is just as problematic as the description theoretic account that he rejects (see chap. 2, n. 6). But since we had no better alternative to offer, we hurried on with our own argument, granting that the decision on whether our premises sustained our conclusion would have to be something of a "judgment call."

I wasn't all that happy with this quick fix, and I resolved that at some point I would try to work out a better theory of reference—one that was more likely to be correct than either Lycan's or the description-theoretic one on which I had been relying. Before I could start on that project, however, there was a prior question to be confronted. If the goal was to produce a correct theory of reference, I would have to get clear on what it is that makes a theory of reference correct or incorrect. What exactly are the facts that a correct theory of reference is supposed to capture? And how can we find out whether a theory has succeeded in capturing those facts? These are the questions I'll take up in section 6. The discussion there follows a line of thought that I developed in a series of papers that have appeared in the last few years (Stich 1991a, 1992, 1993a; Stich and Warfield 1995). But that line kept heading off in a very surprising direction. There are, I think, two quite different stories to be told about what a theory of reference is up to. On one of them, which I'll call the *proto-science* account, the theory of reference is attempting to characterize a word–world mapping that will be useful in one or another empirical discipline such as linguistics, cognitive psychology, or the history of science. According to the other story, which I'll call the *folk semantics* account, the theory of reference is attempting to capture the details of a commonsense theory about the link between words and the world. This latter story appears to be favored, albeit tacitly, by most philosophers. However, as I'll argue in section 7, if this is the view we adopt, then there probably is no correct account of reference for the theoretical terms invoked in a seriously mistaken theory. Reference in these cases is simply indeterminate. Moreover, whether or not I am right about the indeterminacy of reference in these cases, the folk semantics story suggests that reference is a quirky and idiosyncratic relation and that there are lots of alternative relations we might have used in its stead. There is nothing special about reference that distinguishes it from these alternatives. It just happens to be the member of this cluster that our culture has latched on to. If this is right, then the debate over eliminativism begins to look very odd indeed. For, as argued in section 7, if reference is not a particularly interesting or important relation, and if the existence or nonexistence of the posits of folk psychology turns on whether or not the theoretical terms of folk psychology refer, then it seems to follow that the eliminativists' conclusions themselves can't be all that interesting or important. Even if it turns out that the theoretical terms of folk psychology don't refer, just the opposite conclusion might have followed had we inherited a somewhat different notion of reference.

This was a rather radical conclusion to reach. But I had never let that bother me before. Indeed, I confess that I have a certain fondness for such conclusions. And anyhow, that was where the argument seemed to be leading, provided that we opt for the folk-semantics account of the facts that a theory of reference is supposed to capture. Suppose we opt for the other account, the proto-science story? In that case, as noted in section 8, there is no saying what follows from the eliminativists' Premises, since the relevant sciences have not yet determined which word–world relation will be of use to them. And even if we ignore this problem, the proto-science story leads to some pretty bizarre consequences of its own.

So it looked like I was stuck with the conclusion that an issue I had spent much of the last two decades thinking about was either unresolvable or not very interesting and that I'd just have to learn to live with that conclusion. As part of the process, I did what many philosophers do these days: I took my show on the road, trying to defend my new view in front of a variety of audiences. Few were persuaded. But it took John Searle (with some help from Frank Jackson and Christopher Gauker) to convince me that there was something very wrong with the argument I was offering. What persuaded me was Searle's insistence that my argument, if sound, was perfectly general. It applied equally to the posits of folk psychology and to the posits of physics. So if my argument were correct, debates about the existence of black holes or the big bang should also be unimportant and uninteresting. And that is a crazy conclusion, even for someone with my high tolerance for views that fly in the face of conventional wisdom. Now I was in a real pickle. For while Searle and others had persuaded me that there must be something wrong with my argument, none of my critics had a plausible account of *what* was wrong with it. Where, exactly, had the argument gone wrong? I am, I admit, still not completely confident that I know the answer to this question. But in section 9, I'll set out the best analysis I've come up with so far. It's rather a long story, and I won't ruin the suspense by trying to summarize it here. The bottom line, if I'm right, is that the mistake came right at the beginning when we turned to the theory of reference to try to settle whether the eliminativists' Premises supported their conclusions. On the view I'll set out in section 9, the appeal to reference and the strategy of "semantic ascent" are complete nonstarters when it comes to settling ontological questions like those that eliminativists raise.

But if we can't appeal to the theory of reference, what can we do?

How do we settle questions about the existence of things spoken of in theories that we no longer take to be correct? One idea, considered briefly in section 10, is that the notion of a "constitutive" or "conceptually necessary" property will help resolve the issue. That proposal, I'll argue, raises more problems than it solves.

Having reached this point, it seemed prudent to look for some other way of determining what we should conclude from the eliminativists' premises, a way that didn't rely on semantic notions or appeals to conceptual necessity. One idea that seems promising is to look to the history of science in the hope of finding principles of ontological inference that have been used in other cases. If we can locate some candidate principles, perhaps these can then be confirmed by looking at other historical cases and by testing the principles against our intuitions in hypothetical cases. This would, I think, be an intriguing project. But as I argue in section 11, there is no guarantee that it would succeed. For it might well be the case—indeed, I think it *is* the case—that there are no principles in this area that are strong enough to specify what ontological conclusions we should draw when confronted with a seriously mistaken theory. Rather, I maintain, these issues are typically settled through a process of social negotiation in which politics, personalities, and social factors can all play a role. I'm told that makes me a social constructionist, or at least a fellow traveler. But, as I'll argue in section 12, the position I'm advocating can also be viewed as a close neighbor to the versions of pragmatism favored by Quine, Rorty, and others. And ever since I started out in philosophy, I've thought that's the best neighborhood in town.

That brings me to the end of my preview of the current chapter. The rest of the book consists of essays, some of which have been previously published, that were written while I was struggling with the ideas set out in this chapter. Once the fabric of the eliminativist argument started to unravel, new holes seemed to pop up everywhere. On a closer look, some of the arguments aimed at showing that folk psychology was not a very promising theory—arguments that I had once thought quite plausible—now seemed much less plausible. My current view on these arguments is set out in chapters 5 and 6. After a while, even the first step of the eliminativists' argument, the one that claims there is a folk psychological theory that might turn out to be badly mistaken, began to look much less obvious than it once had. Chapter 3 explores some of the reasons why many philosophers and cognitive psychologists have accepted this assumption and sets out some of the ways in which it might turn out to be untenable. Chapter 4 focuses on simulation theory, which is the basis of the most recent attack on the First Premise of the eliminativist argument.

Since most of these essays have more than one author, perhaps this is an appropriate place for a few words about my collaborators. Throughout my professional career, I have been exceptionally fortunate in having the opportunity to interact with many gifted, creative, and enthusiastic students. They have always been my best critics and my best inspiration to explore new ideas and to say things more clearly. Many of them have gotten involved in my intellectual projects, or gotten me involved in theirs, and these interactions, more than anything else, are what makes academic life rewarding for me. All of my collaborators in this volume are my former students. And I owe them all a considerable debt. Without them the book would have been much less interesting to read and much less fun to write. At one time, I planned to combine the material in this chapter with chapter 3, chapter 5, and parts of chapter 4 and publish it all together as a single book-length study. But in each case, my students and I decided it would be best to publish the collaborative work separately. One result of that decision is that there is a bit of overlap in these chapters. Ideas, arguments, and even a few sentences appear more than once.

I've made lots of promises about what I'm going to do in the pages that follow. Now it's time to get to work. But since all work and no play makes for dreary going, let me end this section with a few mischievous observations on how my project in this chapter might be construed. For some years now, deconstructionism has been a pretentious and obfuscatory blight on the intellectual landscape. But buried in the heaps of badly written blather produced by people who call themselves "deconstructionists," there is at least one idea—not original with them—that is worth noting. This is the thesis that in many domains both intellectual activity and everyday practice presuppose a significant body of largely tacit theory. Since the tacit theories are typically all but invisible, it is easy to proceed without examining them critically. Yet once these tacit theories are subject to scrutiny, they are often seen to be very tenuous indeed; there is nothing obvious or inevitable about them. And when the weaknesses of the underlying theories have been exposed, the doctrines and practices that rely on them can be seen to be equally tenuous. If, as I would suggest, this process of uncovering and criticizing tacit assumptions is at the core of deconstructionism, then eliminativism is pursuing a paradigmatically deconstructionist program. However, if I am right, the eliminativist deconstruction of commonsense psychological discourse has itself tacitly assumed a dubious package of presuppositions about the ways language and ontology are related. So if the goal of eliminativism is to provide a deconstruction of the mind, one goal of this chapter is to deconstruct that deconstruction.

2 The First Premise: Folk Psychology Is a Tacit Theory

A central thesis of this chapter is that even if we grant the premises in the eliminativists' arguments, there is no plausible way of getting from these Premises to the ontological conclusions that eliminativists want to establish. In this section, I'll set out one version of the eliminativists'

First Premise, a version designed to make the job of getting from premises to conclusions as easy as possible. There are lots of other ways in
which this premise might be unpacked, and in chapter 3 Ian Ravenscroft and I have tried to explore them in a systematic way; but in
this chapter, I propose to ignore these alternatives. There are also lots
of reasons to suspect that the version of the Premise I'll set out here
might turn out to be false, and some will be considered in chapters 3
and 4; here, however, I will ignore them. Since I want to focus on the
link between Premises and conclusions, I'll just explain what this version of the First Premise claims and then *assume* that it is true.

   It is an easy job to state the version of the First Premise that I think
will give the eliminativists their best shot at drawing the conclusions
they want to draw. Explaining it will take a bit more work. What the
Premise claims is that our folk psychological capacities are subserved by
a theory (I'll call it *folk psychology*) which:

   1. is largely tacit;
   2. is encoded in a declarative linguistic format;
   3. asserts (or presupposes) that beliefs, desires, and other intentional states that it invokes have representational (or semantic)
   properties and that these properties play an essential role in individuating beliefs and desires;
   4. attributes an opulent array of causal powers to beliefs, desires,
   and other intentional states, some of which are dependent on the
   representational properties of those intentional states.

   Obviously, a fair amount of unpacking is in order. Let's start with
the notion of *folk psychological capacities*. This is the term Ravenscroft
and I introduced to refer to a cluster of abilities, including the ability
to make predictions (which often turn out to be correct) about what
people will do; the ability to attribute beliefs, desires, and other intentional states to people in a way that other observers often agree with;
and the ability to construct explanations of people's behavior that are
couched in intentional terms and that other people often agree with. A
number of other abilities might be added to this list (see chap. 3, sec.
4), but for current purposes this should suffice. One of the few claims
that *isn't* controversial in this area is that normal adults in our culture
do indeed have all three of these abilities.

   To explain what I mean when I say that our folk psychological capacities are "subserved" by a theory, it will be useful to consider an
analogy with another capacity, which might be called our *folk physics
capacity*. This capacity, too, consists of a cluster of abilities, including
the ability to make predictions (which often turn out to be correct)
about the movements of middle-sized physical objects (rocks that are
dropped, or thrown, or rolled down hill; boxes that are pushed or
pulled; swinging pendulums) and the ability to offer explanations (that
other people often agree with) of why the objects behave as they do.

How do people go about making these predictions and constructing these explanations? One very plausible answer is that people are relying on a commonsense theory (sometimes called *naive physics* or *folk physics*) that includes principles specifying how objects will move under a variety of circumstances, along with other sorts of information that might be useful. The theory might well include terms for forces or for aspects of situations that are not readily observable and whose existence or magnitude must be inferred. Of course, the hypothesis that people rely on a theory to come up with physical predictions and explanations does not constitute a complete explanation of their folk physics capacity, even if the folk theory is specified in detail. We also need some account of how they use the theory—how they apply it in various situations.

In recent years, cognitive scientists have offered a fair amount of evidence for the hypothesis that people's folk physics capacity is subserved by a commonsense theory. One of the most fascinating findings in this area is that many people seem to base their physical predictions and explanations on a mistaken physical theory that posits an unobservable internal force which, according to Newtonian (and post-Newtonian) accounts of the world, simply does not exist. McCloskey offers the following summary of this "naive theory of motion":

> [The basic theory] makes two fundamental assertions about motion. First, the theory asserts that the act of setting an object in motion imparts to the object an internal force or "impetus" that serves to maintain the motion. Second, the theory assumes that a moving object's impetus gradually dissipates (either spontaneously or as a result of external influences), and as a consequence the object gradually slows down and comes to a stop. For example, according to the . . . theory, a person who gives a push to a toy car to set it rolling across the floor imparts an impetus to the car, and it is this impetus that keeps the car moving after it is no longer in contact with the person's hand. However, the impetus is gradually expended, and as a result the toy car slows down and eventually stops. (1983b, 308)

This basic theory can be elaborated in a variety of ways. One particularly interesting elaboration deals with curvilinear motion:

> Many subjects believe that an object constrained to move in a curved path acquires a curvilinear impetus that causes it to follow a curved trajectory for some time after the constraints on its motion are removed. (311)

Evidence that people rely on this theory comes from a variety of experiments. In one set of experiments, subjects (all of whom were undergraduates at a highly selective American university) were presented with problems like the following:

> Imagine that someone has a metal ball attached to a string and is twirling it at high speed in a circle above his head. In the diagram [figure 1-1a] you are looking down on the ball. The circle shows the path followed by

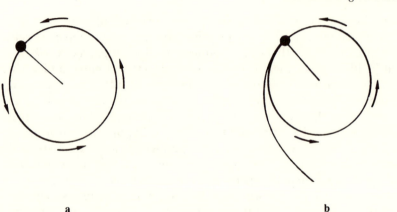

a   b

FIGURE 1-1

the ball and the arrows show the direction in which it is moving. The line
from the center of the circle to the ball is the string. Assume that when
the ball is at the point shown in the diagram, the string breaks where it
is attached to the ball. Draw the path the ball will follow after the string
breaks. (McCloskey 1983b, 301)

Thirty percent of the subjects responded with drawings like figure
1-1b, indicating they believed the ball would continue in curvilinear
motion after the string broke. Moreover, "most of the subjects who
drew curved paths apparently believed that the ball's trajectory would
straighten out" (302). In another experiment, subjects presented with
this and similar problems were interviewed at length about their answers. One subject offered the following explanation for the curved
path that he predicted the ball would follow: "You've got a force going
around and [after the string breaks, the ball] will follow the curve that
you've set it in until the ball runs out of the force within it that you've
created by swinging" (310).

In another problem, subjects were shown figure 1-2a and told that
it represents a side view of a metal ball swinging back and forth at the
end of a string. They are asked to draw the path the ball will follow if
the string is cut when the ball is in the position shown:

> Several subjects indicated that . . . the ball would continue along the
> original arc of the pendulum for a short time, and then would either fall
> straight down [as in Figure 1-2b] or would describe a more or less para-
> bolic trajectory [as in Figure 1-2c]. . . . One subject who made this sort
> of response explained that when the string is cut, the ball has
>> the momentum that it has achieved from swinging through this arc and
>> should continue in a circular path for a little while. . . . then it no
>> longer has the force holding it in the circular path, and it has the force
>> of gravity downward upon it so it's going to start falling in that sort of
>> arc motion because otherwise it would be going straight down. (Mc-
>> Closkey 1983b, 310)

In a separate set of studies, Clement (1983) found that 88 percent of a group of entering freshmen engineering students made similar appeals to an impetus-like internal force in answering questions about the motion of a coin tossed straight up. After taking a freshman level course in mechanics, however, only (!) 72 percent of subjects gave responses that indicated a belief in impetus.

As McCloskey and Clement point out, these subjects have a lot of distinguished company. The claim that the act of setting an object in motion impresses an internal force in the object that serves to keep the object in motion played a prominent role in physical theories from the fourteenth century until the time of Newton. It was clearly endorsed by Galileo in his early writings, and it was invoked by Leonardo da Vinci, who offered the following description of the motion of an object under conditions similar to those in Figure 1-1: "Everything movable thrown with fury through the air continues the motion of its mover; if, therefore, the latter move it in a circle and release it in the course of this motion, its movement will be curved."[2]

These findings certainly make a plausible case for the hypothesis that people's folk physics capacity relies on a commonsense theory. For eliminativists, they offer an added attraction, since modern physics has shown that the theory being exploited by many subjects is simply mistaken. Moreover, one of its mistakes has a distinctly ontological flavor. The impetus theory posits the existence of an internal force in most moving objects, a force which obeys a fairly complex set of laws and which explains why the objects move as they do. But, modern physics assures us, *that force does not exist*. Sensible eliminativists will acknowledge that the facts about folk physics don't by themselves allow us to draw any strong conclusions about the posits of folk psychology, but I think the work on folk physics does make it plausible that the eliminati-

FIGURE 1-2

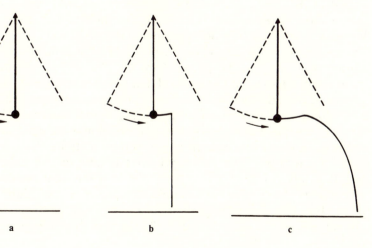

a b c

vists' conclusions *might* be true. It shows that it is possible that in their everyday dealings with the world—dealings which are by and large pretty successful—people rely on commonsense theories which appeal to forces that simply do not exist.

The next bit of jargon that needs explaining in my version of the eliminativists' First Premise is the claim that the theory subserving our folk psychological capacities is "largely tacit." Here another analogy will be helpful, this time an analogy with our linguistic capacities. Native speakers of a language can understand and produce an indefinitely large set of sentences of the language and make a wide array of judgments about the grammatical properties of those sentences. Also, there is an impressive degree of intersubjective agreement on those judgments. According to Chomsky and his many followers, the best explanation for these capacities includes the hypothesis that people have internally represented a generative grammar of their native language and that the internalized grammar is exploited in various ways in producing, processing, and judging sentences.[3] Of course, this internalized grammar is stored in a way that makes it largely (perhaps completely) inaccessible to conscious access. People can't simply introspect and tell us the rules of the grammar they have internalized. If they could, the science of linguistics, which tries to specify the grammars that speakers have internalized, would be a lot easier than it is. Rather, Chomsky maintains, the grammars that people use are "tacitly known." The theory subserving our folk psychological capacities may be a bit more accessible to introspection than the grammar of our language. But there is good reason to think that much of the information (or misinformation) that we use in predicting and explaining people's behavior is stored in a way that makes it inaccessible to conscious access (see chap. 3, sec. 4). And that is what my version of the Premise claims.

Much of the debate in cognitive science over the last three decades has turned on the format in which information of various sorts is represented in the mind. Early on, it was widely assumed that most of the information stored in the mind is represented in linguistic or quasi-linguistic form. Some theorists argued that the natural language a person spoke (or something close to it) would be a suitable medium for storing most of what the person knows, while others maintained that natural languages would not do and that one or more species-wide "languages of thought" had to be posited.[4] But nonlanguage-like competitors were soon suggested, including quasi-pictorial representation, holographic representation, various sorts of mental models, and, most recently, various sorts of connectionist representations.[5] Since eliminativists want to argue that folk psychology is false, it had better be the case that folk psychology is represented in a way that admits of such assessments. And, while various sorts of representations might arguably fit the bill, linguistic representations are the least problematic. So on my version of the First Premise, it's claimed that folk psychology is stored in a linguistic or quasi-linguistic format. Not just any linguistic representation will do, however, for there are lots of linguistic constructions—imperatives, for example, and questions—which can't be straightforwardly evaluated as true or false. Thus, my version of the tacit-theory premise assumes that significant parts of our tacit folk psychological theory is stored declaratively.

According to both eliminativists and their staunchest critics, folk psychology takes beliefs, desires, and other intentional states to be representational states. My belief that Reno is further west than Los Angeles represents the world as being a certain way, and so my belief is true if and only if the world *is* that way. That state of affairs is the *truth condition* of my belief. Desires represent the world as the person with the desire would like it to be. My desire to have sushi for dinner is fulfilled if and only if I *do* have sushi for dinner. That state of affairs is the *fulfillment condition* of my desire. Jargon abounds in this area. Truth and fulfillment conditions are sometimes collectively referred to as *conditions of satisfaction*. Sometimes they are called the *content* of the beliefs and desires that have them. Having a satisfaction condition is sometimes called a *semantic property* or an *intentional property*.

Many philosophers contend that semantic properties play an essential role in folk psychology's scheme for individuating instances (or "tokens") of propositional attitudes and classifying them into types. If we ask when a belief that a person has at a given time is identical with a belief she has at some later time, folk psychology's answer, according to these philosophers, is that the beliefs are identical if and only if they have the same content. Similarly, if we ask when two different people have the same belief (or "believe the same thing"), folk psychology's answer, according to these philosophers, is that they have the same belief if and only if they have beliefs (or "belief tokens") with the same content. Though this account of how folk psychology individuates beliefs is not without its critics, the version of the First Premise that I'm developing takes the account to be correct.

This is far from a complete account of the folk psychological scheme for individuating beliefs, however. To tell a more detailed story, we would have to specify the circumstances under which folk psychology counts two belief tokens as having the same content. And on this point controversy abounds. Some of the arguments surveyed in section 3 assume that folk psychology relies on one set of principles for content identity while other arguments assume that folk psychology relies on quite different principles. In my account of the First Premise, I propose to leave the matter unsettled. So the Premise, as I construe it, is compatible with any reasonable account of how contents are to be individuated.

Much of our ordinary folk psychological discourse can be construed as making causal claims in which intentional states figure prominently. We often say things like "His mother's tone of voice *led* the child to believe that she was angry at him" and "The child looked under the chair *because* he believed his kitten was hiding there." Though terms like "led" and "because" might be interpreted in a variety of ways, it has become commonplace in philosophy to view them as making causal claims. The tone of voice was *the cause* (or at least a cause) of the belief, and the belief *caused* the child to look under the chair. The causal interpretation of such commonsense psychological claims was not always widely accepted by philosophers. I suspect that the two papers that did most to convince philosophers that this was the right interpretation were Brandt and Kim (1963) and Davidson (1963)—they were certainly the two that convinced me. There have always been dissenters, however, and in recent years their ranks have grown as some philosophers have tried to fend off the challenge of eliminativism by denying that commonsense psychology attributes causal properties to beliefs and desires.[6] This is an important debate, and the matter is far from settled. But since my current aim is to set out the version of the eliminativists' First Premise that is most likely to support their conclusions, I will simply assume that the dissenters are wrong and that ordinary folk psychological discourse does indeed make robust causal claims. This assumption does not, by itself, tell us anything about the tacit theory that subserves our commonsense discourse. But one very natural way to explain the fact that we often make causal claims involving intentional states is to suppose that the underlying tacit theory includes nomological generalizations specifying the causes and effects of intentional states and that many of these generalizations are couched in terms of the content of intentional states. On my version, this is what the First Premise in the eliminativists' argument claims.

Horgan and Graham (1990) suggest some vivid terminology that can be pressed into service to characterize competing accounts of folk psychology. Accounts that portray folk psychology as making lots of substantive claims about the nature of intentional states, including lots of nomological generalizations, are *opulent* accounts, while accounts portraying folk psychology as making relatively few such claims are *austere*. Austere accounts have some appeal to those who would challenge the Second Premise in the eliminativists' argument, since the fewer claims a theory makes, the less likely it is to be wrong. But the First Premise of the argument, as I propose to construe it, opts for an account of folk psychology that is at the opulent end of the spectrum. Folk psychology, the First Premise insists, includes many putative laws and makes many claims about intentional states.

3   The Second Premise: Folk Psychology Is a Defective Theory

In the previous section, my goal was to explain the version of the First Premise that I think will give eliminativists their best shot at building an argument from their premises to their conclusions. In this section, my goal is to do the same for the Second Premise. My approach, however, will be quite different. It takes no great effort to state the best version of the Second Premise, and since it is so straightforward, there is no need to explain what it means. What it claims is that folk psychology is a seriously defective theory because many of the claims that folk psychology makes or presupposes are false. What does need some explaining is why eliminativists endorse this claim and why many opponents of eliminativism take it very seriously and feel they have to refute it. To explain that, I will provide a brief tour of what I take to be the most influential arguments aimed at showing that folk psychology is bad psychology. In this chapter, I don't propose to dwell on the details, or to say much about the counterarguments that have been urged by the friends of folk psychology, though in later chapters, I'll return to a few of these arguments and discuss them at greater length. This section is intended mostly for readers who are new to the debate and for those who would like a reminder of how some of the arguments go. The rest of you can scoot ahead to Section 4.

For heuristic purposes, the arguments I'll sketch can be divided into two categories. Those in the first category focus on what might be called the *structural and nomological* commitments of folk psychology—the claims it (allegedly) makes about the structure of the psychological states underlying behavior and about how these states causally interact with one another and with other sorts of states. Arguments in this category typically try to marshal evidence indicating that structures or processes of the sort folk psychology appeals to are not likely to be found in the systems that actually produce behavior. Since the available evidence is often quite fragmentary and inconclusive, these arguments commonly indulge in more than a bit of futurology or science fiction. Arguments in the second category focus on the fact that folk psychology attributes semantic properties to many of the states it invokes and that it exploits these semantic properties in some of its generalizations. These arguments try to show that, for one reason or another, semantic properties are ill suited to the role folk psychology would have them play. Though there is some appeal to science fiction in these arguments too, much of the work is done by metaphysical or methodological principles. There is, I should stress, no sharp divide between these two categories of arguments, and nothing much turns on how an argument is classified. I find that dividing things up in this way is a useful strategy for surveying the literature; I'm sure there are other taxonomies that would do equally well.

Except where explicitly noted, all the arguments I'll sketch work best if folk psychology is assumed to have all the characteristics specified in the previous section. But in many cases, these are not enough. To get the arguments going, it must be assumed that folk psychology has properties in addition to those already specified. I'll note these additional assumptions as we go along. Not surprisingly, all of them are controversial. And one standard strategy used by opponents of eliminativism is to deny that folk psychology has the additional property that the argument at hand needs. Though I'll note some of these controversies, I don't plan to take sides, since it's my view that even if the additional claims about folk psychology are granted, there is *still* no plausible way of getting to the ontological conclusions that the eliminativists want.

3.1   Structural Arguments That Rely on a Sellarsian Account of Folk Psychology

In his seminal paper "Empiricism and the Philosophy of Mind," Sellars (1956) offers a mythical reconstruction of the birth of folk psychological theory. In the myth, a great genius, Jones, puts forward a theory to explain the fact that people behave intelligently even "when no detectable verbal output is present" (317). The explanation Jones offers posits internal events that he calls *thoughts*. And his model for these internal episodes is "overt verbal behavior itself." Thus, for Jones, thoughts are a kind of "inner speech," and the posited processes that produce intelligent behavior are "inner discourse." Since thinking is modeled on overt discourse, it inherits many of the semantic properties that apply to stretches of public language. Individual thoughts have meaning, and sequences of thoughts may be logically related in various ways. Indeed, when things go well, a sequence of thoughts can have the structure of a sound deductive or inductive argument, and these covert, logically sound arguments play a central role in Jones's explanation of intelligent behavior.[7]

It is an impressive testimonial to the importance of Sellars's work that a number of leading figures on *both* sides of the eliminativism debate take this account very seriously. These philosophers agree that folk psychology characterizes thinking and believing on the model of inner speech and that it seeks to explain intelligent behavior by appealing to the logical cogency of covert quasi-linguistic episodes. They disagree totally, however, on the plausibility of this folk psychological theory.

3.1.1   The "Infra-linguistic Catastrophe"

Those who think that Jones and the folk who followed him have got it terribly wrong make much of the fact that nonlinguistic creatures like monkeys, cats, and dogs can behave in strikingly intelligent ways. They also stress that infants achieve some remarkably intelligent feats long before they have begun to talk. If Jones's hypothesis about the covert processes subserving intelligent behavior is plausible for human adults, then, these eliminativists urge, it would be equally plausible for infants and animals. Yet surely, they insist, this is simply too absurd to take seriously. It is preposterous to suppose that science will discover a language in which the family dog thinks, and it is even more preposterous to suppose that our future science will explain Fido's clever behavior by appeal to his covert construction of deductive and inductive arguments.[8]

This sort of *reductio ad absurdum* works, of course, only if it is conceded that the putative implications of folk psychological theory really are absurd. And it is certainly not the case that everyone is prepared to make that concession. Indeed, Jerry Fodor, who has long been one of the staunchest defenders of folk psychology, has advanced some very sophisticated arguments aimed at showing that some of the best of contemporary cognitive psychology presupposes a "language of thought" (1975, chaps. 1, 3, 4). Moreover, since most of the psychological theories on which Fodor bases his arguments are equally applicable to people and their pets, Fodor concludes that some of the best animal psychology also presupposes a language of thought. As for children, here again Fodor and some of his followers are more than prepared to bite the bullet. Children certainly do lots of intelligent things before they learn to talk. Indeed, learning to talk is itself one of their more impressive accomplishments. But, Fodor insists, since the best explanations we have for how children succeed in learning to talk presuppose that they already *have* a language of thought, it must be the case that the language of thought is innate.

3.1.2   The Argument from Neuroscience

A second cluster of eliminativist arguments that rely heavily on Sellars's portrait of folk psychology looks to neuroscience to impugn the folk. If Jones were right, then there would have to be lots of sentence-like states bouncing around in the brain when people do intelligent things. But contemporary neuroscience seems to have little use for states modeled on sentences. And, gazing into their crystal balls, the advocates of this argument do not foresee the neuroscience of the future having any more commerce with brain writing. Patricia S. Churchland, for example, concedes that "there is some sentence crunching, almost certainly" (1986, 396). But she goes on to endorse Hooker's prophecy that "language will surely be seen as a surface abstraction of much richer, more generalized processes in the cortex, a convenient condensation fed to the tongue and hand for social purposes" (Hooker 1975, 217, quoted in P. S. Churchland 1986, 396). In Tim Van Gelder's projection of the course of neuroscience, there is even less place for "sentence crunching." He sees an "intimate association" between various nonsymbolic "distributed" representational systems and "the actual machinery underlying human cognition." This intimate association, Van Gelder maintains,

> stands in plain contrast with the biological remoteness of symbolic representations. Though CTM [the Classical Theory of Mind] demands a lan-

guage of thought, and CTM advocates insist that the expressions of this language are realized in the neural substrate, and consequently predict the eventual discovery of "symbols amongst the neurons," neuroscience has never yet stumbled across syntactically structured representation in the brain. This discrepancy only becomes more embarrassing to CTM as the sum of neuroscientific knowledge increases, and provides at least a prima facie argument in favor of any biologically motivated alternative. (1991, 56)

So if it is granted that intelligent behavior must ultimately be explained by what goes on in the brain, then if these futurologists are right, Jones and the folk were wrong, and so, too, is folk psychology. Of course, those who distrust the neurophilosophers' crystal ball are not much impressed by the argument: "Auntie says that it is crude and preposterous and *unbiological* to suppose that people have sentences in their heads. Auntie always talks like that when she hasn't got any arguments." (Fodor 1985, 23).

Before moving on, we should pause to note that eliminativists who endorse the argument just sketched can't also endorse the version of the First Premise that I set out in section 2. For that version of the Premise stipulates that folk psychology itself is stored in quasi-linguistic form. So if neuroscience does indeed establish that there are no sentences in the head, the First Premise will be undermined. I don't think this is a devastating objection to eliminativists who advocate the argument from neuroscience, since it is open to them to adopt some other account of how folk psychology is stored in the brain. That's a delicate business, however, and not just any account will do. It has to be an account on which it makes sense to say that folk psychology makes claims or asserts propositions. For if folk psychology does not make claims, then it can't make *false* claims, and that *would* undermine the Second Premise. But, as we'll see in chapter 3, there are several options available that might be adopted by eliminativists who are convinced that neuroscience will establish that there are no "symbols amongst the neurons."

3.2   Structural Arguments That Don't Rely on a Sellarsian Account of Folk Psychology

It is conceded on all sides that natural languages are highly structured systems and that well-formed sentences in natural languages must comport with complex syntactic and semantic principles. So, if Sellars is right—if folk psychology really does take natural language as the model on which to base its conception of thoughts and other propositional attitudes—then the commonsense conception of propositional attitudes will view them as highly structured as well. But many defenders of folk psychology would deny that the commonsense conception of propositional attitudes requires them to have syntactic structure (see, for example, Loar 1983 and Stalnaker 1984). And, on the other side of the fence, some of the structural arguments aimed at showing that folk psychology is mistaken do not assume that folk psychology claims propositional attitudes must have internal quasi-linguistic structure.

The argument set out in chapter 2 that Ramsey, Garon, and I developed is an example. That argument says nothing about the internal structure of beliefs. Indeed, as far as that argument is concerned, folk psychology might perfectly well claim that beliefs have *no* internal structure. The only special assumption about beliefs the argument requires is that folk psychology views beliefs as "propositionally modular"—they are semantically interpretable states that can be causally implicated in some cognitive episodes and causally inert in others. If this is right, then not all of our beliefs need be causally implicated in each inference we make. Having tried to make this assumption plausible, the argument then indulges in a bit of science fiction. There is a family of connectionist models capable of storing a set of propositions in a widely distributed way. But these models have no functional parts that can be identified with the storage of individual propositions. Rather, as one critic of our paper put it, "there is a real sense in which *all* the information encoded in the network's connectivity matrix is causally implicated in *any* processing in which the network engages" (O'Brien 1991, 173). Thus when one of these radically holistic models does its thing, it makes no sense to ask which of its encoded propositions were causally active and which were inert. Now, *if* it turns out that models like this provide the best psychological account of human belief or propositional memory, then folk psychology, which rejects this radical causal holism, will have made a pretty serious mistake.[9]

Another argument in which connectionist models play a central role is due to Martin Davies (1990; 1991, 250–55). According to Davies, folk psychology assumes that there is "a single inner state which is active whenever a cognitive episode involving a given concept occurs and which can be uniquely associated with the concept concerned."[10] But many advocates of connectionism take it to be a virtue of connectionist models that their strategy for conceptual representation can be "context sensitive." So, for example, in the sorts of models that Smolensky (1988) favors, the representation of coffee when the coffee is in a cup will be somewhat different from the representation of coffee when the coffee is in a can. And, Davies argues, if this sort of model turns out to be the right account of what goes on in human cognition, then folk psychology's conceptual modularity assumption is mistaken.

Yet another non-Sellarsian structural argument, one that does not appeal to connectionism, exploits some intriguing findings in cognitive social psychology. Those results suggest that, in some cases at least, people's sincere reports about their own mental states and processes do not match up very well with the mental states and processes that are actually responsible for their behavior. Rather, what people report in these cases seems to be driven by socially shared theories about how their behavior is to be explained. A bold hypothesis that has been pro-

posed to explain the experimental results posits two largely independent cognitive subsystems. One of them "mediates behavior (especially
unregulated behavior), is largely unconscious, and is, perhaps, the older
of the two systems in evolutionary terms. The other, perhaps newer,
system is largely conscious, and its function is to attempt to verbalize,
explain, and communicate what is occurring in the unconscious system," on the basis of "theories about the self and the situation" (Wilson
1985, quoted in Stich 1983, 236). To turn this empirical speculation
into an argument against folk psychology, we need an additional premise which claims that folk psychology embraces a more unified picture
of the mind. According to this premise, folk psychology assumes that
beliefs and desires play a central role in the processes guiding our nonverbal behavior *and* in the processes leading to our verbal behavior.
Folk psychology claims that the very same pair of states which lead us
to walk toward the refrigerator also lead us to explain our behavior by
saying, "I want a beer" and "I think there is a beer in the refrigerator."
If our verbal behavior and our nonverbal behavior really are subserved
by independent systems, then this putative presumption of folk psychology is just wrong.[11]

3.3   The Semantic Arguments

The version of the First Premise set out in section 2 included the claim
that many of the nomological generalizations of folk psychology are
couched in terms of content. It also claimed that content plays an essential role in folk psychology's scheme for individuating belief and desire
tokens. A pair of belief tokens or a pair of desire tokens are (type-)
identical if and only if they have the same content. But as we noted,
this is far from a complete account of how folk psychology individuates
propositional attitudes. To flesh it out, we have to say more about how
folk psychology determines sameness or difference of content. The first
of the semantic arguments that I'll sketch assumes that folk psychology
exploits a "wide" account of content identity; the second assumes that
folk psychology individuates contents holistically.

3.3.1   Wide Content and Supervenience

About twenty years ago, Hilary Putnam and Saul Kripke put forward a
famous argument which allegedly showed that "meanings just ain't in
the head."[12] The now-familiar story on which the argument is based
asks that we imagine a planet in some distant corner of the universe
which is all but identical to our own. On this planet each of us has a
twin—a molecule-for-molecule replica. The only difference between
Earth and Twin Earth is that the stuff in their lakes and rivers is not
H_2O but another clear, tasteless liquid, XYZ. Now, it is claimed, when
Twin Stich says "Water is wet" folk psychology takes the content of the

belief he is expressing to be different from the content of the belief that I express when I utter the same sequence of words. My twin's belief is true if and only if XYZ is wet, while mine is true if and only if H_2O is wet. If this is right, then as folk psychology sees it the contents of beliefs and other propositional attitudes do not supervene on the non-relational physical properties of the believer, since *ex hypothesis* my twin and I are identical in all our nonrelational physical properties.[13] In the colorful though occasionally misleading jargon that has become commonplace in the literature, folk psychology's account of content identity is "wide."

To spring their trap, the critics of folk psychology must introduce one additional premise. This one is not a claim about the commitments of folk psychology or folk semantics. Rather, it is a metaphysical thesis (or perhaps it's a *methodological* thesis—I confess that I'm less than clear about where methodology ends and metaphysics begins). What it claims is that the only properties that may legitimately be invoked in scientific explanations of behavior, and thus the only properties that may be legitimately invoked in scientific psychological theories, are properties that supervene on the nonrelational physical properties of the subject.[14] If this is right, then whatever explanation a scientific psychological theory offers for the behavior of an organism will apply as well to the behavior of the organism's physical replicas. There is, to put it mildly, considerable controversy surrounding this thesis. Some writers, myself included (but I was younger and much more naive at the time), have claimed that it is intuitively obvious that scientific psychology should treat organisms that behave in the same way to be psychologically identical. And since Putnamian twins behave identically in all possible settings, psychology should treat them as psychologically identical. Others have tried to defend the thesis by deducing it from other, perhaps less controversial, metaphysical doctrines; still others have claimed that it is simply false.[15] But if it is not clear whether the thesis is defensible, it *is* clear that *if* the thesis is accepted then the argument has all it needs to show that folk psychology is in trouble. For, according to the version of the First Premise set out in Section 2, folk psychology includes lots of nomological generalizations that are couched in terms of the content of intentional states. But the Twin Earth argument (putatively) demonstrates that content does *not* supervene on the nonrelational physical properties of an organism. And the metaphysical principle insists that the properties invoked in the generalizations of scientific psychology *must* supervene. So if scientific psychology has it right, then folk psychology must have it wrong.

3.3.2 Meaning Holism

A second semantic argument begins with the contention that folk psychology takes the content of a propositional attitude to be dependent in part on the network of other propositional attitudes that a person has. Thus, if the doxastic networks surrounding a pair of belief tokens are sufficiently different, the tokens will differ in content. One example that is supposed to illustrate this phenomenon focuses on the case of an elderly woman, Mrs. T, who gradually loses beliefs as the result of some degenerative disease.[16] Before the onset of the disease, she believes that McKinley was assassinated, and she has a whole slew of related beliefs of just the sort one would expect. But as the disease progresses, she loses the belief that McKinley was a U.S. president; then she loses the belief that assassinated people are dead; then she loses most of her beliefs about the differences between the living and the dead— she no longer has any idea what death is. Even at this advanced stage of her disease, she is still capable of answering the question "What happened to McKinley?" by saying "McKinley was assassinated." However, it is claimed, folk psychology does not count the belief that underlies this answer as having the same content as the belief she had before her illness began. She no longer believes *that McKinley was assassinated.* The change in the "doxastic surround" has altered, perhaps even destroyed, the content of the belief that remains.

One way to parlay examples like this into an argument against folk psychology is to add a premise which claims that on the account of psychological state individuation that will be embraced by scientific psychology, the psychological state that causes Mrs. T to say "McKinley was assassinated" need not have changed at all as her disease progressed. To support the premise, a bit of science fiction is required. Imagine it is the case that people store information the way certain computer models do. They have long lists of syntactically complex symbolic structures stored in memory. Imagine further that the causal interactions of these symbol structures are akin to the causal interactions of their analogs in computer memories. These interactions depend only on the "shape" of the individual symbols and on the syntactic properties of the structures into which they are assembled. This story may be wildly mistaken, of course. But it is hardly unfamiliar. On the view of many observers, it is just the sort of account that is presupposed by most computational models in cognitive psychology. As Fodor (1978, 223) has observed, these models are "really a kind of logical syntax (only psychologized)." For our purposes, the essential fact about models of this sort is that their symbol structures are individuated without any appeal to the other structures stored in memory. The same symbol structure might at one time be surrounded by thousands of related structures and at another time be surrounded by only a few related structures, or by none at all. Thus, in models of this sort, symbol structures are *not* individuated in ways that are sensitive to their doxastic surround.

O.K. Now we have all the pieces needed to assemble the argument for the eliminativists' Premise. If we have drawn the right conclusion from the Mrs. T case, then the content of a belief is sensitive to its doxastic surround. When the surround is very different, the content is different. And, since folk psychology assumes that beliefs are individuated by their contents, if the surround is very different, then the belief itself is different. But if the computational paradigm that we've just sketched is on the right track, then the psychological states that actually cause behavior are not individuated in a way that is sensitive to their surround. Since beliefs are individuated in a way that is sensitive to their surround, and the actual causes of behavior are not, beliefs are not among the causes of behavior. Applying this argument to the Mrs. T case may make the point a bit more vivid. Since folk psychological belief individuation is surround-sensitive, none of the beliefs that Mrs. T has when her illness is far advanced can be the same as the beliefs she had before she became ill. But since the individuation of computational symbol structures is not surround-sensitive, Mrs. T may well have some of the same symbol structures in memory before and after her illness. If one of these structures causes her utterances of "McKinley was assassinated" both before and after her illness, then neither of these utterances is caused by a belief. Since folk psychology claims that utterances like these *are* caused by beliefs, folk psychology is wrong.

With a bit of fiddling, this argument can be recast along lines quite parallel to the argument in section 3.3.1: Folk psychology couches many of its nomological generalizations in terms of content, and content is surround-sensitive. The nomological generalizations in computational models of cognition are couched in terms of the syntax of mental symbol structures, and syntax is *not* surround-sensitive. So if the computational models have it right, then folk psychology must have it wrong.

The arguments just sketched rely on some heavy-duty assumptions about the account of psychological state individuation that will be embraced by scientific psychology. For the arguments to work, scientific psychology has to buy into what I have elsewhere called the Syntactic Theory of the Mind (Stich 1983, chap. 8). Other writers have attempted to argue from meaning holism to the conclusion that folk psychology is mistaken without assuming anything as controversial as the Syntactic Theory of the Mind, but these arguments typically rely on a much more virulent version of holism. On the version of holism that is assumed in the Mrs. T example, content identity requires a similar network in the doxastic surround. On the more extreme version of holism, two belief tokens are identical in content only if they are embedded in identical doxastic surrounds.[17] If that is right, then no two people will have beliefs that are identical in content, nor will two time slices of the same person, provided the person is awake and the time slices are separated by a minute or two. But this, the argument continues, would make appeal to content useless in the generalizations of scientific psychology, since the goal of scientific psychology is to find nomological generalizations that apply to many people, or many organisms.[18] So, while the generalizations of folk psychology appeal to content, the generalizations of scientific psychology will have to be stated in content-free terms. And, once again, if scientific psychology is right, then folk psychology is wrong.

3.3.3 The Heterogeneity of the Content Taxonomy

A third semantic argument begins with the premise that the belief tokens that folk psychology classifies as having the same content can be extremely heterogeneous. There are a variety of psychological dimensions on which people can differ enormously and still be classified by folk psychology as having beliefs that share the same content. Perceptual capacities provide one cluster of illustrations of this phenomenon. Some people have sharp vision, others see poorly, and still others are blind. Yet there are circumstances in which folk psychology would attribute the belief that the traffic light has just turned green to all three sorts of people. Even someone like Helen Keller, whose perceptual deficits are quite staggering, might perfectly well believe that the traffic light has just turned green (if she is told that this is the case by someone she trusts, for example, or if she knows that the car she's riding in has been stopped at a red light and she feels it begin to accelerate).

Cognitive skills provide another cluster of illustrations. Some people are swift and agile in reasoning, they see lots of logical connections, and they are quick to draw valid conclusions. Others are much slower and much more prone to logical errors. And there may well be people who, as the result of illness or brain damage, are simply incapable of drawing one or another kind of basic logical inference. Yet, under appropriate circumstances, folk psychology will attribute a belief with the same content to the clever, the retarded, and the brain damaged.[19] Indeed, the premise maintains, folk psychology is often quite comfortable in attributing belief tokens with the same content to both animals and people. The dog and his master may both believe that the stick has been thrown down the hill. In the right setting, folk psychology may even sanction the attribution of beliefs with familiar contents to fish or to bees. So for many propositions, it looks like the class of mental states that folk psychology will count as having content will be very heterogeneous indeed. The neurological states subserving these beliefs will differ drastically, both physically and functionally.

To complete the argument, we need yet another premise speculating about what a mature science of the mind/brain will look like. What it claims is that the heterogeneous content categories invoked in the generalizations of folk psychology, categories that group together belief tokens in Einstein's head, in a brain-damaged person's head, and in a dog's head, will be too inclusive to be of any use in that future science. Sophisticated sciences categorize states in terms of their causal powers, and from that point of view the dog's belief and Einstein's are too different to be grouped together. The nomological generalizations of the cognitive science of the future will invoke much less heterogeneous categories. At best, the premise maintains, folk psychology, with its coarse-grained content-based generalizations, is going to miss most of the interesting generalizations. More likely, it's going to turn out that there are no true content-based generalizations to be found. If that's right, then once again folk psychology will be in conflict with the future science of the mind.

3.3.4 Nonreducibility and Explanatory Exclusion

One of the most widely discussed families of arguments aimed at showing that folk psychology is a defective theory begins by arguing that the intentional properties of beliefs and desires, and the other characteristically "mental" properties invoked by folk psychology, are neither identical with nor reducible to physical properties. There are various routes to this conclusion. Perhaps the most plausible turns on claims about the possibility of multiple physical realizations of beliefs. Humans can think that $2 + 2 = 4$. But surely, the argument insists, there is no reason to be chauvinistic. If Martians exist, they too may be able to think that $2 + 2 = 4$, even if their brains are made of "green slime" whose chemistry is quite different from ours. Computers of the future, like HAL in the movie *2001*, will also be able to think that $2 + 2 = 4$. And it is plausible to suppose that there are indefinitely many physically different ways to build such a computer. Thus, there is a vast, open-ended class of physical systems that could think that $2 + 2 = 4$. Since these systems have different physical properties, no physical property can be identified with thinking that $2 + 2 = 4$. Since the class is vast and open-ended, no reduction of intentional properties to physical properties is possible. This argument has been challenged in various ways (see, for example, Kim 1989b and 1993; Bickle 1992). One strong motive for challenging the argument is that if the conclusion is correct, it can be used in a second argument aimed at showing that intentional properties are causally impotent.

Here is an abridged version of that second argument, modeled on a more detailed exposition due to Robert Van Gulick.[20]

1. *Token physicalism:* Every intentional event token (i.e., every event token having intentional properties) is identical with some physical event token (i.e., some event token having physical properties).

2. The causal powers of a physical event token are completely determined by its physical properties.

3. *The nonreducibility of the intentional:* Intentional properties are neither identical to nor reducible to physical properties.

4. Thus, intentional properties are not causally potent; they are causally irrelevant.

If this is right, and if, as we assumed in the previous section, folk psychology includes an opulent collection of nomological generalizations that are couched in terms of content, then folk psychology must be very seriously mistaken.

3.3.5   Naturalizing Content

For many friends of folk psychology, the last semantic argument that I'll mention is the most worrisome. In some ways, it is also the most puzzling. The premise about content with which this argument begins is the claim that content (and related intentional notions) can't be "naturalized"—there is "no place for intentional categories in the physicalistic view of the world" (Fodor 1987, 98), and they "will prove permanently recalcitrant to integration in the natural order" (Fodor 1984, 32). But, the argument continues, if semantic content can't be naturalized, then it's not real—it doesn't exist at all. Here is how Fodor puts the point:

> It's hard to see . . . how one can be a Realist about intentionality without also being, to some extent or other, a Reductionist. If the semantic and the intentional are real properties of things, it must be in virtue of their identity with (or maybe of their supervenience on?) properties that are themselves *neither* intentional *nor* semantic. If aboutness is real, it must be really something else. (1987, 97)

If it's true that intentional or semantic properties can't be naturalized, Fodor would insist, it follows that they can't be "reduced" to nonintentional, nonsemantic properties. And if that's right, then they are not "real properties of things" at all.

To conclude the argument, we need only recall that, according to the version of the First Premise set out in section 2, folk psychology assumes that propositional attitudes do have semantic content, views sameness of content as a necessary element in individuating propositional attitudes, and couches many of its generalizations in terms of content. Plainly, if content is not a real property of things, then folk psychology has got all this pretty badly garbled.

Before accepting that conclusion, however, there are at least three clusters of questions that need answering. First, what exactly would be required to "naturalize" content? In the brief passage I've quoted from Fodor, he mentions reduction, supervenience, and property identity. In another paper, he specifies that naturalizing content requires providing nonintentional necessary and sufficient conditions for the application of intentional predicates. And in still other places, he says that sufficient conditions will do. Until we get a lot clearer on what "naturalizing" comes to, the remainder of the argument is going to be all but impossible to evaluate. A second set of questions focuses on the relation between naturalizing and being real. Why, one would like to know, would the fact that intentional properties can't be naturalized entail that they are not real properties of things? Is everything real reducible to (or supervenient upon, or definable in terms of) the physical (or the nonintentional, or the natural)? If the answer is yes, what's the argument that makes this answer plausible? A third group of questions takes aim at the premise with which the argument begins. What reason do we have to think that content can't be naturalized? Is it simply that no one has figured out how to do it (whatever exactly *it* turns out to be)? If so, then it may well be that content has lots of company, since there are lots of things for which no one knows how to provide a reduction (or definition) or an account of how it supervenes on the physical. Are all of them unreal?

Good questions, these, but not easy ones. To address them seriously would require a whole paper. And, as it happens, Stephen Laurence and I have written just such a paper. It is reprinted as chapter 5 in this volume.

This completes my brief survey of arguments aimed at showing that folk psychology is a seriously defective theory. It isn't intended to be an exhaustive survey; there are a number of other arguments to be found in the literature. I've focused on arguments that at one time or another I myself have been tempted to endorse. Nor do I claim to have presented the most subtle or persuasive version of each argument. Where brevity and subtlety conflict, I often opted for brevity. Still, I hope that some of these arguments strike you as plausible. For argument's sake, I'm going to assume that at least some of them are sound, and thus that some of the central claims made or presupposed by folk psychology are indeed mistaken. That assumption sets the stage for the questions I want to ask next: If folk psychology is a seriously mistaken theory, what conclusions ought we to draw about the existence or the scientific utility of intentional states? Should we conclude that a mature science of the mind/brain will not invoke beliefs and desires? Should we conclude that beliefs and desires are like witches and phlogiston—they do not exist at all?

4   From Premises about Folk Psychology to Conclusions about the Existence of Beliefs and Desires: Lewis's Strategy

Eliminativists, of course, answer both these questions in the affirmative, and, as I noted earlier, by and large their opponents seem to agree. Most authors on both sides of the debate think that the battle over the virtues and shortcomings of folk psychology will be the decisive one. If folk psychology really is a seriously mistaken theory, then the eliminativists will have won.[21] But why is this conditional so widely accepted? Why, exactly, does the falsity of folk psychology lead to the eliminativists' conclusions? There is remarkably little sustained discussion of this question in the literature on eliminativism. So, rather than trying to extract an answer from the literature, I propose to take a different tack. In this section, I'll try as best I can to reconstruct the considerations that once persuaded *me* that if folk psychology is very wrong, then there are no such things as beliefs. Having said why I once accepted this crucial step in the eliminativists' argument, I'll go on in section 5 to recount how I came to doubt it, and I'll explain why I no longer find the line of argument set out in this section to be very persuasive.

It's my guess that the cluster of views I'll recount in this section has been widely, though often tacitly, accepted by lots of authors on both sides of the debate.[22] These views are the tacit theory that is most often lurking in the background when people impugn or defend the virtues of folk psychology and then draw ontological conclusions. I may, of course, be quite wrong about this. It may be that others saw (or thought they saw) some quite different link from premises about the shortcomings of folk psychology to conclusions about the nonexistence of beliefs, desires, and the like. I know of only two other likely candidates, however. I'll discuss one of them in section 10 and the other in sections 11 and 12.

For me the essential element linking the falsehood of folk psychology to the nonexistence of the states it invokes was a theory about the meaning and reference of theoretical terms. Versions of the theory have been suggested by a number of distinguished philosophers including F. P. Ramsey and Rudolf Carnap, but the version that most influenced me was the one put forward by David Lewis. In a series of elegant and important papers, Lewis developed an account according to which a theory typically provides an "implicit functional definition"[23] of the terms it introduces. His "general hypothesis about the meanings of theoretical terms" is that "they are definable functionally, by reference to causal roles" (1972, 207).

To make his hypothesis plausible, Lewis offers the following illustration:[24]

> We are assembled in the drawing room of the country house; the detective reconstructs the crime. That is, he proposes a *theory* designed to be the best explanation of the phenomena we have observed: the death of Mr. Body, the blood on the wallpaper, the silence of the dog in the night, the clock seventeen minutes fast, and so on. He launches into his story:
>> X, Y and Z conspired to murder Mr. Body. Seventeen years ago, in the gold fields of Uganda, X was Body's partner. . . . Last week, Y and Z conferred in a bar in Reading. . . . Tuesday night at 11:17, Y went to the attic and set a time bomb. . . . Seventeen minutes later, X met Z in the billiard room and gave him the lead pipe. . . . Just when the bomb went off in the attic, X fired three shots through the French windows. . . .
> And so it goes: a long story. Let us pretend that it is a single long conjunctive sentence.

The story contains three names, X, Y and Z. The detective uses these new terms without explanation, as though we knew what they meant. But we do not. We never used them before, at least not in the senses they bear in the present context. All we know about their meaning is what we gradually gather from the story itself. Call these *theoretical terms* (*T-terms* for short) because they are introduced by a theory. Call the rest of the terms in the story *O-terms*. These are all the *other* terms except the T-terms. They are the *old, original* terms we understood before the theory was proposed. . . . (1972, 208)

In telling his story, the detective set forth three roles by X, Y and Z. He must have specified the meanings of the three T-terms 'X', 'Y' and 'Z' thereby; for they had meanings afterwards, they had none before, and nothing else was done to give them meanings. They were introduced by an implicit functional definition, being reserved to name the occupants of the three roles. . . . (209)

Suppose that after we have heard the detective's story, we learn that it is true of three people: Plum, Peacocke and Mustard. If we put the name 'Plum' in place of 'X', 'Peacocke' in place of 'Y', and 'Mustard' in place of 'Z' throughout, we get a true story about the doings of those three people. We will say that Plum, Peacocke and Mustard together *realize* (or are a *realization* of) the detective's theory. . . . (208–9)

I claim [that] the T-terms are definable as naming the first, second and third components of the unique triple that realizes the story, . . . [and thus] the T-terms can be treated like definite descriptions. (209)

On Lewis's view, the moral to be drawn from this example applies quite generally. Theoretical terms are "defined as the occupants of the causal roles specified by the theory . . . ; as *the* entities, whatever those may be, that bear certain causal relations to one another and to the referents of the O-terms" (211). For Lewis, we have specified the sense of a term when we have specified its denotation in all possible worlds. And "in any possible world, [T-terms] . . . name the components of whatever uniquely realizes [the theory] in that world" (1970, 85).

Two further features of Lewis's account deserve special emphasis. The first is the strategy Lewis urges for dealing with terms introduced by mistaken theories. Theoretical terms, Lewis tells us, are implicitly defined by the causal patterns specified in the theory that introduces the terms. Thus, if no set of entities exhibits the specified causal patterns—if the theory has no realization—then the theory is mistaken. When this happens, Lewis maintains, the theoretical terms themselves will lack a denotation—they will refer to nothing:

If we learnt that no triple realized the [detective's] story, or even came close, we would have to conclude that the story was false. We would also have to deny that the names 'X', 'Y' and 'Z' named anything; for they were introduced as names for the occupants of roles that turned out to be unoccupied. (1972, 209)

Now, as Lewis goes on to note, this is a rather extreme doctrine, for it entails that if a theory makes even a small mistake, then all of its theoretical terms will be denotationless. To make the view more palatable, Lewis offers "a complication":

> What if the theorizing detective has made one little mistake? He should have said that Y went to the attic at 11:37, not 11:17. The story as told is unrealized, true of no one. But another story is realized, indeed uniquely realized: the story we get by deleting or correcting the little mistake. We can say that the story as told is *nearly realized,* has a unique *near realization.* (The notion of a unique near realization is hard to analyze, but easy to understand.) In this case the T-terms ought to name the components of the near realization. More generally: they should name the components of the nearest realization of the theory, provided there is a unique nearest realization and it is near enough. Only if the story comes nowhere near to being realized, or if there are two equally near nearest realizations, should we resort to treating the T-terms like improper descriptions. (210)

So it is only in those cases where the theory is *very* wrong that the theoretical terms refer to nothing. When the theory is only a little bit wrong, the theoretical terms will still denote (provided there isn't more than one equally near "nearest realization").

Lewis does not say much about the boundary between these two sorts of cases. He makes no serious effort to specify *how* wrong a theory has to be before its theoretical terms fail to denote because it has no unique nearest realization that is "near enough." In the sentence following the passage just quoted, he tells us that "scientific theories are often nearly realized but rarely realized, and that theoretical reduction is usually *blended* with revision of the reduced theory" (1972, 210 [emphasis added]) This suggests that he thinks the boundary between theories that have near enough nearest realizations and those that do not is a blurry one, and perhaps that it has little theoretical significance. But, of course, in the context of arguments for and against eliminativism, the boundary is of *enormous* significance since, if we accept Lewis's account, it is the boundary that separates those false theories whose theoretical posits exist from those whose posits do not exist. If the boundary is a blurry one, then it may well turn out that even after all the scientific facts are in, both about the mind/brain and about what folk psychology claims, there will be no way of determining whether or not the eliminativists' thesis is correct. The truth or falsehood of eliminativism may simply be indeterminate.[25] But even if it turns out that there is no sharp boundary between false theories whose posits exist and false theories whose posits do not exist, Lewis's account might still provide an essential step in arguments aimed at establishing that the entities invoked in one or another false theory do not exist. For the fact that a boundary is vague or indeterminate is fully compatible with there being clear cases on both sides of the divide. There is, after all, no sharp or principled divide between bald and hairy people, yet some people are clearly bald, while others are unmistakably hairy. So if Lewis is right about theoretical terms, then to show that the posits of a theory do not exist, it will suffice to show that the theory is *very* wrong and not just a little bit mistaken.

The second point about Lewis's account that merits special emphasis is that if we "think of commonsense psychology as a term-introducing scientific theory, though one invented before there was any such institution as professional science" (1972, 212), then everything he has claimed about theoretical terms in general can be applied straightforwardly to the theoretical terms of commonsense psychology. Moreover, on Lewis's view, this is the right way to think of commonsense psychology:

> Imagine our ancestors first speaking only of external things, stimuli, and responses—and perhaps producing what we, but not they, may call *Äusserungen* of mental states—until some genius invented the theory of mental states, with its newly introduced T-terms, to explain the regularities among stimuli and responses. But that did not happen. Our commonsense psychology was never a newly invented term-introducing scientific theory—not even of prehistoric folk-science. The story that mental states were introduced as theoretical terms is a myth.
>
> It is, in fact, Sellars' myth. . . . And though it is a myth, it may be a good myth or a bad one. It is a good myth if our names of mental states do in fact mean just what they would mean if the myth were true. I adopt the working hypothesis that it is a good myth.[26]

Putting together the two points that I've been emphasizing gives us just the link that the eliminativist needs to go from claims about the shortcomings of commonsense psychology to the conclusion that the posits of commonsense psychology do not exist. "If the names of mental states are like theoretical terms, they name nothing unless the theory . . . is more or less true" (Lewis, 1972, 213). Indeed, if we suppose that commonsense psychology is an integrated theory containing or entailing claims about causal relations among various different kinds of psychological states, then, if Lewis's account is correct, problems in one part of commonsense psychology put our *entire* mental ontology in jeopardy: "On my version of causal definability, the mental terms stand or fall together. If common-sense psychology fails, all of them alike are denotationless" (214). So, on Lewis's view, if folk psychology turns out to be seriously mistaken, it's not just beliefs and desires that will have to be dropped from our ontology. Pains, pleasures, and other conscious states will have to go as well. Lewis himself sees little chance that things will work out this way. He identifies commonsense psychology with the psychological "platitudes which are common knowledge among us—everyone knows them, everyone knows that everyone else knows them, and so on" (212).[27] And he has no doubt at all that most of these platitudes will turn out to be correct. But we have been assuming that folk psychology is more than a collection of commonly accepted platitudes. My version of the eliminativists' First Premise takes folk psychology to be a largely tacit, opulent, internally represented theory. And if we grant that some substantial subset of the arguments set out in section 3 are sound, then by any reasonable standard folk psychology will turn out to be pretty badly mistaken. So, it appears that Lewis's account of the meaning and reference of theoretical terms provides eliminativists with an attractive way of getting from the premises of their argument to the conclusions.[28]

5   A Challenge to Lewis's Strategy—or How Bill Lycan Woke Me from My Dogmatic Slumbers

In my own case, I blush to admit, Lewis's account was so attractive that until recently I was barely aware of how heavily I was relying on it. It had become one of the unnoticed and unquestioned assumptions on which the more controversial and fussed-over parts of my philosophical view were built. But, as our deconstructionist friends are fond of noting, when the foundations are hidden, so too are the cracks.

All this began to change, for me, while Ramsey, Garon, and I were at work on the paper that is reprinted as chapter 2 in this volume. At that time, as luck would have it, I was asked to review Bill Lycan's book *Judgement and Justification*. And while rereading the essays in that volume I was brought up short by several brief passages that were not at all central to Lycan's projects. In those passages, Lycan notes that most eliminativists seem to presuppose something like Lewis's theory about the meaning and reference of theoretical terms, and he emphasizes that this is not an assumption that one gets for free. Accounts like the one Lewis develops are *not* the only game in town. Indeed, in the recent philosophy-of-language literature, they are not even the most popular game in town. On the very different account of reference that Lycan favors, premises detailing untenable features of the commonsense conception of beliefs and desires simply do not support the sort of ontological conclusions that eliminativists are wont to draw. Here are a couple of passages in which Lycan sets out his view:

> I incline away from Lewis's Carnapian . . . cluster theory of the reference of theoretical terms, and toward Putnam's causal-historical theory. As in Putnam's examples of 'water,' 'tiger,' and so on, I think the ordinary word 'belief' (qua theoretical term of folk psychology) points dimly toward a natural kind that we have not fully grasped and that only mature psychology will reveal. I expect that 'belief' will turn out to refer to some kind of information-bearing inner state of a sentient being, . . . but the kind of state it refers to may have only a few of the properties usually attributed to beliefs by common sense. (1988a, 32)

> I am entirely willing to give up fairly large chunks of our commonsensical . . . theory of belief or of desire (or of almost anything else) and decide that we were just wrong about a lot of things, without drawing the inference that we are no longer talking about belief or desire. (31–32)

There are several points suggested in these passages that I want to emphasize and endorse. First, Lycan is certainly right to note that description-based accounts of reference of the sort offered by Carnap and Lewis are not the only option available.[29] Putnam, Kripke, Devitt, and others have suggested a quite different family of theories about reference which many philosophers find more plausible. According to these causal-historical accounts, the reference of a term is determined by the appropriate sort of causal chain connecting users of the term with previous users from whom they acquired the term and ultimately proceeding back to an event or series of events in which the term is introduced to refer to a certain object or kind. Since serious alternatives to description theories have been proposed and defended with considerable ingenuity, eliminativists surely cannot legitimately do what I did for many years. They cannot simply take some version of the description theory for granted. If they are going to rely on it to get from their Premises to their conclusions, they will have to *defend* it against the competition. It is Lycan, I think, who deserves the credit for starting the deconstruction of the eliminativists' deconstruction by stressing that eliminativists themselves are relying on a barely acknowledged theory of reference that might well turn out to be unacceptable.

Second, Lycan is quite right in claiming that causal-historical theories will not sustain an argument from premises about the falsehood of folk psychology to conclusions about the nonexistence of the mental states that folk psychology invokes. Indeed, it is one of the selling points of causal-historical theories that they do a much better job than description theories at handling what Devitt and Sterelny call the problem of error (1987, secs. 3.3, 4.2, 5.1, 5.2). One way to explain the problem is to imagine a community of ancient stargazers who have what we now know to be wildly mistaken views about the objects visible in the night sky. They think that most of them are holes in a black and otherwise solid celestial dome through which we can see the light in the heavenly region that surrounds the dome. But even though their theory about the stars is about as mistaken as it is possible to get, it seems to make perfectly good sense to say that when these ancients spoke about the objects in the night sky, they were talking about stars. It is plausible to suppose that there was a term in their language that referred to stars, and they sometimes used that term to make profoundly mistaken claims about stars. Now, as advocates of causal-historical accounts of reference often note, cases like this pose a serious problem for description based accounts of reference, for on description-based accounts, it seems to follow that the ancients in our little tale aren't talking about stars at all. Since their theory is so seriously mistaken, description theories will entail that the astronomical terms used by the ancients refer to nothing— they are, as Lewis might say, denotationless. Causal-historical accounts, by contrast, do not entail this sort of counterintuitive conclusion. If one of the ancients' astronomical terms was introduced in settings that provided the right sort of causal links to stars, and if the history of transmission of that term was of the right sort, then their term refers to stars no matter how badly informed they may be about what stars really are. Thus, as Lycan rightly notes, causal-historical accounts of reference will not enable eliminativists to get from their premises to their conclusions.

These considerations are a clear indication that eliminativists have some work to do. But they do not suffice to show that the eliminativists' argument can't ultimately be made to work. While the "problem of error" argument certainly casts some doubt on description theories of reference, it is not, by itself, enough to show that description theories are untenable. Nor does it show that some causal-historical theory of the sort that Lycan favors is correct—for those theories seem to have problems of their own, and in just the opposite direction. If description theories sometimes make it too hard to refer, causal-historical theories sometimes make it too easy. To see the point, consider some of the parade cases of ontological elimination that eliminativists are fond of citing. There are no witches, and there is no such thing as phlogiston. So when our forebears used the words 'witch' and 'phlogiston,' they were referring to nothing. But if Lycan is right about reference, it's hard to see how this claim could be sustained. If the term 'witch' was introduced and transmitted in the right way, then it actually refers to certain women who behaved in strange or socially unacceptable ways. Of course, witches "may have only a few of the properties usually attributed to [them] by common sense." And the term may "dimly point toward a natural kind that we have not fully grasped." If we follow Lycan's lead, we should be "entirely willing to give up fairly large chunks of our commonsensical . . . theory . . . and decide that we were just wrong about a lot of things," without drawing the inference that 'witch' is a term that fails to refer. And, of course, the same can be said, mutatis mutandis, for phlogiston. These conclusions are no less counterintuitive than the conclusion that the ancient stargazers were not talking about the stars. So, Lycan and other opponents of eliminativism can't simply assume that some version of the causal-historical theory of reference is correct and thus that terms like 'belief' and 'desire' refer, no matter how wrong we ultimately discover folk psychology to be.

Where does all of this leave us? Here's one assessment of the situation: The most promising way for eliminativists to get from their Premises to their conclusions is to invoke a theory of reference. And one well-worked-out theory (Lewis's) will do just fine. But there are problems with that theory and with other versions of the description theory as well. They seem to entail some quite counterintuitive claims. Moreover, there is another widely accepted family of theories about reference on the market, causal-historical theories, and theories in that family will not enable eliminativists to get from their Premises to their conclusions. Causal-historical theories have problems of their own, however; they too seem to entail some quite counterintuitive claims. So, it looks like both eliminativists and their opponents would be well advised to turn their attention to the theory of reference. They have to determine which sort of account of reference is right and find some plausible way of explaining away the objections to that account. Or perhaps the objections indicate that neither description theories nor causal-historical theories are right and that some new, better theory[30] of reference is needed. In any event, the theory of reference has now moved to center stage. Before we can determine whether the eliminativists' Premises support their conclusions, we're going to have to settle which account of reference is correct.

6   What Is a Theory of Reference? Two Proposals

At this juncture, many philosophers who were trained to do philosophy the way I was would be tempted to roll up their sleeves and jump into the fray—constructing new theories of reference (or fine-tuning old ones), exploring the consequences of these theories, developing arguments, looking for counterexamples. That's what we do for a living; it's how the game is played. So, having persuaded myself that the assessment offered at the end of the previous section was correct, I set to work looking for a better theory of reference. But after lots of work and very little progress, I gradually became convinced that this is the wrong way to proceed. What changed my mind was not that it was hard to come up with alternative theories of reference—quite the opposite, it was actually quite easy. I have a notebook full of them. But as my list of alternatives grew, I found that I got less and less clear about how I was supposed to evaluate these alternatives. How could I tell which one was the right one?

At first I assumed that the problem I was confronting was just another case of a familiar epistemic problem that has to be confronted by theory builders in almost every domain. Very few areas of inquiry have anything even close to established decision procedures for determining whether or not a theory is correct. There may be no obvious or generally accepted set of procedures for evaluating alternative theories of reference, but much the same can be said for theories in physics or biology or archeology, as well. Gradually, however, I became convinced that the problem I was having in evaluating theories of reference was deeper than this, for in trying to assess theories of reference, the familiar epistemic problem is exacerbated by a quite basic methodological problem (or perhaps it's really a metaphysical problem—I've already confessed that the distinction is one I have trouble drawing). Other domains may not be entirely free from this methodological problem, but in the theory of reference it arises in a particularly acute form. In just about every area of inquiry, it's hard to determine whether a given theory is successful in capturing or explaining the facts that it is intended to capture or explain. That's what I've been calling the *epistemic* problem. But in most parts of physics or biology or archeology it is pretty clear what the theory is expected to do; though there may be a bit of squabbling about it from time to time, there is typically considerable agreement about the sorts of facts that a theory is expected to describe or explain. By contrast, it is far from clear what sorts of facts the theory of reference is supposed to account for. Indeed, it is my suspicion that, while the issue is only rarely a topic on which they have explicitly formulated views, different writers have quite different expectations. And, no doubt, some of the disagreement about which theories of reference are most promising can be traced to this underlying, largely tacit, disagreement about the job that a theory of reference is expected to do. Other writers have no coherent views at all about what a theory of reference is expected to do. It is not surprising that they have a particularly hard time figuring out which theory is best. My problem, in attempting to evaluate my growing collection of alternative theories, was that, without being clearly aware of it, I fell squarely into this latter category: I didn't know what a theory of reference was supposed to do.

When all of this finally came into focus, I decided to put my collection of theories on the back burner for a while and attend, instead, to the methodological question that had to be clarified before I could make any progress in assessing alternative accounts of reference. So, I started thinking about the sorts of projects people might have in mind when they debate the virtues of various theories of reference. The decision to concentrate on the methodological question turned out to be a pivotal step in the intellectual adventure (or misadventure) that I'm recounting in this chapter, for it ultimately led me to the conclusion that my entire conception of the eliminativism debate was radically mistaken. But here I am getting way ahead of myself. To explain how I reached that conclusion, I'll start by sketching the most plausible answers I have come up with to the question about what a theory of reference is supposed to do.

6.1   Theory of Reference as an Account of Folk Semantics

One family of answers begins with the observation that appeal to people's spontaneous judgments, or their intuitions, as philosophers often call them, seems to play a central role in many debates about the virtues of competing theories of reference. Sometimes, the intuitions invoked concern actual cases of language use, but often they are intuitions about hypothetical or imaginary cases, some of which can be more than a bit bizarre. We have already seen several examples of the way in which intuitions are invoked in these debates. In explaining "the problem of error" argument, I imagined a community of ancient stargazers who had a seriously mistaken theory about the objects visible in the night sky. Description theories, I noted, typically entail that terms embedded in seriously false theories don't refer to anything and thus if description theories are right, then the ancients aren't actually referring to the stars. But this, the critics of description theories insist, is counterintuitive. Our intuitions tell us that the ancients *were* referring to the stars, and this conflict with our intuitions poses a problem for description theories. Similarly, the intuition that 'witch' does not refer to anything played a crucial role in the objection I offered against Lycan's views on reference.

In his famous monograph *Naming and Necessity,* Saul Kripke sets out a number of cases designed to bring out our intuitions about the reference of proper names. With a bit of familiar elaboration, one of these cases might be put as follows: Suppose that in biblical times there really was a man who survived for three days and three nights in the belly of a great fish. After escaping from the fish, he was killed by bandits, and his memory has vanished without a trace. Suppose also that at roughly the same time there was another man who did not endure any such exciting adventure but about whom, for some reason, people told increasingly tall tales. Over the years, one of these tales evolved into the biblical story of Jonah, which has been passed down from generation to generation. Now if this is really what happened in history, to which of these men do readers of the Bible refer when they ask questions or make claims about Jonah? Description theories will typically claim they refer to the first man, since most of the claims they would make using the name 'Jonah' are true about him. But, many philosophers maintain, our intuitions support the opposite judgment. If the facts are as stipulated in the story, our intuitions tell us that when a reader of the Bible asks questions in which the name 'Jonah' is used, the name refers to the second man, and thus most of what the Bible says about Jonah is false. Examples like this convinced many philosophers that description theories of the reference of proper names were wrong and that causal-historical theories were more plausible.[31]

Clearly, appeal to intuitions plays an important role in debates about the theory of reference. But why? Why should these intuitions be at all relevant to questions about the correctness or incorrectness of a theory of reference? A variety of answers might be offered here, but the most straightforward answer is that intuitions are relevant because capturing the relevant intuitions is what a theory of reference is supposed to do—producing a theory that entails the intuitions is one of the goals of the theory of reference. This answer can be elaborated in two different ways. To pull them apart, it will help to consider the analogy between the theory of reference and grammatical theory.

In grammar, too, intuitions play a central role. They are far and away the most important source of data for the descriptive grammarian. One attempt to explain the role of intuitions in grammatical theory urges that a correct grammatical theory *just is* an idealized theory of grammatical intuitions. The goal of grammatical theorizing, on this account, is to produce the simplest and most elegant theory that captures most of a native speaker's grammatical intuitions.[32] An alternative account of the role of intuitions in grammatical theory urges that the real goal of the theory is not to capture intuitions but to characterize the grammatical principles used by the psychological mechanism that gives rise to the intuitions. This view typically assumes that there is a distinct underlying psychological mechanism that subserves grammatical processing and that this same mechanism plays a central role in the production of grammatical intuitions. The grammar mechanism interacts with other components of the mind, including perceptual processors, attention mechanisms, short-term memory, etc., and together these mechanisms produce the linguistic intuitions that people report. Thus, the intuitions are a good source of evidence about the grammatical principles used by the mechanism. But they are not an infallible guide, since memory limitations, failures of attention, and other factors may produce various sorts of "performance errors," including intuitions that fail to reflect a speaker's underlying "grammatical competence."[33]

Now one way to elaborate on the idea that the goal of a theory of reference is to capture the relevant reference intuitions is to view the theory of reference as analogous to the grammatical theory on the first account of grammar sketched in the previous paragraph. On this view, a theory of reference *just is* an idealized theory of reference intuitions. The theorist's goal is to produce the simplest and most elegant set of principles that captures most of the intuitions that people have about reference.[34]

The other way to develop the idea is to suppose there is a systematic body of information or a set of principles stored in the mind which plays a central role in producing reference intuitions. The goal of a theory of reference, on this view, is to give an accurate account of those mentally represented principles, or of the word–world mapping that they specify. In order to produce intuitions, the mentally represented principles must interact with other components of the mind, including those responsible for attention, inference, and short-term memory. Thus, the intuitions that people offer will not always be accurate reflections of the principles, though they will be a rich source of data for a theorist to use in trying to determine what those principles actually are. On this account, theories of reference have much the same status as theories about people's internally represented folk physics discussed in section 2. In both cases, the goal is to describe an internally stored body of information, and in both cases people's spontaneous judgments or intuitions provide a rich, though occasionally misleading, source of data for the theorist to use. Theories about folk physics and theories of reference, on this account, are both descriptive psychological theories. The theories are correct if they accurately describe the principles of an internally represented commonsense theory. So on this view, it seems natural to think of the theory of reference as an account of another sort of folk theory which might be called *folk semantics*.[35]

6.2 *Theory of Reference as Proto-Science*

The analogy between theories of reference and theories about folk physics and the analogy between theories of reference and grammatical theories are both useful in explaining the view that the goal of the theory of reference is to correctly describe our tacit folk semantics. But there is an important distinction between these two analogies, and elaborating on that distinction will set the stage for a quite different account of the job of the theory of reference. To see the distinction I want to draw, it is crucial to keep in mind that in both grammar and folk physics there are *two* theories to keep track of. A researcher who is interested in characterizing the folk physics used by a group of subjects wants to describe a theory that is represented in the minds of her subjects. Her *description* of that theory is itself a theory—a theory about what's represented in her subjects' heads. And, of course, her theory about what's in her subjects' heads might be wrong. It is also possible that the *subjects'* theory might be wrong. Indeed, the work on folk physics recounted in section 2 indicates that the physical theory inside the heads of many subjects *is* wrong. Now let's consider grammar. Here, too, there are *two* theories to keep track of. The descriptive grammarian is attempting to specify a set of principles that are represented in the minds of speakers of the dialect the grammarian is concerned with. The specification that the grammarian offers is thus a theory about the principles her subjects are using. And, just as in the case of folk physics, the grammarian's theory may be wrong. She may mischaracterize the principles in her subjects' heads. Moreover, as in the case of folk physics, the principles inside the subjects' heads can themselves be regarded as a theory, since (we have been assuming) one of the things they do is entail lots of claims about the grammatical properties of sentences in the speakers' dialect.

Now we can raise the question that brings out the important distinction between grammar and folk physics: Can the grammatical theory inside the speaker's head be wrong in the way that folk physics can? Is it possible, for example, for a speaker's internalized grammar to entail that a sentence in the speaker's dialect is grammatical when it isn't? The answer to this question turns on the sort of answer we accept to a cluster of further questions about the nature of grammatical properties themselves: What is it for a sentence in a dialect to be grammatical? In virtue of what does a sequence of phonemes count as a grammatical sentence? Various answers might be explored here. The one Chomsky and some other leading figures in linguistics seem to favor is that a sequence of phonemes is grammatical in a dialect if and only if it is classified as grammatical by the grammar inside the heads of the speakers. It is the grammar itself that determines whether or not a phoneme sequence is grammatical. If this is right, then it follows that the answer to the questions at the beginning of this paragraph is "no." The grammatical principles inside a speaker's head can't be wrong in the way that folk physics can be wrong, for what makes it the case that a phoneme sequence is grammatical is that it is classified as grammatical by the rules or principles inside the speaker's head. Of course, it is possible that a member of some community might have a set of grammatical rules inside his head that is slightly different (or very different) from the rules inside the heads of other members of the community. If this happened, it might well be the case that the nonconforming grammar classified as grammatical some phoneme sequences that the grammars inside other heads classified as *un*grammatical. But, on the account of grammatical properties that I am attributing to Chomsky, this would not count as an *error* on the part of the nonconforming speaker or his grammar. Rather, it would be the case that the nonconforming speaker spoke a different dialect. Perhaps he is the only speaker of the dialect, in which case it is best described as an *idiolect*. However, the claims entailed by the speaker's internalized grammar cannot possibly be wrong about sentences in his own idiolect, since the grammatical properties in that idiolect are determined by the internalized grammar of the idiolect.[36]

Let's return, now, to the theory of reference and the analogies with grammar and with folk physics. Obviously, if the job of a theory of reference is to describe an internalized folk semantics, then any particular account that a theorist gives may be mistaken. The theorist may misdescribe the folk semantic theory inside people's heads. But what about the folk semantic theory itself? Can *it* be mistaken? Here, as before, the answer turns on what we say about some further questions— this time questions about the nature of semantic properties (or relations): What is it for a term in a language to refer to an object? In virtue of what does a term count as referring to an object? If we push the analogy with the Chomskian account of grammatical properties, the answer is that it is the internalized folk semantic theory which specifies the conditions a term must meet if it is to refer to an object. The reference relation just is whatever the internalized folk semantics says it is. And if that's right, then of course the internalized theory can't be mistaken. If two people have different internalized folk semantic theories, then the notions of reference that they are using are simply different. When they use the term 'refer', they are talking about different relations. Occasionally, such people may *appear* to be disagreeing about what refers to what in a particular case; but actually, they are not disagreeing at all. Rather, their situation is much the same as the situation of people who speak different idiolects who appear to be disagreeing about the grammaticality of a particular sentence: They are also not disagreeing at all. Assuming their judgments accurately reflect their internally represented theories, they are both right.

Suppose, however, that the right analogy to push is not the one between theory of reference and grammar but rather the one between theory of reference and folk physics. In that case, there will be no guarantee that our internalized folk semantic theory is correct. Folk semantics, on this view, is just a collection of commonsense beliefs about reference and what determines reference, and the real facts about reference, like the real facts about physics, are as they are quite independently of what our folk theory may say about them. So, if folk semantics is like folk physics, then our attempt to describe the commonsense theory of reference may be an interesting bit of psychology, but there is no reason to suppose that it will tell us much about reference. If we want to learn about the laws governing motion, we don't study what ordinary folks think; rather, we study the science of physics. And if we want to learn about the nature of various diseases, we don't study folk theories of disease,[37] we study medicine and pathology. So, if folk semantics is like folk physics, then if we want to learn about reference, we shouldn't study the folk conception of reference. Rather, we should study the science that tells us about reference. But, it would seem, at just this point the analogy between folk semantics and folk physics hits a snag. For while there is a well-developed science of physics for the person interested in the laws of motion to study, and a well-developed science of pathology for the person interested in disease to study, it is not clear that there is any science at all whose business it is to investigate the real nature of reference.

It might be thought that this shows that the analogy between folk semantics and folk physics is indefensible and the analogy with grammar is the only tenable one. But I am inclined to think this conclusion might be too hasty. For while it is true that the notion of reference plays no role in any well-developed science, it might well be the case that one or another reference-like word–world mapping relation will prove to be of considerable importance in various domains of empirical investigation. Perhaps linguistics will be able to make good use of such a relation; or perhaps parts of cognitive psychology or evolutionary biology will find a need for such a relation. Or, turning to very different domains of inquiry, perhaps anthropology or history and sociology, particularly the history and sociology of science, will find an explanatory use for a word–world mapping that's not too different from the intuitive notion of reference. There is no way of knowing a priori whether any of these possibilities will pan out. The only way to find out is to elaborate various word–world mapping relations and then try to put them to use in one or another scientific or historical project. The job of hunting for scientifically useful word–world relations is, of course, not distinct from actually doing the science in question. Rather, it is best thought of as an activity that might be pursued in the early stages of the development of the science, a sort of proto-science, if you will. So the alternative to viewing the theory of reference as attempting to characterize a relation specified by folk semantics is to view it as a kind of proto-science which tries to find or construct word–world relations that will be useful in some explanatory project or other.

Perhaps I am being too cautious here. I have met a few philosophers who think that there already are up-and-running sciences that invoke the notion of reference. Linguistics is the candidate most often mentioned, though various parts of cognitive psychology are sometimes mentioned as well.[38] I am inclined to be more than a bit skeptical about the claim that any of these areas of inquiry make genuinely explanatory use of a reference-like word–world relation. But for present purposes there is no need to enter into a debate on the matter. For if it is true that linguistics or parts of cognitive psychology or some other discipline already exploits a notion of reference, then the project for the theory of reference can be viewed as providing an explicit description or explication of the reference relation that these disciplines are using. This sort of project is quite familiar in the philosophy of science. Even in well-developed sciences, it is sometimes the case that researchers will use a concept quite productively without providing a fully explicit or philosophically satisfying account of the concept. In these cases, philosophers of science sometimes step in and try to make the notion in question more explicit. In recent years, there have been illuminating studies of fitness, space-time, grammaticality, and a host of other notions.[39] Part of this work can be viewed as straightforward conceptual description, where the concepts being characterized are those of working scientists. Often, however, philosophers of science discover that the concepts they are studying and the theories in which they play a role are uncomfortably vague or obscure in various ways. When this happens, it is not at all uncommon for philosophers of science to propose improvements in the concepts and theories they are describing. Typically, it is no easy matter to say where description stops and construction begins, and for most purposes it hardly matters. Nor is there any clear boundary between this activity and the sort of proto-science described above. In both activities, the goal is to provide explicit accounts of kinds or properties or relations that will be (or already are) useful in some scientific project. The proposal I'm offering in this section is that building a theory of reference might be taken to be an activity of just this sort.

If this proposal is accepted, then the appeal to intuitions that plays such a large role in the philosophical literature on reference will have to be viewed with considerable skepticism. For our intuitions are, at best, an indicator of our current commonsense conception of the reference relation and of the theory in which that conception is embedded. This may be a reasonable place to start in trying to construct a scientifically useful account of reference—we have to start somewhere, after all. But on the proto-science view, the fact that a proposed account of the nature of reference flies in the face of our intuitions provides little reason to reject it, just as the fact that the layperson finds a proposed account of the nature of space or disease or water to be counterintuitive provides little reason to reject that account.

Finally, before turning to other matters we should note that there is no a priori reason to suppose that the proto-scientific project of characterizing scientifically useful word–world relations will yield a *unique* result. It may turn out that the word–world mapping useful in linguistics is different from the one useful in cognitive psychology and that both of these are different from the one useful in anthropology or in the history and sociology of science. Or it may turn out that two or more word–world relations are explanatorily useful within the same science in much the same way that the premodern notion of speed divided into the Newtonian notions of velocity and acceleration.[40]

7 Using the Folk Semantics Account of Reference to Assess the Eliminativists' Argument: Some Surprising Results

Let's pause for a moment to take stock of where we are, how we got there, and where we might go from here. In sections 1–3, I sketched the overall structure of the eliminativists' argument and explained how I thought the Premises might be most charitably construed. In section 4, we saw that one way in which the eliminativists' Premises might lead to their conclusions would be to invoke an additional premise—a description-theoretic account of reference. But in section 5, we saw that this additional premise is not one that the eliminativists get for free. There are other accounts of reference to be reckoned with, and which account is correct is a hotly contested issue. Moreover, as we saw in section 6, it is far from clear what would settle the dispute between advocates of various theories of reference, since it is not clear what a correct theory of reference is supposed to do. Two possibilities were proposed. On one, the theory of reference aims at describing the principles underlying our intuitions about what refers to what in various cases. On the other, the theory of reference aims to specify a word–world relation that will be useful in some scientific project. That's where we are, and how we got there. Where should we go from here?

It looks like the most reasonable next step is to use our two accounts of what a theory of reference is supposed to do in order to assess alternative theories of reference. The theory of reference that comes out looking most promising can then be plugged into the eliminativists' argument, and, if we're lucky, it will tell us whether or not the conclusions actually do follow from the premises. When I reached this point in my own thinking, that's just what I decided to do. It might seem that the existence of two quite different accounts of what a theory of reference is supposed to do would have posed a problem for this strategy. But actually it didn't—at least not for me. For on the proto-science account, there is no saying what reference is until we have made some progress at building a science in which a reference-like word–world mapping plays a role. And as I have already noted, I don't think there is anything around that fills that bill, nor do I have any idea how to construct such a science. So, from a practical point of view, the only way to make progress is to concentrate on the account that views a theory of reference as an attempt to describe the intuitive reference relation, the one specified by folk semantics. That's the way I decided to proceed.

My approach was as direct and head-on as it could be. The question that concerned me was what the tacit theory that guides our folk semantic intuitions entails about the reference of terms that are embedded in theories which we now take to be seriously mistaken. To answer the question, I set out constructing examples designed to elicit the relevant intuitions. Some of the examples were comic book versions of actual events in the history of science:

> Here's what Democritus said about atoms (or what Mendel said about genes): . . .
>
> Here's what modern science says about atoms (or genes): . . .
>
> If we assume that modern science is correct, was Democritus actually referring to the same things that modern science is? (Or, . . . was Mendel actually referring to the same things that modern science is?)

Others were completely fictional:

> The Tuoba people in the Highlands of Papua New Guinea have the following theory about the cause of a certain set of symptoms (or about what sometimes causes the moon to go dark in the clear evening sky, or . . .): . . .
>
> Modern medicine (or astronomy, or . . .) explains these symptoms (or these eclipses, or . . .) as follows: . . .
>
> If we assume that modern medicine (or astronomy, or . . .) is correct, is it the case that the Tuoba word '———' actually refers to what contemporary scientists call '***'? (Or, . . . is it the case that what the Tuoba call '———' is the same thing as what modern scientists call '***'?)

Generating a range of quite varied examples proved to be a fairly easy task. A rainy afternoon yielded several dozen. As I was constructing the examples, however, I was struck by the fact that I myself had no firm intuitions about most of them. Initially, this was no great cause for concern, since it often happens in linguistics that when one plays with sample sentences long enough, one develops a sort of grammatical tin ear and can no longer tell which ones sound grammatical and which do not. To get around the problem of my tin ear, I presented the examples to several of my graduate students and several of my colleagues. This was not a great success. Many of them claimed to have no firm intuitions, either, although in some cases, some people claimed to have firm intuitions in favor of an affirmative answer, while others claimed to have firm intuitions in favor of a negative answer. That was a bit of a bother, of course, but it wasn't a surprise. On questions like this, one expects to find philosophy departments full of people with tin ears, particularly a department like mine. So, I resolved that I would have to do it the hard way and run a little experiment with naive subjects. Fortunately, we have lots of them available at my university; our introduction to philosophy classes are very popular. Thus, I wrote up a pilot version of a questionnaire containing various fictional examples of the sort displayed above, and asked students in several classes to fill them out at the beginning of the class period. After doing some preliminary analysis on about a hundred responses, however, I decided to drop the project, for what I found was that the intuitions of these naive subjects were no more firm or consistent than those of my graduate students and colleagues. There was little agreement on the cases; some students protested that they really didn't know what to say; and small variations in the wording of the questions seemed to produce a substantial shift in the sorts of answers I got. Perhaps there were some systematic and widely shared principles about reference underlying the very messy data that I was collecting, but if there were, I couldn't find them. My conclusion from this little pilot study was that there probably are no systematic, widely shared principles that guide people's judgments when they are presented with questions about the reference of terms in mistaken theories.

I don't pretend for a moment that the little bit of data I've collected is sufficient to establish my conclusion. And I would certainly be pleased to see the results of a much more serious and careful study. However, it is perhaps worth noting that it would not be at all anomalous if the facts about people's intuitions are as I believe them to be. The assumption on which my experiment was based is that the judgments people offer are guided, in part, by a largely tacit theory (folk semantics), in much the same way that commonsense intuitions about the motions of middle sized physical objects are guided by a largely tacit theory. And, as noted earlier, it is far from obvious that this assumption is correct (see n. 35). But even if it is correct, there is certainly no a priori reason to suppose that the theory must entail some definite judgment about every imaginable case. Lots of theories, tacit and explicit, are incomplete and say nothing at all about some range of cases. Indeed, commonsense theories should perhaps be expected to remain silent on cases that are far removed from the workaday situations in which such theories earn their keep. Where nature doesn't itch, folk theory has no need to scratch.

Suppose I am right and that the commonsense theory underlying

our intuitions about reference says little or nothing about the reference
of terms embedded in theories that we take to be seriously mistaken.
What follows about the debate over eliminativism? If we assume, as I
have been, that terms like 'belief' and 'desire' can be viewed as part of
the theoretical vocabulary of an opulent, largely tacit, commonsense
theory and that the theory is seriously mistaken in a variety of ways,
then if I am right about folk semantics, it follows that questions like:

Does '_____ is a belief' refer to anything?

will not be answered either positively or negatively by folk semantics.
Folk semantics leaves these questions unsettled. But now, if we also assume that what folk semantics says about reference is all there is to say
about the matter, in much the way that what the grammar of an idiolect
says about grammaticality in the idiolect is all there is to say about the
matter, it follows that claims like:

'_____ is a belief' refers to X

and

'_____ is a belief' refers to something

are simply indeterminate—they are neither true nor false. And that
looks like bad news for *both* sides in the eliminativism debate, since beliefs exist if and only if '_____ is a belief' refers to something. So, the
upshot of the argument seems to be that the eliminativists' basic ontological claim—the claim that beliefs and desires do not exist—is neither
true nor false: It simply has no determinate truth conditions.[41] Since I
had spent a good part of my time over the last two decades trying to
determine whether eliminativism was true or false, this was a rather
startling conclusion. And there were more surprises to come.

Some years earlier, while working on a book concerned mainly with
issues in epistemology, I had elaborated an argument aimed at showing
that the reference relation favored by our intuition is just one rather
idiosyncratic member of a large family of more or less similar relations.[42] The fact that our intuitions pick out that particular relation
rather than one of the other members of the family is, I argued, little
more than a historical accident. As the indeterminacy argument
sketched in the last few paragraphs was taking shape, I began to realize
that if my claim about the idiosyncrasy of reference was correct, it
might have some quite unexpected implications for the eliminativism
debate. For the idiosyncrasy of reference suggests that even if I am
wrong about the *indeterminacy* of the eliminativists' thesis, the thesis may
nonetheless turn out to be idiosyncratic and uninteresting. To explain
how I reached that conclusion, I'll have to begin by summarizing the
argument for the idiosyncrasy of the intuitive reference relation.

That argument starts with a hunch, albeit a widely shared one.
While there are lots of theories of reference on the market these days,
my hunch is that the accounts that do the best job at capturing people's
relatively firm and stable intuitions about reference are not those that

follow the path staked out by Ramsey and Lewis but those that tell what Lycan calls a causal-historical story. The basic idea of these theories, as we saw earlier, is that words get linked to things in the world via causal-historical chains. The first step in creating such a chain is a *grounding* or a *reference fixing*—an event or process (or, more commonly, an array of such events or processes) in which a term is introduced into a language to designate an object or a kind of objects. Following this, there is a series (often a very long series) of reference-preserving transmissions in which the term is passed from one user to another, preserving the reference that was fixed when the term was introduced. But, of course, not just any way of introducing a term into a language will count as grounding the term on a particular object or kind of objects, and not just any way of passing a term from one user to another will count as a reference preserving transmission. The legitimate groundings and transmissions will be those embedded in causal-historical chains that are sanctioned by intuition. When one looks carefully at the class of groundings and the class of transmissions that pass this test, however, it appears that in each class the allowable events are a mixed bag, having at best a loosely knit fabric of family resemblances to tie them together. The grounding of 'water' (or some ancestor of the term) on water was surely markedly different from the grounding of 'helium' on helium. The heterogeneity of intuitively acceptable groundings looks even more extreme when we consider the various ways in which predicates like 'kangaroo', 'asteroid', 'mutation', 'electron', 'quark', 'superconductivity', and 'strange attractor' were introduced. The class of intuitively acceptable reference-preserving transmissions is comparably diverse. What ties all the reference-determining causal-historical chains together is not any natural property that they share, but simply the fact that commonsense intuition counts them all as reference-fixing chains.

If it is indeed the case that common sense groups together a heterogeneous cluster of causal-historical chains, then obviously there are going to be lots of equally heterogeneous variations on the commonsense theme. These alternatives will depart from the cluster favored by common sense, some in minor ways and some in major ways. They will link some words, or many, to objects or extensions different from those assigned by commonsense intuition. In so doing, they will characterize alternative word–world links, which we might call REFERENCE*, REFERENCE**, REFERENCE***, and so on. And the only obvious complaint against these alternative schemes for nailing words onto the world is that they do not happen to be the schemes sanctioned by our commonsense intuition. Thus, the word–world mapping that will be captured by the correct theory of reference will be a highly idiosyncratic one. It will be one member of a large family of word–world mappings, a member that stands out from the rest only because it happens to be favored by intuition.

The rather arbitrary contours of the intuitively sanctioned reference relation may come into sharper focus if we reflect on the prove-
nance of our semantic intuitions. We have been assuming that our intuitions are largely determined by a set of tacit principles. If this is right,
where did those principles come from? The short answer is that no one
really knows. But it is a good bet that these principles, like principles
underlying our intuitions about grammaticality or morality or politeness, are culturally transmitted and acquired by individuals from the
surrounding society with little or no explicit instruction. Though the
range of principles people can acquire may be genetically constrained,
there is every reason to suppose that other cultures could perfectly well
internalize different principles of folk semantics, just as they may internalize different principles of grammar or politeness or morality. Thus,
the fact that our intuitions pick out the particular word–world relation
that we call *reference* rather than one of the many others in the envelope
of genetic possibility is largely the result of historical accident, in very
much the same way that details of the grammar of our language or
elements of our principles of politeness are in large measure the result
of historical accidents.

That's the end of my summary of the argument that convinced me
that the intuitive reference relation is idiosyncratic and arbitrary. Suppose the conclusion is correct. What implications would it have for eliminativism? The answer that I once found convincing ran as follows: The
central claim of eliminativism is that beliefs and other intentional states
do not exist. But that claim is true if and only if predicates like '___ is
a belief' refer to nothing. Well, suppose that '___ is a belief' doesn't
refer to anything. How interesting a result would this be? Would it be
anything to worry about? To think that it would, we must suppose that
there is something interesting or important about *reference*—the intuitively sanctioned word–world mapping. For surely there are lots of alternative word–world mappings on which predicates like '___ is a belief' *are* related to something ontologically unproblematic. So, even if
'___ is a belief' refers to nothing, it may well REFER* (and REFER**,
and REFER***) to lots of things. If the difference between reference
and REFERENCE* is simply that one of these idiosyncratic mappings
happens to have gotten itself embedded in our folk semantics, while
the other has not, then it's hard to see why we should care whether or
not the extension of '___ is a belief' is empty. If the only thing that
distinguishes reference from REFERENCE**, REFERENCE***, and
various other word–world mappings is an historical accident, then the
fact that '___ is a belief' refers to nothing just isn't very interesting or
important. But if *that* isn't interesting, then neither is the fact that beliefs don't exist.

The point can be put in a slightly different way by considering a
family of doctrines that are related to eliminativism. On the account we

have been working with, eliminativism is true if and only if '_____ is a belief' refers to nothing. Let ELIMINATIVISM* be a doctrine that is true if and only if '_____ is a belief' REFERS* to nothing; let ELIMI-NATIVISM** be a doctrine that is true if and only if '_____ is a belief' REFERS** to nothing; and so on. Clearly, some of these ELIMI-NATIVISM-stars are bound to be true, while others will be false. Suppose that ELIMINATIVISM***** happens to be one that turns out to be true. Is that anything to worry about? It's hard to see why it should be. But unless there is some interesting and important difference between reference and REFERENCE*****, it is hard to see why eliminativism should be any more worrisome than ELIMINATIVISM*****. If, as I have argued, the only noteworthy difference between reference and various of the REFERENCE-stars is that the former happens to be sanctioned by our intuitions, then eliminativism is neither a troublesome doctrine nor a particularly interesting one.

I confess that I was never entirely comfortable with this argument. The conclusion seemed rather wild, even by my very permissive standards. But since I couldn't see anything clearly wrong with the argument, I decided to write it up, read it around, and see if my colleagues could convince me that I had made a mistake.[43]

8 More Implausible Consequence

Objections to the arguments that I sketched in the last section weren't long in coming. The one that I found most unsettling I heard first from John Searle; it was reinforced, in a slightly less strident tone of voice, by Christopher Gauker. Searle and Gauker focused on the second argument, the one that starts with the claim that the intuitive reference relation, is an idiosyncratic relation and concludes that eliminativism is an uninteresting doctrine not worth worrying about. What Searle and Gauker pointed out was that this argument seems to be generalizable in a way that leads to *lots* of strikingly implausible conclusions. As I set it out, the argument is aimed at propositional-attitude eliminativism—the claim that beliefs and desires don't exist. But consider some claims that have been hotly debated in other intellectual domains. Most physicists, I gather, accept the claim that the big bang occurred and the claim that black holes exist, though there are a few who deny one or the other of these. Those who deny them advocate ontological views that are analogous to eliminativism; indeed, we might well label their views big-bang eliminativism and black-hole eliminativism. Now, as Searle and Gauker noted, for each of these eliminativist doctrines we can construct an argument entirely analogous to the argument that allegedly showed that propositional-attitude eliminativism is nothing to worry about. For just as the REFERENCE-star relations (REFERENCE*, REFERENCE**, etc.) can be used to formulate a family of claims parallel to propositional-attitude eliminativism, so, too, they can be used to formulate a family of claims parallel to black-hole eliminativism:

> Black-hole eliminativism is true if and only if '_____ is a black hole' refers to nothing.
>
> Black-hole eliminativism* is true if and only if '_____ is a black hole' REFERS* to nothing.
>
> Black-hole eliminativism** is true if and only if '_____ is a black hole' REFERS** to nothing.

And so on. According to the argument that Searle and Gauker were criticizing, there is nothing special about the reference relation. It's just a historical accident that our intuitions happen to favor reference rather than one of the equally idiosyncratic REFERENCE-stars. If that's sufficient to show that propositional-attitude eliminativism isn't interesting or worth worrying about, then it looks like we should draw exactly the same conclusion about black-hole eliminativism (and about big-bang eliminativism, and while we're at it, we might as well throw in God eliminativism, also known as atheism). But this, Searle and Gauker insisted, is just *mad*. If it really is the case that black holes don't exist, or that the big bang didn't occur, it would be enormously interesting and would pose a major challenge to contemporary physics. Of course it is worth worrying about!

In most areas of intellectual activity, there is a fair amount of disagreement about how puzzling or implausible the consequences of a view must be in order to constitute a *reductio ad absurdum* of the view. And in philosophy, more than in most other disciplines, one person's *modus ponens* is another person's *modus tolens*. As will come as no surprise, I tend to be on the *ponens* end of the spectrum. If there is a plausible argument in favor of a doctrine, it requires a substantial collection of implausible consequences before I'm convinced that the doctrine producing those consequences should be rejected. But the Searle/Gauker argument pushed me passed my limit. Clearly, something had gone very wrong. This conviction that there must be some major mistake in the way I was thinking about these issues was reinforced by another objection to my views suggested by Frank Jackson.

As I interpreted it, Jackson's objection focused on the first of the two arguments developed in the previous section. That argument starts with the claim that our intuitions about the reference of terms embedded in theories that we now take to be mistaken may simply be indeterminate, because the folk semantic theory that underlies our intuitions has nothing to say about such cases. From this, it concludes that if folk psychology is indeed a mistaken theory, then the eliminativists' ontological claims are also indeterminate. Claims like: "There are no such things as beliefs" are neither true nor false. What Jackson noted is that there is something rather odd about the way in which our semantic intuitions get to play a central role in determining whether or not beliefs exist. For, if beliefs do in fact exist, then no doubt they have been around for a very long time—probably far longer than people have *had* semantic intuitions. To drive home the point, Jackson also suggested an analogy between propositional-attitude eliminativism and big-bang eliminativism. Suppose it turns out that our current theory about the big bang is wrong in various ways. If so, then by an argument parallel to the first argument in the previous section, it seems to follow that if our semantic intuitions remain silent on such cases, then whether or not the big bang occurred is indeterminate. If, on the other hand, our semantic intuitions are determinate about cases like this, then the big bang really did occur, or (if the intuitions go the other way) it really did not. But this, Jackson protested, is a very strange conclusion. For if the big bang *did* occur, it occurred billions of years before there was anything around that had semantic intuitions. So any view that entails that *our* semantic intuitions play a central role in settling whether or not the big bang occurred is at least a bit paradoxical.

Various moves might be made in response to the argument I'm attributing to Jackson, and thus I don't think the argument is as compelling as the one offered by Searle and Gauker.[44] One reason I found Jackson's argument particularly interesting, however, is that it can be generalized in a way that challenges those whose view on what a theory of reference is supposed to do follows the proto-science line that I sketched in section 6.2. On that view, it will be recalled, our semantic intuitions and the folk semantic theory that underlies them do not play a central role in determining the correct account of reference. Rather, the reference relation is whatever reference-like word–world relation that turns out to play an important explanatory role in linguistics (or perhaps in some other area of science). Suppose this is right. How would it connect with the eliminativism debate? Well, eliminativism as we have been construing it is the view that beliefs (and other propositional attitudes) don't exist. And that's true if and only if '_____ is a belief' refers to nothing. Now let's suppose, as we have been throughout, that terms like '_____ is a belief' are embedded in an opulent tacit theory (folk psychology) and that this theory turns out to be mistaken in lots of ways. Do beliefs exist? It looks like the answer is that we don't know yet, since our colleagues in the linguistics department have not yet settled what reference is. They haven't determined which word–world relation it is that is going to prove useful in their explanatory endeavors. Nor has there been any resolution of the matter in other parts of the university. Cognitive psychologists, anthropologists, historians of science, and others who may invoke the reference relation are in no better position to set out the details of the word–world relation that will facilitate their inquiries. Optimists may think that linguists or others have at least a rough and ready story to tell about the reference relation. But even if that's right (and I rather doubt it), they haven't settled on enough of the details to say when or whether terms embedded in false theories succeed in referring. Until they do, the findings of psychologists, neuroscientists, metaphysicians, and others who (allegedly) have shown that folk psychology is seriously mistaken won't be enough to settle whether '_____ is a belief' refers. And thus we won't know whether or not beliefs exist.

Now, at this point one can well imagine someone who has heard Jackson's argument protesting that something has gone disastrously wrong here. Linguistics, particularly that part of the discipline that deals with reference, is a tiny twig on the tree of science. Yet if the line of thought in the previous paragraph is correct, then this twig on the tree of science (or perhaps some other twig) gets to play a fundamental role in determining whether beliefs exist. Moreover, the oddness generalizes just as it did in Jackson's argument. For it is entirely possible, indeed quite likely, that at some point in the future physicists will become convinced that some important claims in the currently accepted theory about the big bang are mistaken. Some of these physicists may begin thinking that perhaps the big bang did not occur at all. How should they settle the matter? Well, if we adopt the strategy set out in the previous paragraph, it looks like they should take their best available theory, troop down to the linguistics department, and wait patiently until the linguists have reached some firmer view on what reference really is. Needless to say, this is a hopelessly implausible scenario. The scenario is even more peculiar if, as is entirely possible, it turns out that different disciplines find different word–world relations to be most useful to their projects. If linguistics explicates reference in one way, and anthropology (or sociology of science, or . . .) explicates it in a different way, then it may turn out that the physicists in our little story will get conflicting advice. If they listen to the anthropologists, they will have to conclude that the big bang did occur; if they listen to the linguists, they will have to conclude that it didn't. Once again, it looks like we've ended up with a singularly implausible conclusion.

The upshot of all of this is that when plugged into the overall account of the eliminativism debate that I have been working with, *both* accounts of what a theory of reference is supposed to do that were developed in section 6 lead to consequences that strain credulity (at least *my* credulity) to the breaking point. Having reached this point in my own thinking, I could no longer suppress the conclusion that there was a quite catastrophic mistake lurking somewhere in the views I had been defending. Unfortunately, however, while both the Searle/Gauker argument and the Jackson argument make it clear that something has gone wrong, neither the arguments nor the philosophers who suggested them could offer a convincing diagnosis of where exactly the mistake had occurred. Nor, at first, could I. After a while, however, I began to suspect that the real source of my difficulties was to be found in a place I'd never thought of looking.

9 The Ontological Irrelevance of Semantics: Why Semantic Ascent Can't Be Used to Solve Ontological Problems

As I now see it, the crucial mistake in the line of reasoning that I've been recounting in this essay—the misstep that ultimately led to the quite preposterous consequences encountered in the previous section— was one that was taken very early on. It was the step in which I proposed that questions about the existence of entities posited by false theories could be productively addressed by focusing on what the theory of reference tells us about the terms used in such theories. This strategy of trading substantive scientific or metaphysical questions concerning the nature or the existence of entities (questions in the "material mode" as Carnap used to say) for apparently equivalent semantic questions concerning the terms we use in talking about those entities (Carnap's "formal mode" questions) is sometimes called the strategy of *semantic ascent* (see Quine 1960, sec. 56). Resorting to semantic ascent was the crucial error that ultimately led to disaster. More accurately, it was half of the crucial error. The other half was to pay insufficient attention to the distinction between deflationary and nondeflationary accounts of reference. On my current view, semantic ascent and appeal to the theory of reference can be of no help at all in addressing ontological issues. Since eliminativism is an ontological doctrine, appeal to the theory of reference can play no role in determining whether the doctrine is true.

Obviously, this new view of mine will require some unpacking. Let me start by focusing on the strategy of semantic ascent. The general form of the principle that justifies semantic ascent (for reference— there's an analogous story to be told about truth) might be put roughly as follows:

(1) (x) Px iff 'P_____' refers to (or is satisfied by) x.

Less formally, what (1) says is that an entity is a P if and only if the predicate 'P_____' refers to it. (1) can be viewed as an axiom schema whose instances include claims like:

(2) (x) x is a black hole iff 'black hole' refers to x.

and

(3) (x) x is a belief iff 'belief' refers to x.

Obviously, (2) and

(4) ~(∃x) 'black hole' refers to x

entail

(5) ~(∃x) x is a black hole.

Similarly, (3) along with

(6) ~(∃x) 'belief' refers to x

entail

(7) ~(∃x) x is a belief.

So, if we have a theory of reference which tells us that terms in seriously mistaken theories do not refer, and if we are prepared to grant that 'belief' is such a term, then these claims along with (3) will entail that beliefs don't exist. And that is pretty much the way my ill-fated line of reasoning began.

But what about (3) and the other instances of (1). What justification do we have for them? No justification was offered on the many occasions when I've invoked (or presupposed) instances of (1) in my arguments, either in this chapter or elsewhere. I've always simply assumed that instances of (1) are so obvious that they need no justification; indeed, they hardly need to be stated. But are they? As I now see it, the answer turns on whether or not the notion of reference being invoked is a deflationary notion. If it is, then instances of (1) are indeed trivial. But if reference is understood as a deflationary notion, then instances of (1) are also quite useless for our purposes. They provide no help at all in determining whether theoretical terms embedded in a seriously mistaken theory refer to anything. If, on the other hand, reference is taken to be a nondeflationary notion, then instances of (1) may well be helpful in settling whether or not terms in a mistaken theory refer. But on nondeflationary accounts of reference, (1) and it's instances are themselves problematic. If they are true, they are not obviously true. They aren't premises we get for free. So if we are going to invoke them in arguments for or against eliminativism, we are going to need an argument that supports them. And I, for one, haven't a clue about what the argument might be.

In defending this cluster of claims, I'll begin by elaborating a bit on what I mean by *deflationary* accounts of reference. These accounts, which are modeled on deflationary accounts of truth, take terms like 'refers' 'denotes' and 'designates' to be quasi-logical devices that earn their keep by facilitating semantic ascent and descent. On these accounts, the schema (1) or something like it captures the entire meaning of 'refers'. It tells us all there is to tell about the nature of the reference relation. So, on these accounts (3) and its kin really are trivial and obvious; indeed, on some versions of the deflationist story, they are analytic.[45] Thus, if 'refers' is read in a deflationary way, then if we can establish that 'belief' refers to nothing [= (6)], we can infer that there are no beliefs. But of course, on a deflationary story, reference is not determined by a complex causal chain or by any other empirically investigatable "naturalistic" relation. So we can't attempt to determine whether 'belief' refers by exploring whether anything lies at the other end of an appropriate reference fixing causal chain. Rather, (3) itself provides us with our only way of finding out whether 'belief' refers to anything. The answer is yes if and only if something is a belief. But now what shall we say about brain states (or functional states, or dispositional states, or whatever else you might fancy) that have some but not all of the features attributed to beliefs by folk psychology? Does 'belief' refer to *them*? The only answer we get from deflationary accounts of reference is that it does *if and only if they are beliefs*. Obviously, there is no hope of making progress here. We are tugging at our own bootstraps.

Let's turn, now, to nondeflationary accounts of reference. For our purposes, any account of reference that isn't deflationary will be nondeflationary. This includes causal-historical accounts, description accounts, and perhaps others as well. Some of these accounts seem to offer a promising way of breaking out of the circle sketched in the previous paragraph. If reference is some naturalistic relation, then we can try to use the techniques of science and history to determine whether or not a problematic term refers to something. But it's my contention that on nondeflationary accounts we need some argument for accepting (3) and other instances of (1). We don't get them for free.

Perhaps the easiest way to make the point is to focus on causal-historical accounts of reference, though everything I say in the next few paragraphs could be recast, mutatis mutandis, if we were to focus instead on description-based accounts. As we saw in section 7, given any detailed specification of a causal-historical reference relation—a relation mapping words on to entities and classes or kinds in the world—it is an easy matter to construct alternative relations that map words to the world in a different way. By fiddling with the specification of what counts as an acceptable grounding, or with the specification of what counts as a reference preserving transmission, or by making various other modifications, we can generate an array of word-world mapping relations (REFERENCE*, REFERENCE**, etc.) that differ from the specified relation. Some of the alternatives may depart from the specified relation in only one case, some in a few cases, and still others may depart massively. Let us call the causal-historical relation that, according to our favorite theory, determines the actual reference relation "C-H-link-r". Also, let's use "C-H-link-R*" as a label for the causal-historical relation that determines REFERENCE*, "C-H-link-R**" as a label for the relation that determines REFERENCE**, etc. Using this terminology, (1) is equivalent to:

(C-H 1) (x) Px iff C-H-link-r ('P___', x).

Less formally, what this says is that an entity is a P if and only if it stands in the C-H-link-r relation to the predicate 'P___'. But, of course, for each of the alternative word–world mappings, there is a schema analogous to (C-H 1):

(C-H 1*) (x) Px iff C-H-link-R* ('P___', x).

(C-H 1**) (x) Px iff C-H-link-R** ('P___', x). etc.

Clearly, it can't be the case that *all* these schemata are correct. Since C-H-link-r and C-H-link-R* are different relations, there is at least one predicate, 'P___', and one entity, x, such that if 'P___' stands in the C-H-link-r relation to x, then 'P___' does not stand in the C-H-link-R* relation to x, or vice versa. Why, then, should we suppose that

(C-H 1) is correct and that all the others are mistaken? Surely, it is not *obvious* that, for example, all and only pigs stand in the C-H-link-r relation to the predicate '_____ is a pig'; nor is it *obvious* that all and only black holes stand in the C-H-link-r relation to the predicate '_____ is a black hole'. Let me stress that I am not claiming that these instances of (C-H 1) aren't true. It is, I suppose, entirely possible that they are. My claim is simply that we need an argument to show us that they're true. Contrary to what I once assumed, these claims are far from trivial.

Presumably, a plausible argument aimed at establishing the truth of instances of (C-H 1) would rely heavily on one or the other account, sketched in section 6, of what it is to get a theory of reference right. For it is these accounts that show us how to justify the claim that C-H-link-r is to be identified with reference. Those who favor the account in section 6.1 will try to show how the fact that C-H-link-r is sanctioned by intuition (or folk semantics) can be used to establish that all instances of (C-H 1) must be true. While those who favor the account in section 6.2 will try to show how the fact that C-H-link-r is central to the explanatory purposes of linguistics (or anthropology or cognitive psychology) guarantees that all instances of (C-H 1) are true. Unfortunately, I know of no argument along these lines that is even remotely plausible. And without such an argument, the attempt to use semantic ascent to determine whether or not the entities invoked in false theories exist grinds to a halt.

During a seminar on these matters, Hartry Field suggested what might seem to be a tempting strategy for dealing with the difficulty. The basic idea is to make the semantic-ascent principle[46] a constraint on any acceptable nondeflationary account of reference. Thus, for example, a theorist who accepts the account in section 6.1 might say that the right word–world relation (the one that really is reference) is the one that meets a pair of constraints. First, it must be a relation that does a good job at capturing our intuitions about a wide range of cases, and, second, it must satisfy the semantic-ascent principle. Any relation that doesn't satisfy that principle just will not count as the reference relation. The imposition of this constraint might itself be justified by appeal to intuition, since (1) is arguably the most intuitively obvious fact about reference. Theorists who accept the account in section 6.2 can make much the same move. On their view, it is the sciences (linguistics or anthropology or what have you) that get to say which word–world relation reference is. But there is a constraint on their endeavors. Whatever relation they come up with must satisfy the semantic ascent principle. If it doesn't, then it isn't the reference relation. This move has the added attraction of ending the worry that different sciences might find different word–world relations important in their explanatory pursuits. This could still happen, of course. Linguistics might characterize its favored word–world relation in one way, and anthropology could characterize its favored relation in a very different way. However, the relations characterized will not count as reference unless they both satisfy the semantic-ascent principle. And if they both satisfy the principle, then, since relations are individuated extensionally, *they are the same relation*. The relation may be described or picked out very differently in different sciences. But if the relations favored in different sciences all satisfy (1), then for any given term the favored word–world relations must all pick out exactly the same referents. Problem solved!

Well, not quite. For as Field also pointed out, the strategy of building in semantic ascent as a constraint on reference really just hides the problem, it doesn't solve it. Perhaps the easiest way to see the point is to consider a situation in which a pair of theorists agree about the premises of the eliminativists' argument but disagree about the conclusion. Theorist A grants that folk psychology is mistaken in various ways and thus that there is nothing in the world that has all of the properties that folk psychology attributes to beliefs. But theorist A does not think this shows that beliefs don't exist. For theorist A also has a theory of reference which specifies a relation, R (for concreteness, we can imagine it is a causal-historical relation of the sort championed by Lycan). In addition, theorist A has a pretty persuasive argument that the predicate '_____ is a belief' stands in the R relation to certain neurophysiological states (or functional states, or whatever). "So," he argues, "we can conclude that beliefs do exist, since 'belief' stands in the R relation to these neurophysiological states, and R is the reference relation, and the reference relation satisfies the principle of semantic ascent. Q.E.D." Theorist B, an eliminativist, is not persuaded. "Look," she replies, "all you've done is establish that R is not the reference relation. It can't be, because, as you have shown, 'belief' stands in the R relation to these neurophysiological states, and these neurophysiological states *aren't beliefs*. Thus, your R relation fails to satisfy semantic ascent. So, it's not reference. Q.E.D. to you too!"

Obviously, this dispute isn't going to get settled until we determine whether or not the neurophysiological states are beliefs. And appeal to the theory of reference is going to be of exactly no help in that since we can't tell whether the proposed reference relation satisfies the semantic-ascent constraint unless we already know whether the neurophysiological states are beliefs. I think the moral to be drawn from this little tale is clear. If satisfying semantic ascent is proposed as a requirement that any acceptable account of reference must meet, then appeal to the theory of reference can be of no help in resolving contested ontological questions. For without some independent way of settling these contested ontological questions, we have no way of knowing whether the principle of semantic ascent is satisfied. And if we *have* some independent way to resolve contested ontological questions, we don't *need* the theory of reference.[47]

10   *Another Approach: The Appeal to "Constitutive" Properties*

In my own earlier work, and in the work of most other authors who were (or still are) seriously tempted by eliminativism, the strategy of semantic ascent and an explicit or implicit appeal to description-based theories of reference played a central role in getting from the Premises of the eliminativists' argument to the conclusions. A central goal of the last six sections has been to explain why I now think this route is singularly unpromising. My project of deconstructing the eliminativists' deconstruction is not yet complete, however, for in some of the literature on eliminativism, there are hints of a very different strategy for filling the gap between the eliminativists' Premises and their conclusions. Rather than relying on a theory of reference, this alternative strategy invokes the notion of *constitutive* or *conceptually necessary* properties. The central idea is that some of our concepts require, as a matter of logical or conceptual necessity, that any object to which the concept applies must have certain properties. We would not apply the concept to an object or count the object as falling within the category that the concept specifies (or, at least, we *ought* not to do so) unless the object has the constitutive properties. Thus, for example, it might be urged that being unmarried and being male are constitutive properties for the concept of a bachelor, or that having a negative charge is constitutive for the concept of an electron. So, if something is not male and unmarried, then it *can't* be a bachelor, and if something does not have a negative charge, then it *can't* be an electron. Both of these would be "conceptually impossible."[48]

It's easy to see how the notion of a constitutive property might be used to fill the gap between the Premises and the conclusions in the eliminativists' argument. If it can be shown that a certain property is conceptually necessary for having beliefs, or for having propositional attitudes in general, and if science (or philosophical argument) can demonstrate that no one has that property, it follows that no one has beliefs or propositional attitudes. However, it's my view that this strategy is even less promising than the one that relies on description theories of reference. My skepticism is based on a pair of distinct though related considerations.

The first is that it is far from obvious how a theorist who wants to invoke this strategy could establish that one or another property is indeed conceptually necessary for something to count as a belief or for someone to count as having beliefs. Obviously, the mere fact that lots of people think, or claim, or presuppose that all beliefs or believers have a certain property is not enough to show that the property in question is conceptually necessary. Nor would it be sufficient to show that many people would refuse to apply the term 'belief' to a state that lacked the property. For it might simply be the case that most people (or indeed all people) happen to have some strongly held opinions about beliefs and that these opinions are false. There was, after all, a time at which most people would have refused to apply the term 'star' to an object that did not have the property of rotating around the earth. But as we now know, they had some deeply entrenched false opinions about stars and about the earth, and it was these opinions rather than any conceptual impossibility that was responsible for their refusal.

Actually, if we look at the literature in which the notion of conceptually necessary properties is invoked, there is no serious effort to establish what most people claim about beliefs, nor is there any evidence offered about the percentage of speakers who are willing or reluctant to apply the term 'belief' to particular cases. What we find instead are just assertions that one or another property strikes the author as essential or constitutive. Here is a typical example from Andy Clark:

> It is plausible to require that any being who can be said to grasp a concept C must be capable of judging that she has made a mistake in some previous application of C. . . . It seems to me conceptually impossible for a being to count as grasping a concept and yet be incapable of ever having any conscious experience involving it. That is, part of what we *mean* when we say that someone grasps the concept 'dog' is that, on occasion, the person has conscious mental experiences which involve that very concept. . . . If I am right, the very idea of a True Believer thus builds in two demands (consciousness and the ability to issue genuine judgements about its own past performance) which scientific investigations might reveal not be met in specific cases. (1993, 216–18)[49]

In another publication, where he offers a rather different account of what is conceptually necessary for having a thought or a belief, Clark launches his defense of his proposal as follows: "It remains to pump our intuitions. Here are mine" (1991, 217).

Now the striking thing about these claims and the intuitions that putatively support them is how little agreement there is among the theorists offering them. Some writers maintain that "rationality" and the potential for "logical combination" are essential (Rey 1991). Others deny it.[50] Some insist that "causal efficacy" or having "causal powers" is essential.[51] Others insist that it is not.[52] Some writers agree with Clark's consciousness requirement, though many others find it to be intuitively implausible. And I have yet to find anyone whose intuitions match Clark's in requiring "the ability to issue genuine judgements about its own past performance," since, as Clark readily acknowledges, it is almost certainly the case that household pets and other nonhuman animals fail to satisfy this requirement. Thus, the condition would rule that it is "conceptually impossible" for the family dog to have beliefs!

Since appeal to intuition seems to be the preferred methodological option for those attempting to justify the claim that one or another property is constitutive or conceptually necessary for belief, the existence of widely divergent intuitions obviously poses a major obstacle for anyone who hopes to use the strategy we're considering for linking the Premises of the eliminativists' argument with the conclusions. But I am inclined to think that this practical problem is actually just a symptom of a much deeper theoretical problem. In the current philosophical environment, the very existence of properties that are constitutive or conceptually necessary for the application of one or another concept is hardly an assumption that can be taken for granted. For if some properties are constitutive for a concept, and others are not, and if, as Clark and others suggest,[53] claims about concepts are interchangeable with claims about what our words mean, then it seems there must also be some sentences that are true entirely in virtue of meaning and others whose truth or falsity depends in part on the way the world is. That is, there must be some sentences that are *analytic* and others that are *synthetic*. If, for example, being unmarried is constitutive or conceptually necessary for being a bachelor, then presumably "All bachelors are unmarried" is analytic. And if having causal potency is conceptually necessary for being a belief, then "All beliefs are causally potent" is analytic. Starting more than forty years ago, however, Quine and others offered some enormously influential arguments aimed at showing that the analytic/synthetic distinction is untenable.[54] On Quine's view, and on the view of many other philosophers as well, there are no sentences that are true solely in virtue of their meaning. If this is right, then there are no constitutive or conceptually necessary properties. So it is hardly surprising that those who think that there are conceptually necessary conditions for being a belief or a believer have trouble agreeing about what they are.

I don't propose to review the arguments against the existence of the analytic/synthetic distinction in this essay. Indeed, for current purposes I don't even need to assume that the conclusion of those arguments is correct, though as it happens I think it is. All that is needed here is the observation that the very existence of analytic truths, and thus of constitutive or conceptually necessary properties, is hotly disputed and highly problematic. So, those who want to fill the gap in the eliminativists' argument by invoking the notion of constitutive properties owe us some further argument. They must either make it plausible that the arguments against the existence of the analytic/synthetic distinction are mistaken or that the notion of a conceptually necessary property can be made sense of without presupposing or entailing the existence of analytic sentences. Having done that, they must go on to defend specific claims about the properties that are conceptually necessary for beliefs, and (if it turns out that intuitions are relevant—it's far from obvious that they are) they must explain away the intuitions of those whose intuitions run counter to these claims. Obviously, accomplishing all of this would be no easy task. If there are philosophers who

chose to follow this path in defending eliminativism, I certainly wish
them well. But I don't propose to hold my breath until they succeed.[55]

11   Starting Over: Normative Naturalism and the Search for Principles of Rational Ontological Inference

From the eliminativists' point of view, the results that we've reached so
far have been entirely negative. Even if we grant the most promising
version of the eliminativists' Premises, I've argued, the conclusions
don't follow. Nor is it likely that we can fill the gap by appealing to a
theory of reference or by invoking the notion of a constitutive property.
But, of course, the fact that the eliminativists' conclusions don't follow
from their Premises doesn't indicate that those conclusions are wrong.
Moreover, it hardly seems plausible that the eliminativists' Premises are
totally irrelevant to claims about the existence or nonexistence of beliefs
and other propositional attitudes. Surely, if it is the case that our folk
theory about the propositional attitudes is seriously mistaken, that is
something that should be taken into account in determining whether
propositional attitudes exist. But how? This is, of course, just a special
case of a much more general question that has now moved to center
stage in our exercise in deconstruction: How are we to go about deciding whether or not the entities posited by *any* false theory exist? If we
can't turn to the theory of reference or exploit claims about constitutive
properties, how are these ontological issues to be settled?

11.1   The Normative-Naturalist Strategy

An answer that might seem attractive at this point is suggested by a
strategy that has been much discussed in the philosophy of science in
recent years. What we need is some way to determine whether or not it
would be rational to conclude that a given type of entity exists, in the
face of various sorts of findings about the shortcomings of the theories
in which entities of this type play a role. One way to proceed would be
to see if we can extract some normative principles—principles of rational ontological inference or decision making—from a study of actual
historical cases in which these sorts of decisions have already been
made.

Here's how this project might unfold. We begin by assembling a
collection of historical cases in which it was ultimately decided that the
posits of mistaken theories did not exist and another collection of historical cases in which it was decided that the posits of mistaken theories
did exist, despite the mistaken claims that the theories had made about
them. Caloric, phlogiston, Vulcan, and witches might be plausible candidates for the first set; stars, atoms, planets, and brains might be candidates for the second. With these two sets of cases in hand, we can begin
to look for salient similarities and differences. Are there apparently rel-

evant features of the defective theory, or of the problematic posit, or of the relation of the theory to other theories, that are present in most or all the cases in one set and absent in most or all the cases in the other? If the answer is yes, we can use these features to formulate candidate principles specifying when it is rationally appropriate to retain items in the ontology of a mistaken theory and when it is appropriate to "eliminate" them. The tentative principles can then be tested against additional historical cases that were not part of the original data base. If the principles endorse the decisions that were actually made in these additional cases, this will count in favor of the principles. If the principles endorse the opposite decision in one or more of these cases, it will indicate that we should make some adjustments in the principles and try again. Once we have formulated a reasonably robust set of principles that handles lots of the clear historical cases, we could set about testing the principles against our intuitions about a range of hypothetical cases, provided of course that we have such intuitions and are inclined to trust them. In pursuing this strategy, we need not always modify our principles when they come into conflict with an actual historical case. If a given set of principles for rational ontological decision making does a good job at capturing most actual cases, we may decide that in a few historical cases people made the wrong decision; their ontological inference was not a rational one. Similarly, we need not always modify our principles when they come into conflict with a firmly held intuition about a hypothetical case. Rather, we may decide that our intuition in that case is misguided.

The strategy set out in the previous paragraph is something of a hybrid. The part of the story that relies on intuitions resembles the "reflective equilibrium" account of the justification of inferential principles that was given its most famous formulation by Nelson Goodman.[56] The part that attends to actual historical cases is modeled on the strategies for uncovering normative principles of scientific reasoning and inquiry that are sometimes labeled *normative naturalism*.[57] Obviously, there is room for many variations on the pattern that I've sketched, some stressing historical cases and downplaying the role of intuition, others going in just the opposite direction.[58] Some researchers have used a normative-naturalist strategy to test discursively formulated methodological principles,[59] while others, most notably Herbert Simon and his colleagues, have attempted to produce computer simulations of the reasoning processes that have led to important discoveries in the history of science.[60] Also, as Simon and his coworkers have urged, there are ways to supplement the largely historical approach to locating principles of scientific reasoning with experimental studies in which scientists are asked to solve unfamiliar problems (see, for example, Qin and Simon 1990 and Dunbar 1989).

There has been relatively little work along normative naturalist lines aimed explicitly at uncovering principles of rational ontological inference that might be useful in assessing the eliminativists' argument.

The most interesting study I know of in this area is Robert McCauley's exploration of the way in which tensions between theories at the same and at different "levels of analysis" lead to theoretical and ontological elimination. McCauley offers no detailed definition of "level of analysis," though the intuitive idea is familiar enough. "Broadly speaking, chemistry is a higher level of analysis than subatomic particle physics, ... biology is an even higher level, and psychology higher than that" (1986, 72). Building on the work of Wimsatt (1976a; 1976b), McCauley reviews various episodes in the history of science and offers an interesting and provocative conclusion. When a new theory comes into conflict with an older one at the same level of analysis, and when the new theory is better than the old one, "the superior theory eliminates its competitor (and its ontology)" (1986, 75). However, when theories at different levels of analysis come into conflict, the story is quite different. *"The history of science reveals no precedent for theory replacement or elimination in interlevel contexts"* (79–80; emphasis in original). On McCauley's view, this finding has clear implications for the version of the eliminativist argument offered by Paul Churchland. Both commonsense psychology and cognitive psychology *"operate at different levels of analysis"* from neuroscience (79; emphasis in original). Thus, even if it does turn out, as Churchland insists it will, that neuroscience and common sense psychology are "incommensurable," it would, McCauley maintains, be incorrect to "conclude . . . that such incommensurability requires the elimination of one or the other" (79).

I am not entirely comfortable with McCauley's analysis of the historical record since he is often less careful than one might wish about distinguishing between the "elimination" of theories and the "elimination" of their ontology. But that's not a worry I propose to pursue here. For current purposes, what's important about McCauley's work is that it illustrates the way in which a normative naturalist might begin to make progress in determining what conclusion it would be rational to draw from the eliminativists' Premises. If McCauley is right, and if the eliminativist defends the Second Premise by arguing for a "radical incommensurability" or "logical inconsistency" (1986, 77) between neuroscience and folk psychology, no elimination of the ontology of folk psychology is rationally warranted. This is, of course, only one among many ways in which eliminativists might try to defend the Second Premise. So there's lots more work to be done. Still, one might hope that for each sort of defense that eliminativists offer for the Second Premise, normative naturalists could determine whether the eliminativists' argument, fleshed out in that way, rationally supports the ontological conclusion that eliminativists wish to draw.[61]

11.2   *Two Reasons for Skepticism*

The normative-naturalist strategy that I've been recounting is certainly an intriguing one, and perhaps it will ultimately succeed. But for two rather different reasons, I am inclined to be more than a bit skeptical. The first reason for my skepticism turns on the normative status of the principles of reasoning (or inference or inquiry) that the normative naturalist strategy sanctions. If normative naturalists are right, then the principles produced by the process they recommend are *rational* principles; the conclusions to which the principles point are conclusions we *ought* to accept, provided of course that we accept the premises. But why, exactly, ought we to accept them? What gives these principles their normative force? This is a complex issue on which there has been some vigorous debate in recent years.[62] Since I have staked out my own position elsewhere (Stich 1990, chap. 6; 1993b), I'll restrict myself to two brief observations. First, it is a mistake to ask why *the* normative-naturalist strategy yields principles of rational inference since there isn't *one* normative-naturalist strategy, there are *many* whose relation to one another is best viewed as a loose family resemblance. And while it may be the case that all of these strategies will converge in sanctioning some principles, it is very likely indeed that there will be other principles on whose normative status they will disagree. So, a serious defense of the normative naturalist strategy must say why *one specific member* of this family of strategies is the right one—the one that can be counted upon to produce principles of reasoning that we ought to accept. And that, needless to say, is no easy task. My second observation is that some attempts to defend the normative credentials of normative-naturalist procedures (including Laudan's and my own) have a decidedly relativist flavor. The principles sanctioned by normative naturalism are claimed to be hypothetical imperatives. They are principles that we ought to follow *if* we have certain goals. If our goals are different, the normative-naturalist procedure may well sanction different principles. However, in many intellectual controversies, including the debate over eliminativism, it is far from clear that all parties to the dispute share the same goals. And if they don't, then normative naturalism may recommend different conclusions to different people. I am inclined to think that these two observations justify at least a bit of skepticism about the normative-naturalist approach in general.

My second reason for being skeptical about the normative-naturalist strategy focuses more sharply on what we can expect normative naturalism to tell us about patterns of ontological inference, including the sort of inference that could get us from the eliminativists' Premises to their conclusions. Even if we grant that the output of the normative-naturalist procedure will be principles that rational people ought to follow, it is important to realize that there is no *guarantee* that this approach will succeed in resolving our problem about what to conclude from the eliminativists' Premises. For it is entirely possible that there simply are no normative principles of ontological reasoning to be found, or at least none that are strong enough and comprehensive enough to specify what we should conclude if the Premises of the eliminativists' arguments are true. We might well find that in many cases in which ontological inferences have been made, there are no features of the theories involved, the sorts of errors they make, or the properties attributed to the items in their ontology that are systematically correlated with the ontological conclusions that have been accepted in the history of science. We might also find that facts about the defective theory and its problematic posits do not suffice to generate clear and intersubjectively consistent intuitions about how the ontological decision ought to go. In those historical cases in which widely accepted ontological conclusions were drawn, it is reasonable to suppose that there must be *some* explanation for which way the decision went. And if, in some of those cases (or many), normative principles remain silent, then other factors must have been involved. But these additional factors may be significantly different in different cases. Moreover, in some cases it might turn out that the outcome was heavily influenced by the personalities of the people involved or by social and political factors in the relevant scientific community or in the wider society in which the scientific community is embedded. If this is right, then the normative-naturalist strategy may well fail to produce principles of reasoning that tell us what ontological conclusion to draw about entities invoked in mistaken theories.

While I don't pretend to have enough evidence to mount a conclusive case, it is my bet that this outcome is exactly what we would find if we launched a serious and systematic study of the relevant historical cases. Here is a brief and admittedly speculative list of some of the kinds of cases that I suspect a careful scrutiny of actual examples will uncover.

1. *Don't cares.* In some cases, it just doesn't much matter to anyone whether theorists conclude that some of the entities invoked in a mistaken theory really do exist, though their properties are quite different from those attributed to them by the old theory, or whether they conclude that there are no such things—that some of the theoretical terms in the old theory didn't refer to anything—and that the phenomena that need explaining are best explained by invoking different theoretical entities. In these "don't care" cases, the decision will be made more or less arbitrarily. This may well be what happened with electrons, which were, according to Fine (1975, 24ff.), originally conceived of not as particles but as units of quantity of electric charge. It may also be what is happening now with genes. Modern molecular genetics recognizes nothing that has all of the important properties attributed to genes by Mendel, De Vries, T. H. Morgan, Muller, and the other pioneers of modern genetics. Should we conclude that there are no such things as genes? Or should we conclude that genes do exist, though Mendel and others were seriously mistaken in many of the claims they made about them? There has, it seems, been no firm decision reached in the relevant scientific communities. Eventually, one suspects, the

matter will be resolved, though it may be that little hangs on the issue, and no one much cares which way the decision ultimately goes.[63]

2. *Implicit previous agreements.* In some cases, there may be an implicit agreement in the relevant scientific community that some property or set of properties are the essential ones for some posited entity and that if it turns out that nothing has those properties, then everyone in the community would agree that the entity doesn't exist. I used to think that the history of the aether might well be an example of this sort of case. What was important about the aether, I thought, was that it was uniform and stationary, and thus could provide "the fundamental frame for inertial systems" (Gillespie 1960, 509). So, when Michelson and Morley showed that this conception of the aether was untenable, everyone would agree that there is no aether. It appears, however, that the historical situation was actually considerably more complicated and that some theorists advocated retaining the aether, even though they agreed that it was "undetectable in principle" (510). So, perhaps this case is not a good example of a widely shared implicit agreement.

3. *Social and political factors internal to the relevant science.* According to Kim Sterelny, Elliott Sober once conjectured that had Lavoisier wished to be viewed less as a radical innovator and more as a conservative, he might have retained a venerable old term rather than introducing a new one. And rather than maintaining that there is no such thing as phlogiston, he might instead have claimed that Priestley, Stahl, and earlier theorists were simply mistaken about lots of the properties they attributed to phlogiston. So, if Lavoisier had a somewhat different personality, what we now call "oxygen" would be called "phlogiston" instead.[64] I have no idea whether Lavoisier's temperament and the pragmatic or political consequences of being thought to be radical or conservative played any significant role in this case. (I've checked with Sober, and he doesn't have any evidence bearing on the case; indeed, he can't recall making the comment.) But it is my guess that personalities and the micropolitics of scientific communities often play an important role in situations like this.[65] In some situations, it is easier to get a grant or a promotion or to enhance one's reputation in the scientific community by announcing the discovery of a new entity or denying the existence of one previously claimed to exist. In other situations, it is more politically expedient to conclude that entities of a certain sort don't have some of the properties previously attributed to them and that experimental results or other phenomena can best be explained by attributing some rather different properties to those entities. Which conclusion the scientific community ultimately accepts may well be determined, in some cases, by factors like these.

4. *Broader social and political factors.* During the last decade or two, a growing number of serious and well-educated people have claimed that witches really did exist at the time of the Inquisition and that they still do. However, they also maintain that witches make no pact with the

devil, cast no evil spells, and do not practice black magic (or ride on broomsticks!). These allegations are myths, misunderstandings, or slanders spread about witches by people who know little about witchcraft and also, less innocently, by religious and political enemies. Contemporary people who take themselves to be witches claim that they, like witches in earlier centuries, are practitioners of

> an ancient nature-religion . . . in which the earth [is] worshipped as a woman under different names and guises throughout the inhabited world. . . . [Witches] try to create for themselves the tone and feeling of an earlier humanity, worshipping a nature they understand as vital, powerful and mysterious. . . . Above all, witches try to 'connect' with the world around them. Witchcraft . . . is about the tactile, intuitive understanding of the turn of the seasons, the song of the birds; it is the awareness of all things as holy, and that, as is said, there is no part of us that is not of the gods. . . . The Goddess, the personification of nature, is witchcraft's central concept. . . . The Goddess is very different from the Judeo-Christian god. She is in the world, of the world, the very being of the world. . . . Witchcraft is a secretive otherworld, and more than other magical practices, it is rich in symbolic, special items. (Luhrmann 1989, 45–48)[66]

Modern witches practice some rather unusual rituals, which they believe to be similar to rites practiced by witches in earlier centuries. Most of them are performed in the nude (48–49). It is hardly surprising that these people have a penchant for secrecy, since their neighbors tend to view such behavior as bizarre, immoral, or threatening. Many of those who practice these rituals also maintain that some of the women who were burned at the stake as witches very likely were witches, though they had not had any commerce with the devil and had not done any harm to anyone. Others who were burned as witches probably were not witches at all, they contend, but simply demented old women or victims of various social or political vendettas.

In the liberal democracies of the late twentieth century, the assertion that witches exist and that some of the people who were executed for being witches really were witches, though they had harmed no one and made no pact with the devil, is no doubt a rather eccentric thing to say, though the consequences of saying it are (one hopes) likely to be benign. In sixteenth-century Europe, however, the consequences of making the same statement might well have been very different. At that time, people who held the view that none of the women accused of being witches had made a pact with the devil or caused any harm, and that these women ought not to be tortured or put to death, might be much more effective if they insisted that witches are myths—that they simply do not exist—and thus that all of the women accused of being witches are falsely accused. That, near enough, is what many of them did say and what most of us say as well.

Similar sorts of political considerations color the contemporary debate over homosexuality. While no one denies that same sex sexual activity occurs, there is some reason to believe that many widely held beliefs about sexual preference, homosexuality, and homosexual people are false. This has led some to conclude that there is no such thing as homosexuality or that there are no homosexual people. Others (including some gay and lesbian activists) argue that this is exactly the wrong conclusion to draw. Rather, they insist, homosexuality and homosexuals do indeed exist, though many claims made about them are false. I think it is pretty clear that this dispute is in large measure a political dispute. Both sides agree that there is no kind or condition that has all the features commonly attributed to homosexuality. What is really in dispute is how hatred, prejudice, and discrimination in this area are best confronted and overcome.[67]

The skeptical conjecture that I've been trying to make plausible in the last few pages is that the normative-naturalist strategy will not uncover principles of rational ontological inference that are rich enough to tell us, in lots of the most interesting cases, what ontological conclusions we ought to draw when we come to believe that some previously accepted theory is seriously mistaken. In support of this conjecture, I've suggested that in many historical cases the resolution of ontological questions can be explained in part by the personalities of those involved or by social and political factors in the relevant scientific community or in the surrounding society. This is a descriptive claim about the ways in which ontological questions have in fact been resolved. One might, however, be tempted to think that there is also a normative conclusion to be wrung from this descriptive claim. And since I find such temptations hard to resist, let me sketch how the argument might go.

Suppose it is the case that social and political negotiations of the sort I've been sketching played an important role in determining the ontological conclusions that were accepted, in the history of science, about atoms, stars, electrons, and brains and about caloric, phlogiston, and the aether. Surely, it is rational for us now to believe that stars and electrons, etc., exist and that caloric and phlogiston, etc. don't. But if it is rational for us to hold these beliefs, and if social and political negotiations played an essential role in determining what we now believe, then such negotiations are sometimes an important part of the process leading to rational scientific belief. Moreover, it seems plausible to assume that any process that leads to the formation of a rational belief counts as a rational process. If that's right, then social negotiations are sometimes an important part of the rational process of belief revision in science.

I am, I hasten to add, not entirely comfortable in urging this conclusion, since the argument that supports it helps itself to lots of assumptions about rationality, and I have no idea how those assumptions could be defended.[68] Indeed, I suspect that debates about assumptions like these are best viewed as moves in the vehement social and political negotiations over the role and authority of science in contemporary society. But that's a theme I will have to save for some other occasion.

11.3   Eliminativism and Politics

I don't think that the brief and rather breezy discussion of the previous section comes at all close to establishing my skeptical thesis about normative naturalism. Indeed, the only way to make a persuasive case for (or against) my claim that the naturalist strategy will not produce principles of ontological inference that are powerful enough to assess eliminativist arguments is to do lots of careful historical research and lots of detailed cognitive modeling. And that's a project for scholars with skills very different from mine. But suppose it turns out that I'm right. What then?

Well, if there are no principles of rational ontological inference to guide us in deciding what to conclude from the eliminativists' Premises, then the question will have to be settled in some other way. It is my guess that a good deal of the debate over what conclusion to draw about the existence or nonexistence of the posits of commonsense psychology is best viewed as falling under heading 3 in my list in section 11.2. Support for this view can be found in some surprising places. Here is a passage in which Patricia Churchland, widely regarded as a leading advocate of eliminativism, is discussing how it is decided whether to retain or eliminate the entities and properties invoked by a theory, when that theory is reduced to a theory in a more basic science:

> If a reduction is smooth, in the sense that most principles of T_R [the theory that is to be reduced] have close analogues in T_B [the more basic reducing theory], then the matching of cohort terms denoting properties can proceed and identities can be claimed. Informally, a similarity-fit means that property P_R of the reduced theory has much the same causal powers as the cohort property P_B of the basic theory.
>
> Determining when the fit is close enough to claim identities between properties and entities of the old and those of the new is not a matter for formal criteria, and the decision is influenced by a variety of pragmatic and social considerations. The whim of the central investigators, the degree to which confusion will result from retention of the old terms, the desire to preserve or to break with past habits of thought, the related opportunities for publicizing the theory, cadging for grants, and attracting disciples all enter into decisions concerning whether to claim identities and therewith retention or whether to make the more radical claim of displacement. (P. S. Churchland, 1986, 283–84)[69]

I am also inclined to think that some of the debate over commonsense psychology falls under heading 4 since the conclusions that scientists and scholars advocate about the existence or nonexistence of commonsense mental states may well have a very significant impact on broader political and social issues. Consider, for example, the question

of how to treat people who are mentally or emotionally ill. Making a persuasive political case for public funding of various forms of psychotherapy, particularly "cognitive" psychotherapy with its focus on removing false beliefs and changing unrealistic expectations, will be significantly more difficult if leading scientists and philosophers insist that there are no such things as beliefs and expectations or that they play no role in a suitably scientific understanding of the causation of human behavior. On the other hand, those who would urge the wider use of psychoactive drugs in treating mental and social problems may find their case significantly easier to make if the eliminativists succeed in persuading lots of people that commonsense mental states are myths.[70]

If the account of ontological decision making that I've been sketching is on the right track, and if, as we have been assuming, commonsense psychology turns out to be mistaken in important ways, then, for a while at least—and perhaps for a very long while—indeterminacy looms. The question we have been pursuing since the end of section 3—"What conclusion should be drawn about the existence of intentional states?"—will have no determinate answer until the political negotiations that are central to the decision have been resolved. When those negotiations are finished and we have reached a broad social consensus, the conclusion that wins will have much the same status as the conclusions that were reached in the case of stars or atoms or phlogiston.[71] If, in the spirit of the argument at the end of section 11.2, we are prepared to say, in retrospect, that the conclusions reached about the existence of stars, atoms, and phlogiston are the ones that rational people should accept, then the same will be true for the conclusion reached about the existence of intentional states, whatever that conclusion turns out to be. I've been warned more than once that the view I'm urging makes me a "social constructionist"—or something dangerously close. If so, so be it. However, as I will argue in the section to follow, it also situates me squarely within the pragmatist tradition that runs from Peirce to Quine to Rorty. And, like Brer Rabbit in the briar patch, that's a place where I feel right at home.

12   *Two Reactions*

Earlier versions of the ideas sketched in the previous section have been tried out in a variety of forums over the last few years. In this final section, I'll try to clarify my position by considering two very different reactions that it has provoked. One of them maintains that my thesis about the role of politics and personalities in resolving scientific disputes is dangerously radical—or would be if it weren't simply absurd. The other suggests that the role played by social and political factors in resolving ontological questions, though real enough, is utterly innocuous—hardly more than a platitude. I think the right reaction is somewhere in between.

Those who are most alarmed by my view claim that it is antirational, nihilistic, and ultimately self-defeating. If political, social, and psychological factors, rather than evidence and principles governing rational reasoning, can determine what conclusion we accept about the existence or nonexistence of intentional states (or phlogiston, or stars), the critics ask, then why don't the same factors determine the answers to questions like: Does smoking cause cancer? or Did millions of people die in the Nazi death camps? or Is the earth more than 10,000 years old? And if political and social factors *do* determine the answers to these questions then it seems that for all questions, about the way the world is, might makes right and there can be no objective or rational inquiry. Nihilism reigns! Moreover, as one critic went on to note, if political and social factors really did determine the conclusions we should accept about all these questions, they would determine the conclusions we should accept about the correctness of the view I am advocating. So, if someone wished to refute my view, he could do so by mounting a smear campaign, or making large and prestigious grants to those who opposed it, or just hiring some hit men to kill those who are sympathetic to the view and burn their manuscripts!

Fortunately, the Orwellian nightmare that the critic is conjuring can be traced to a misunderstanding of the view I am proposing. I am not a thoroughgoing skeptic about the normative naturalist strategy—quite to the contrary. I think that over the centuries scientists have developed an increasingly sophisticated and powerful set of strategies for going about the business of reasoning and inquiry in various domains and that conveying these strategies from teachers to students is one of the fundamental functions of education and apprenticeship in science. But expertise in this area, like expertise in most other domains, is largely tacit. The aim of normative naturalism, as I construe it, is to make explicit the strategies of reasoning and inquiry that underlie good scientific practice. I suspect that there are going to be lots of such principles. And, for those with the appropriate goals, the principles have real normative clout, since they are the best strategies of reasoning that our species has yet developed for pursuing those goals.[72] Moreover—and this is my direct response to the accusation of nihilism—I think these principles are rich and detailed enough to provide normative guidance on lots of questions. My skepticism about normative naturalism is focused quite sharply on its capacity to produce principles of rational ontological inference that are strong and detailed enough to dictate what we should conclude about the entities invoked by a theory when we come to believe that the theory is seriously mistaken. In particular, I very much doubt that the principles that the normative-naturalist process will uncover will tell us what ontological conclusions to draw if the premises in the eliminativists' argument turn out to be correct. But in claiming that normative naturalism will not produce comprehensive principles that specify a determinate answer in all cases, I am most emphatically *not* claiming that the principles of reasoning these strategies yield will be so radically incomplete that they will yield no determinate answer on any question, or on most. So much, then, for the accusation of nihilism.

The second reaction I want to consider is set out with great clarity in a recent paper by David Papineau. Papineau agrees that ontological questions of the sort we've been considering may well be "indeterminate," and he agrees that in many cases "scientific decisions are inevitably determined by sociological factors" (forthcoming, sec. 2). However, on his account there is little to be concerned about in all of this, since sociological factors and "scientific politics" "only come into play when a scientific term . . . turns out to be vague in a way that requires remedying." Since "there is generally no objective reason to refine [the definition of the term] in one direction rather than another," political and sociological factors are free to step in. But there is nothing of empirical substance at stake when such questions arise. They are really just linguistic questions. "It is simply a matter of deciding how to use words" (sec. 7). This is a refreshingly down-to-earth view of the situation, one which I wish I could accept. To explain why I can't, I'll have to back up a bit and sketch the argument that Papineau offers in support of his view.

Papineau begins with the assumption that the Ramsey/Carnap/Lewis account of the meaning and reference of theoretical terms is on the right track and thus that Putnam-style causal-historical accounts are mistaken. As we saw in section 4, the Ramsey/Carnap/Lewis view claims that the meaning of theoretical terms can be captured by definite descriptions of a certain sort and that these descriptions determine the reference of the term. For Lewis, whose statement of the view Papineau takes to be "definitive," theoretical terms are "defined as the occupants of the causal roles specified by the theory . . . ; as *the* entities, whatever those may be, that bear certain causal relations to one another and to the referents of O-terms [the *old, original* terms we understood before the theory was proposed]" (Lewis 1972, 211, 298). A bit more formally, the meaning of a theoretical term, F_1, can be given by the following definition:[73]

$$F_1 = df\ (\imath x)\ (T(x))$$

where "$T(F_1)$ is the set of assumptions [of the theory] involving F_1 that contribute to its definition" and "$T(x)$ is the open sentence that results from $T(F_1)$ when F_1 is replaced by the variable x, and $\imath$ is the definite description operator" (Papineau forthcoming, sec. 2). If, as is likely, $T(F_1)$ invokes other theoretical terms, say $F_2, \ldots F_n$, these can be handled by existentially quantifying into the positions they occupy, yielding:

$$F_1 = df\ (\imath x_1)\ (\exists! x_2, \ldots, x_n)\ (T(x_1, \ldots, x_n))$$

"This says that F_1 refers to the first in the unique sequence of entities which satisfies $T(x_1, \ldots, x_n)$, if there is such a sequence, and fails to refer otherwise (where $T(x_1, \ldots, x_n)$ is the open sentence which results when we replace $F_1, \ldots F_n$ by $x_1, \ldots, x_n$ in F_1's defining theory)" (sec. 30). As Papineau notes, one important consequence of this view is that theoretical terms are eliminable: "any claims formulated using such terms are simply a shorthand for claims that can be formulated without such terms." Thus, "we can *eliminate* theoretically defined terms from any claims in which they appear" (sec. 3).

This bare-bones version of the Ramsey/Carnap/Lewis story requires some embellishments, since, as noted in section 4, without them it is implausibly holistic and implausibly stringent. *All* of a theory's causal claims play a role in the definition of *all* of the theory's theoretical terms. So if any of the theory's causal claims turns out to be mistaken, all of its theoretical terms will fail to denote. One way to avoid the problem would be to distinguish sharply between those theoretical claims that contribute to the definition of the term and those that do not. But, in agreement with Quine, Papineau maintains that "there is no obvious feature of scientific or everyday thinking which might serve to underpin this distinction" (forthcoming, sec. 1). Like Quine, he thinks "there is no fact of the matter, for many theoretical assumptions, whether they are definitional or not" (sec. 6). Papineau's agreement with Quine is really quite limited, however, for, unlike Quine, he thinks that there typically are some "core assumptions" of the theory that "unquestionably *do* contribute" to the definition of each theoretical term, while other assumptions of the theory "unquestionably do *not* contribute" (sec. 4). He also thinks that there will typically be some theoretical assumptions whose definitional status is indeterminate. Papineau uses the handy notation T_y, ("y" for yes), T_n ("n" for no) and T_p ("p" for perhaps) to label these three sets of assumptions. Since the definitional status of T_p is unsettled, the definitions of theoretical terms are imprecise.

The central point of Papineau's paper is that in many cases "the imprecision does not matter."

> [If a theoretical term, F,] has this kind of imprecise definition, with T_y strong enough to ensure a unique referent and T_y-plus-T_p not too strong to rule out a referent entirely, . . . [then] *F would end up referring to the same entity however the imprecision were resolved.* Given this, there is no need to resolve the imprecision. Understand F as you will, consistently with your definition including T_y and excluding T_n, and you will be referring to the same thing.

Since this sort of imprecision or vagueness "does not necessarily imply any indeterminacy of reference, it does not automatically follow that any sentences involving F will lack determinate truth conditions" (forthcoming, sec. 4).

Papineau recognizes that things need not always work so nicely, however. His account of why problems arise, how they can be resolved, and why the resolution need not be disquieting is worth quoting at some length.

I admit that there are also cases where such definitional imprecision *does* lead to claims which lack determinate truth-conditional content. When this happens, our discourse is flawed. So when we identify such cases, we ought to remedy the imprecision. . . .

There are two dangers a theoretical definition of some term F must avoid, if it is to yield a term that is useful for stating truths. It must not make the definition so weak as to fail to identify a unique satisfier. And it must not make the definition so strong that it rules out satisfiers altogether. The special risk facing imprecise definitions is that the indeterminate status of the assumptions in T_p can make it indeterminate whether these two dangers have been avoided. Thus, to take the first danger, T_y might be too weak to ensure a unique satisfier by itself, but may be able to do so if conjoined with some of the assumptions in T_p. Then it will be indeterminate whether F refers uniquely. Second, it may be that nothing satisfies all of T_y-plus-T_p, but that there would be satisfiers if we dropped some of the T_p assumptions from this conjunction. Then it will be indeterminate whether F refers at all.

Cases of the second kind are perhaps more familiar. The example of *belief* . . . fits this bill. Suppose that the assumption that beliefs have internal structure is in the T_p of "belief"'s definition. And suppose further that the connectionists are right to deny that the entities which satisfy the undisputed criteria for being beliefs ("belief"'s T_y) have internal structure. . . . Then it would be indeterminate whether "belief" refers to those entities or not, since it would be indeterminate whether their lack of causal structure disqualifies these entities from being beliefs. It is plausible that many cases from the history of science and elsewhere have the same structure. Does the failure of "caloric is a fluid" mean that there is no caloric? Does the failure of "straight lines are Euclidean" mean that there are no straight lines? Does the failure of "witches have magic powers" mean that there are no witches? Does the failure of "entropy invariably increases in a closed system" mean that there is no entropy? And so on.

There are also plausible cases of the other kind, where the indeterminacy of T_p makes it indeterminate which entity, if any, some term refers to. Thus modern microbiology tells us that various different chunks of DNA satisfy the undisputed criteria for "gene", and that further assumptions are needed to narrow the referent down. . . .

In both these kinds of cases, some new discovery makes it manifest that the looseness in the definition of some term F is not benign after all. . . .

The obvious remedy in this kind of situation is to refine the definition so as to resolve the question. . . .

Is there anything which makes it right to go one way rather than another in such cases? I doubt it. Certainly if we look at the history of science, there is no obvious principle which decides whether in such cases scientists concluded that there are no F̱s, or, alternatively, that there are F̱s, but the assumption at issue is false of them. Consider the different fates of the terms "caloric" and "electric". Originally both of these were taken to refer to a fluid that flowed between bodies. . . . Later it was discovered that neither quantity is a fluid, and that the appearance of flow is in both cases a kinetic effect. The two cases are structurally similar. Yet we now say that electricity exists, but that caloric fluid does not.

If there is a pattern governing which way the terminology goes in such cases, it is probably one involving the micro-sociology of the thinkers responsible for the relevant theoretical revision. Theorists who want to present themselves as merely continuing the tradition of those who have previously studied F̱s will retain the term F for the thing satisfying the basic criteria T_y but not the newly revised part of T_p. On the other hand, theorists who want to distance themselves from the existing theoretical establishment will urge that F̱s do not exist, and that their new assumption identifies a hitherto unknown entity G. . . .

The idea that scientific decisions are inevitably determined by sociological factors seems antithetical to any realist attitude to science. . . .

However, the limited role I have ascribed to sociological factors has no such implication. For I am suggesting only that sociological factors come into play when a scientific term that was hitherto thought to have a determinate reference turns out to be vague in a way that requires remedying. When the meaning of a vague term needs refining, there will generally be no objective reason to refine it in one direction rather than another. It is simply a matter of deciding how to use words, given that our previous practice with these words has proved inadequate. So the intrusion of sociological factors at this point need cause no disquiet to the realist. (forthcoming, sec. 7)

To get a bit clearer on the implications of Papineau's position for the issues that are central to this chapter, let's focus on the problem facing theorists (like the eliminativists) who come to believe that some of the claims in a previously accepted theory are mistaken. Suppose that F is a theoretical term in the old theory. What ought the theorists to conclude about the existence of F̱s? According to Papineau, these theorists may be in one of three quite different situations.

In the first situation, one or more of the claims that the theorists now take to be mistaken are part of T_y—the set of "core assumptions" that "unquestionably *do* contribute to the definition" of F. In this case, according to Papineau, the definition requires the theorists to conclude that there are no F̱s. If for some reason the theorists are disinclined to say "There are no F̱s," they might also decide to change the meaning of F by reassigning the rejected assumptions to T_n. They could then go on saying "F̱s exist." But in saying this they would not be denying what, prior to the change, someone could have asserted by saying "F̱s do not exist."

In the second situation, all of the mistaken assumptions are in T_n. Here, the appropriate conclusion is that there are F̱s, though the old theory made some mistaken claims about them. As in the previous case, theorists who are so inclined are perfectly free to change the meaning of F in a way that makes one of the rejected assumptions part of T_y. They could then say "Fs do not exist." But this is perfectly compatible with their earlier assertion, "Fs exist."

Finally, in the third situation, one or more of the mistaken assumptions is in T_p, though none is in T_y. In this case, the imprecision in the definition of F leads to indeterminacy. Claims that invoke F, including the claim that Fs exist, have no determinate truth value. Since the imprecision matters in this case, something must be done to remedy the problem. There are two obvious options. Theorists can either decide to reassign one or more of the mistaken assumptions to T_y, in which case they will say "Fs don't exist," or they can decide to reassign all the mistaken assumptions to T_n, in which case they will say "Fs do exist." But whichever option they adopt, the claims they make after the decision to adopt it will neither deny nor affirm what they were saying when they uttered "Fs exist" or "Fs don't exist" prior to the decision. For psychological or political reasons, different theorists may prefer different decisions. But there is no factual issue at stake in these disputes. One way to make this obvious relies on the fact that, on Papineau's account, theoretical terms are eliminable. Imagine that there are two theorists, one of whom wants to continue saying "Fs exist" while the other wants to say "Fs don't exist." We need only invite each of them to restate their claims without invoking the term F, by using the Ramsey-sentence strategy. Since the two theorists have revised the old definition in different ways, the result will be two quite distinct sentences, both of which both theorists should be happy to accept. The only real dispute between them is a dispute over how to redefine the term F. Though Papineau does not make the point, his story even has a nice explanation of why, once the political dust has settled, we all *ought* to conclude that Fs (read: 'atoms' or 'electrons') do exist, or that Fs (read: 'phlogiston' or 'witches') do not exist. It's not because there was a correct conclusion that the political negotiations inevitably reached. It's simply that the political negotiations are the process by which we decide how to reform our language. And once a consensus has been reached, we ought to abide by it for much the same reason that we ought to use the word 'dog' when we want to say something about dogs, not the word 'cat'.

Papineau's paper offers an attractive and very reassuring package. His view is well informed and crystal clear, and the account it provides of the role of political and psychological factors in scientific decisions is much easier to live with than the one I've proposed. It's not a package that I think we ought to buy, however, since the philosophical price we'd have to pay for the reassurance it offers is far too high. In order to make his position plausible, Papineau must help himself to a pair of very fundamental assumptions. Characteristically, he is completely up front about their status as *assumptions;* he doesn't pretend to offer any serious arguments for them. On my view, neither of the assumptions is defensible.

The first assumption is that a description theory, something at least roughly similar to the account offered by David Lewis, is the right theory of reference for theoretical terms. As we noted in section 5, many philosophers reject this account of reference for theoretical terms and favor instead a Putnam-style causal-historical account. More recently, the deflationary disquotational account championed by Brandom, Horwich, and Field has also won some converts. So the truth of the description theory is hardly an assumption we should grant to Papineau without argument. But, as I explained in section 6, my own reservations about the description theory go deeper than this. I don't think it makes much sense to debate which theory gives the right account of reference for theoretical terms until we get a lot clearer on what it is that the "right" theory of reference is supposed to do. Moreover, as I argued in sections 6 and 7, there is a sensible answer to this question on which it's entirely possible that there is *no* correct account of reference for terms in a mistaken theory and another sensible answer on which there may be several quite different theories of reference, all of which are equally correct. So my complaint about Papineau's first assumption is twofold. First, he has assumed a controversial account of the reference of theoretical terms. Second, his assumption presupposes that there *is* a correct theory of reference for various sorts of terms. And that presupposition is one I have taken pains to undermine.

The second assumption that underlies Papineau's position is that there is a philosophically defensible way to draw an analytic/synthetic distinction. The distinction he needs is not quite the traditional analytic/synthetic distinction since Papineau does not claim that all declarative sentences are either analytic or synthetic. He allows—indeed insists—that there are some sentences whose status is indeterminate. But for Quine, and for most other critics of the analytic/synthetic distinction, the existence of indeterminate cases is of little moment. What Quine and those who follow him deny is that there are any sentences whose truth depends on nothing apart from their meaning. And on Papineau's view, there are going to be lots of these sentences. Each member of T_y for a given theoretical term F (i.e., each of the "core assumptions" that "unquestionably do contribute to F's definition") generates an analytic truth. If T_{y1} is one of the core assumptions for F, then (8) is true by definition:

(8) For all x, if x is $\underline{F}$ then x is $\underline{T}_{y1}$.

It is analytic truths like these that mandate a negative ontological decision when one of the assumptions in T_y turns out to be mistaken. Papineau also thinks that when indeterminacy becomes problematic, we sometimes *make* sentences like this true (indeed, analytically true) by stipulating a revised definition of F. Once that's done, we can't rationally reject the sentence without again changing the meaning. For

Quine, by contrast, there are no cases of this sort. As science evolves, every sentence in a theory is a potential candidate for revision or rejection, whether or not it was originally introduced as a stipulation, and there is no principled distinction between revising a sentence that was originally a definition and revising any other sentence. Indeed, this egalitarian attitude that grants no sentence special privileges because of its meaning or its history is one of the central strands in Quine's version of pragmatism.

It would be easy enough to set out lots of other illustrations of the fact that Papineau's view clashes head-on with Quinean skepticism about analyticity. But there is no need, since the point is both obvious and uncontested. Papineau himself is quite explicit about the matter. He recognizes that "many of the objections to a simple analytic-synthetic distinction apply equally to my tripartite division of theoretical assumptions into analytic, synthetic and indeterminate." He is untroubled by this, however, since he thinks those objections are unconvincing and that it is a straightforward matter to determine empirically whether various sentences are analytic, synthetic, or indeterminate in a given linguistic community (forthcoming, sec. 6).

Where does all this leave us? Well, if you're prepared to accept a description theory of reference for theoretical terms, along with a version of the analytic/synthetic distinction that allows for indeterminate cases, then Papineau's view provides an account of the role of politics and personalities in scientific decision making that few will find disquieting. It also provides an attractive strategy for answering our question about the right conclusion to draw if the eliminativists' Premises are right: First, we do some meaning analysis to determine which of the three situations distinguished above obtains. If it's the first, then the eliminativists get to draw their conclusion; if it's the second, they don't. And if it's the third, then the conclusion itself is defective—it's vague in a way that prevents it from having a determinate truth value. So we can sit back and let the political dust settle, confident that the only real issue is how to redefine our propositional attitude terms. On the other hand, if you're not prepared to accept Papineau's assumptions, and if I'm right in guessing that normative naturalism won't produce principles that are strong enough to be of help, then until the social negotiations reach a consensus there is no determinate answer to the question of what to conclude if the eliminativists' Premises are correct. And there is more at stake in these debates than how to redefine a word. What's at stake is whether or not we ought to accept the existence of propositional attitudes.

Let me close with a few brief historical observations that may help to locate my view in philosophical space. My disagreement with Papineau is in many ways quite similar to Quine's dispute with Carnap over the role of language in settling ontological questions.[74] On Carnap's view, scientific inquiry, when rationally reconstructed, can be divided into two quite different sorts of activities. One of these is the choice (or sometimes the construction) of the language or "linguistic framework" in which our inquiry will be conducted. Within a given framework, certain ontological claims (like "Numbers exist" or "Propositions exist") will be trivial analytic truths. Frameworks will also include "meaning postulates" which specify or entail analytic conditionals [like (8)] stating necessary and/or sufficient conditions for being an entity of a certain sort. When a framework has been adopted, there will remain lots of questions, including lots of ontological questions, that are far from trivial and must be resolved by empirical or logical investigation. Those investigations constitute the second stage of scientific inquiry, whose job it is to develop and test hypotheses or theories within the linguistic framework that has been chosen. Sometimes, as science progresses, it may turn out that the linguistic framework being used is awkward or inconvenient or perhaps even defective. When this happens, investigators may decide to adopt another linguistic framework. The question of which linguistic framework to adopt is not a "theoretical" question, according to Carnap. It is "a matter of a practical decision concerning the structure of our language. We have to make the choice whether or not to accept and use the forms of expression in the framework in question" (1950, 207). Thus, for example, to accept a linguistic framework containing the apparatus for talking about the familiar, "spatio-temporally ordered system of observable things and events" is "to accept rules for forming statements and for testing, accepting, or rejecting them." And "the efficiency, fruitfulness, and simplicity of the use of the thing language may be among the decisive factors" in deciding whether to accept it (208). "The acceptance cannot be judged as being either true or false because it is not an assertion. It can only be judged as being more or less expedient, fruitful, conducive to the aim for which the language is intended" (214). But, as we've seen, the acceptance of a framework commits us to accepting lots of sentences, including both existential claims and conditionals like (8). On Carnap's view, we accept these because the framework that they are part of is useful for our purposes. Other statements that the framework makes available we accept or reject on the basis of evidence, along with the framework's rules for testing, accepting, and rejecting such statements.

As I read Quine, the central thesis in his critique of Carnap is that this distinction between two different kinds of statements—those that are mandated by our choice of linguistic framework, which we accept because the framework is useful, and those that are not mandated by the framework and that we accept on the basis of evidence—is not a distinction that can be drawn in a principled way when we look at the history of science or at the evolution of our own beliefs. If we could draw this distinction in a principled way, we would have all that is needed to distinguish the analytic from the synthetic. Or, going the other way round, if we could distinguish analytic from synthetic statements, there would be little problem in distinguishing between those scientific developments that count as changes in language from those that count as changes in theory. But, Quine maintains, we can do neither:

> Carnap . . . and others take a pragmatic stand on the question of choosing between language forms, scientific frameworks; but their pragmatism leaves off at the imagined boundary between the analytic and the synthetic. In repudiating such a boundary I espouse a more thorough pragmatism. Each man is given a scientific heritage plus a continuing barrage of sensory stimulation; and the considerations which guide him in warping his scientific heritage to fit his continuing sensory promptings are, where rational, pragmatic. (1936b, 46)

It will come as no surprise that I side with Quine in this controversy, while Papineau's view is much closer to Carnap's. But there is one respect in which my pragmatism may be more radical than Quine's. In talking about the factors that "influence our inclinations to adjust one strand of the fabric of science rather than another," Quine mentions "conservatism," "the quest for simplicity," and "the continuing barrage of sensory stimulation" (46). But there is no mention of the role of psychological and political considerations in determining either the inclinations of an individual or the ultimate consensus in a community. I have argued that both of these factors often do play important roles in inquiry. I have also argued, more tentatively, that at least sometimes they ought to.

Notes

Parts of section 10 in this chapter are borrowed from Stich and Warfield (1995).

1. Philosophers are not the only ones to advocate eliminativism, nor were they the first. J. B. Watson, one of the founders of behaviorism in psychology, disparaged the mental states mentioned in commonsense psychological explanations, states like beliefs and desires, as "medieval conceptions" and "heritages of a timid savage past," of a piece with "superstition," "magic," and "voodoo" (1930, 2–5). B. F. Skinner, perhaps the most famous behaviorist, tells us that "mental life" is an "invention" and that "mental or cognitive explanations are not explanations at all" (1974, 114–15).
2. Quoted in McCloskey (1983a, 124). For a quotation from Galileo's *De Motu*, written in about 1590, see McCloskey (1983a, 127).
3. See, for example, Chomsky (1965, chap. 1; 1975).
4. For the former view, see Harman (1973); for the latter, see Fodor (1975).
5. For quasi-pictorial representations, see Kosslyn (1994); for holographic representations, see Eich (1982) and Metcalf (1989); for mental models, see Johnson-Laird (1983); for connectionist representations, see Hinton, McClelland, and Rumelhart (1986).
6. The most explicit example I know is Andy Clark's recent proposal that in order to counter the eliminativists we should "reject outright the idea that

folk psychology is necessarily committed to beliefs and desires as being straightforwardly causally potent" (1993, 211). Others who suggest similar moves include Jackson and Pettit (1990; forthcoming) and Horgan and Graham (1990).

7. For a more extended discussion of Sellars's "myth of Jones," see chapter 3, section 2.

8. See, for example, P. S. Churchland (1980; 1986, 386–99).

9. A precursor of the Ramsey, Stich, and Garon argument can be found in Stich (1983, 237–42). However, back in those days there were no up-and-running radically holistic models of memory.

10. The quotation is from a useful summary of Davies's argument in Clark (1993, 197). Clark calls this assumption "the demand for *conceptual modularity*." Conceptual modularity certainly does not entail a full-fledged Sellarsian language of thought, though perhaps it comes closer than the propositional modularity invoked in Ramsey, Stich, and Garon's (1990) argument.

11. For a critique of this argument, see Horgan and Woodward (1985).

12. The quotation is from Putnam (1975); for Kripke's arguments see Kripke (1972).

13. Roughly speaking, one set of properties supervenes on another if the presence or absence of properties in the first class is completely determined by the presence or absence of properties in the second. For a detailed discussion of various ways in which this account can be made more precise, see chapter 5, section 4.

14. This is, near enough, the "principle of psychological autonomy" that I advocated in Stich (1978a). For some additional discussion of the principle, see Stich (1983, chap. 8).

15. Fodor defends the thesis in both, (1987), chap. 2, and (1991), though as he notes, the arguments in these two sources are very different. Those who claim it is false include Burge (1986); Van Gulick (1989); and Von Eckardt (1993, chap. 7).

16. See Stich (1983, chap. 4). For a critique of this argument, see Fodor (1987, chap. 3).

17. Or, on a slightly different version of the view, only if they have identical inferential properties. This is, needless to say, a very demanding condition to impose on content identity. Indeed, it is so demanding that Jones, Mullaire, and Stich (1991) claimed it was a straw man—a view that no one had ever really held. But, as Michael Devitt (forthcoming, chap. 1) has recently demonstrated, we were wrong. Harman (1973, 14) clearly asserts the view, and both Papineau (1987, 98) and Block (1991, 260) come very close indeed.

18. For one widely discussed version of this argument, see Fodor (1987, chap. 3).

19. For some detailed examples, see Stich (1983, 66–72; 1982, 185–88).

20. Van Gulick (1993). See also Kim (1989a) and (1989b). Both Kim and Van Gulick are critical of the argument, though their objections are quite different.

21. Perhaps this is a good place to note that some authors use the term *eliminativism* for the view that folk psychology is a seriously mistaken theory rather than for either of the ontological theses that I take to be eliminativism's central claims. Other authors seem to slide back and forth between the "ontological" reading and the "badly mistaken theory" reading, a practice that is easy to understand if they think the former reading follows straightforwardly from the latter.

Yet another distinction worth noting separates two versions of ontological eliminativism, one of which claims that *beliefs* (and other propositional attitudes) don't exist, while the other claims that *believers* (and *desirers*, etc.) don't exist. If we assume that beliefs are a sort of internal state, and that someone is a believer if and only if she has some beliefs, the distinction is of no importance. However, some writers reject this account of what it is to be a believer because they think it is a mistake to view propositional attitudes as states or "entities." Of course, these writers do not deny that humans and other organisms are entities. So eliminativists can pose their challenge in a way that is acceptable to these writers by claiming that no humans or other organisms are believers or desirers—that predicates of the form '_____ believes that p' and '_____ desires that q' are never true of them. For more on this distinction, see Stich (1991a, sec. 3) and O'Leary-Hawthorne (1994, sec. 1).

22. For a bit of evidence in support of this guess, see n. 28.

23. Lewis (1972, 209). The other papers include Lewis (1966, and 1970).

24. This is the second time I've quoted this passage from Lewis. The first time was in Stich (1983, 15–16), where I was laying the groundwork for a series of arguments for eliminativism.

25. The idea that the eliminativists' claim may be indeterminate even when all the scientific facts are in will become something of a leitmotif in this chapter. It arises in another context in section 7 and gets a rather radical twist in section 11.

26. Lewis (1972, 212–13). It might be thought odd that Lewis treats all mental state terms (indeed all theoretical terms) as names rather than predicates or functors. But as he notes:

> No generality is lost, since names can purport to name entities of any kind: individuals, species, states, properties, substances, magnitudes, classes, relations, or what not. Instead of a T-predicate 'F _____', for instance, we can use '_____ has F-hood'; 'F-hood' is a T-name purporting to name a property, and '_____ has _____' is an O-predicate. It is automatic to reformulate all T-terms as names, under the safe assumption that our O-vocabulary provides the needed copulas. (1970, 80)

27. For more on this view of folk psychology, see chap. 3.

28. Though I may have been the only person tempted by eliminativism who relied explicitly on Lewis's account, other writers clearly favor similar accounts. According to Paul Churchland:

> Our common-sense terms for mental states are *theoretical terms* of a theoretical framework (folk psychology) embedded in our common-sense understanding, and the meanings of those terms are fixed in the same way as are the meanings of theoretical terms in general. Specifically, their meaning is fixed by the set of laws/principles/generalizations in which they figure. (P. M. Churchland 1984, 56)

Similarly, Patricia Churchland writes:

> The meaning of an expression for an individual is a function of the role that expression plays in his internal representational economy—that is, of how it is related to sensory input and behavioral output and of its inferen-

tial/computational role within the internal economy. Sparing the niceties, this is the *network theory of meaning*, otherwise known as the *holistic theory* or the *conceptual-role theory*. (P. S. Churchland 1986, 344)

This sort of account has also been influential among authors on the other side of the issue, who are not in the least tempted by eliminativism. Here's an example from Colin McGinn:

> It is very plausible that the platitudes of commonsense psychology, as they relate mental states to each other and to behavior, *implicitly define* the terms contained therein: it is thus a necessary, indeed analytic, truth that entities are mental if and only if they satisfy those platitudes. In consequence if *(per impossibile)* the commonsense theory should be false, then mental states would simply not exist—for the corresponding terms have no meaning, and hence no denotations, beyond their role in that theory. (1978, 150)

29. Lewis offers his theory as an account of both the reference and the *meaning* of theoretical terms, and this is certainly the most natural way to construe it. Causal-historical theories, by contrast, are generally offered only as accounts of reference. So one might try to preserve something like Lewis's account of meaning and add on a causal-historical account of reference. This is, near enough, the strategy pursued in dual-factor theories. Since reference rather than meaning does all the work in eliminativists' arguments, I won't have much to say about theories about the meaning of theoretical terms.

30. Or theor*ies*—since it might turn out that different accounts of reference are appropriate for different sorts of terms.

31. The inspiration for this example is in Kripke (1972, 282), though Kripke does not include the bit about the fellow who actually was swallowed by a big fish. I'm not sure who first added this wrinkle to the tale, though if memory serves, I first heard it from Kripke.

32. See Stich (1972 and 1975), and Soames (1984). The inspiration for this account of syntax can be found in Quine (1953a). There is, of course, no guarantee that there will be a unique simplest way to capture speakers' intuitions. If there are several equally simple theories, then on this view of grammar they are all correct.

33. For more on these two views of grammar, see chapter 3, sec. 4.

34. This account is similar to "external" accounts of folk psychology discussed in chapter 3. The closest analog is the view second from the left in the box in figure 3-1.

35. It is important to note that there is a substantive empirical assumption lurking in the background here. If we adopt the view that the job of a theory of reference is to describe the tacit theory that characterizes a word–world mapping and plays a central role in producing our intuitions about various examples, then we are assuming that ordinary folk actually have an internally represented theory of reference guiding their intuitions. And there is certainly no guarantee that this assumption is correct. It might be the case that our intuitions about the sorts of examples that philosophers are wont to discuss (Jonah, witches, stars, and the rest) are guided by a heterogeneous set of principles about translation, paraphrase, charitable interpretation, historiographical convenience, inferential practice, and a host of other considerations. If I under-

stand him correctly, this is the view urged by Rorty (1979, 284–95) who maintains that reference "is not something we have intuitions about" (292). I am inclined to think that Rorty may be right and thus that much recent philosophical work on reference is built on a foundation of quicksand. But that's a topic for another occasion.

Some passages in Field (1994, sec. 4) might be interpreted as agreeing with Rorty and denying that we have intuitions about reference; however, Field tells me that his view is rather different from Rorty's. For more on Field's view, see n. 47.

36. The best sustained statement and defense of this view of grammar is in Laurence (1993). For Chomsky's view, see Chomsky (1965; 1975; 1992).

37. Though there is a fascinating literature on this topic. See, for example, Murdock (1980).

38. The most explicit endorsement of this view that I've found is in Devitt and Sterelny (1987, 170): "Just as it is the task of economics to explain such properties as price and value, . . . it is the task of linguistics to explain such properties as truth and reference." In the next paragraph, they describe "the semantic properties of linguistic symbols" as "the properties *revealed* by linguistics" (emphasis mine). Unfortunately, they offer no references to the work of linguists in which the nature of semantic properties is revealed. More recently, Devitt (1994 and forthcoming) seems to have adopted a less sanguine view of what linguistics has revealed about the nature of semantic properties.

39. For fitness, see Sober (1984); for grammaticality, see Fodor (1981b) and Laurence (1993); for space-time, see Sklar (1974).

40. Cummins (1989, chaps. 1 and 2) argues persuasively that different branches of cognitive science will require different "representation" relations. This is not quite the same point I'm making here, since the representation relations that Cummins has in mind are mind–world mappings, not word–world mappings. But the points are closely related, and I am indebted to Cummins for getting me to see this possibility more clearly.

41. Much the same follows for the claim that believers and desirers don't exist—i.e., that no one believes or desires anything. See n. 21.

42. Stich (1990, chap. 5). I am indebted to Peter Godfrey-Smith, who was, I think, the first to stress that the reference relation picked out by our intuition is a quite "baroque" and idiosyncratic word–world mapping. See Godfrey-Smith (1986).

43. For much the same arguments in a more confident tone of voice, see Stich (1991a and 1992).

44. Perhaps the most persuasive response to the Jackson argument would be one which adopted the general outlines of Papineau's position, which is discussed at length in section 12.

45. "Generally speaking, any expression of the form " ' . . . ' designates . . . " is an analytic statement provided the term " . . . " is a constant in an accepted framework. If the latter condition is not fulfilled, the expression is not a statement" (Carnap 1956, 217). For some very sophisticated recent discussion of the deflationary account, see Brandom (1984), Field (1986; 1994), and Horwich (1990).

46. I.e., (1) or something like it. For obvious reasons, this schema is also sometimes called the disquotation principle.

47. I'm grateful to Hartry Field for much helpful conversation on these issues.

This might be an appropriate place to say a bit more on how I interpret Field's current view about reference. As noted in n. 35, there are passages in Field (1994) which suggest that Field, like Rorty, denies that ordinary folk have any intuitions about reference. However, Field tells me that this is not what he intended in those passages. Rather, he is inclined to think that people generally do have a tacit internalized theory of reference, but that this theory is really quite minimal. It contains little more than the semantic-ascent (or disquotation) schema and also, perhaps, some information on how to use it. This internally represented schema underlies lots of intuitions about reference. But the intuitions in question are the "trivial" ones—i.e., the ones that are just instances of the schema, like (2) and (3). In the philosophical literature on reference, by contrast, the focus is on a quite different set of intuitions which are evoked by setting out a scenario like the story about Jonah recounted in sec. 6.1 or like Kripke's scenario in which we discover the following fact:

> (F) The incompleteness theorem was proved by a man baptized "Schmidt" and who never called himself anything other than "Schmidt"; a certain person who called himself "Gödel" and who got a job under that name at the Institute of Advanced Study stole the proof from him. (Field 1994, 261)

Against the background of stories like these we are asked: "Who is it natural to say that we have been referring to when we use the name 'Gödel'?" On Field's view, our answers to such questions

> *aren't at the most basic level about reference but about our inferential practice.* That is, what Kripke's example really shows is that we would regard the claim (F) as *grounds for inferring* "Gödel didn't prove the incompleteness theorem" rather than as grounds for inferring "Gödel was baptized as 'Schmidt' and never called himself 'Gödel' ". Reference is just disquotational. It does come in indirectly: from (F) I can indirectly infer
> "Gödel" doesn't refer to the guy that proved the incompleteness theorem.
> But that isn't because of a causal theory of reference over a description theory, but only because I can infer
> Gödel isn't the guy that proved the incompleteness theorem
> and then "semantically ascend." (Field 1994, 261–62)

In claiming that "reference is just disquotational," Field is not merely claiming that our internalized theory of reference is exhausted by something like (1). For he *also* holds that the disquotational account of reference is the only notion of reference that we really need in the sciences (including semantics and logic). So, on Field's view, it doesn't much matter whether we answer the question posed in section 6 by appeal to folk semantics (as in 6.1) or by appeal to proto-science (as in 6.2). In both cases, we will get the same, disquotational, account of reference.

48. As Michael Devitt has pointed out to me, it looks like the strategy of semantic ascent, or something very much like it, is lurking in the background

here, too, linking claims of the form 'We ought not *apply the concept* C to an object lacking some property that is constitutive for that concept' to claims of the form 'The object in question *can't be* a C.'

49. For some other examples, see Davies (1991, 239ff.); Evans (1981, 132); Rey (1991, 221).

50. Fodor denies that rationality is essential for having a belief. Indeed, he writes: "I accept—in fact, welcome—what amounts to the conclusion that people can believe things that are *arbitrarily* mad" (1987, 88). Clark apparently denies that "logical combination" is conceptually necessary.

51. Fodor (1987, Chap. 1); Clark (1991); Egan (1995); and perhaps Dretske (1989, 1). Clark is clearest in claiming that causal potency is a conceptual necessity. Fodor tells us that it "seems to me intuitively plausible" that having causal powers is an "essential property of the attitudes" (1987, 10). Dretske and Egan both think that folk psychology is committed to causal potency, though it's not clear that they think it is conceptually necessary. There is also an extensive literature attempting to say what the causal potency requirement comes to. See, for example, LePore and Loewer (1987); Fodor (1989); Horgan (1989) and (1993); Heil and Mele (1993).

52. Jackson and Pettit (1988; forthcoming). Clark seems to have changed his mind on this one. See the quotation from Clark (1993) in n. 6.

53. See the quotation displayed two paragraphs back.

54. See, for example, Quine (1953b); White (1950); Goodman (1949); and Harman (1967). In reading the books and articles of those who invoke the notion of a constitutive property, it is easy to get the feeling that one has fallen into a time warp. These philosophers write as though the notion of constitutive properties were entirely unproblematic, and they give no indication that they have ever heard of Quine and his assault on the analytic/synthetic distinction. There is, for example, not a single reference to Quine in Clark (1989; 1989/90; 1991; 1993), or in Davies (1990; 1991).

55. It's perhaps worth noting that throughout this section there is a sense in which I have been stacking the deck in favor of the eliminativist, since I have identified constitutive properties with conceptually necessary properties. If eliminativists can show that there are some properties that are conceptually necessary for having beliefs, and if they can show that people fail to have one or another of these properties, then the eliminativists win. But if they can't show that there are any conceptually necessary properties for having beliefs, then since we have been assuming that the Second Premise of the eliminativists' argument is correct (i.e., that folk psychology is a seriously mistaken theory), the issue remains unsettled. For the opponents of eliminativism to win using an analogous argument, they would have to defend the claim that there are properties that are *conceptually sufficient* for having beliefs and that some people have these properties. Needless to say, I don't recommend holding one's breath until the project succeeds in this case, either.

56. Goodman (1965). The term 'reflective equilibrium' is due to Rawls (1971). For further discussion of the reflective-equilibrium strategy, see Daniels (1979) and (1980), Cohen (1981), Stich (1988; 1990, chap. 4), and Stein (forthcoming).

57. I believe that the term 'normative naturalism' was first introduced by Larry Laudan, though I use the label rather more broadly than Laudan does. See Laudan (1987; 1990) and Laudan, Laudan, and Donovan (1988). For an

excellent discussion of the historical roots of normative naturalism and its relation to other projects in the naturalized epistemology tradition, see Philip Kitcher (1992).

58. For a discussion of some of these alternatives, see Philip Kitcher (1992). Thagard (1988, chap. 7), proposes an integrated strategy in which intuitions and historical studies both play a role.

59. E.g., the "rule of predesignation," which requires scientists to "prefer theories that make successful surprising predictions over theories which explain only what is already known," or the Popperian principle that requires scientists to "propound only falsifiable theories." Both of these are discussed in Laudan (1987). The most systematic and impressive effort to determine which discursively formulated principles have actually been adhered to in the history of science is the project proposed in Laudan et al. (1986). The results are reported in Donovan, Laudan, and Laudan (1988).

60. See Simon (1966; 1973) and Langley et al. (1987). Thagard (1988; 1992) has developed a rather different approach to the computer simulation of episodes in the history of science.

61. For another interesting illustration of the normative-naturalist strategy applied to ontological questions, see Enç (1976). On Enç's view, there is an important distinction to be drawn between terms that purport to refer to ostensible objects (i.e., objects that it is possible to point to) and terms that do not purport to refer to ostensible objects. 'Gold' and 'magnet' are examples of the former; 'electron' and 'phlogiston' are examples of the latter. According to Enç, "the burden of reference for [nonostensible theoretical terms] will be carried by the kind-constituting properties attributed to the object and by the explanatory mechanism developed in the theory" (271). Scientists will deny that a nonostensible object or kind exists if and only if it turns out that nothing has all of the kind-constituting properties. Macdonald (1995) proposes that we can use Enç's analysis to assess eliminativist arguments. But I am more than a bit skeptical, since I have no idea how we determine which properties of intentional states are the "kind-constituting properties." I also have my doubts about the correctness of Enç's account itself since, so far as I can see, it entails that scientists should have decided that atoms and electricity don't exist.

62. See, for example, Doppelt (1990), Giere (1985), Philip Kitcher (1992), Laudan (1990), Nickles (1986), Rosenberg (1990), and Thagard (1988).

63. For an interesting discussion of this case, see Philip Kitcher (1982; 1984, 343ff.) and Waters (1994).

64. As Enç notes (1976, 267), advocates of the Kripke-Putnam account of reference might well be committed to saying that phlogiston is oxygen, since the term 'phlogiston' was a term originally introduced to refer to the substance (or "principle") that is responsible for combustion and calcination (the process in which a heated metal loses its metal-like properties like its brilliance and its cohesiveness). And oxygen *is* the substance that is responsible for both of these phenomena. In his interesting attempt to model the conceptual changes in chemistry from Stahl to Lavoisier, Thagard (1992, chap. 3) points out that the stuff we would call "oxygen" and that Priestley sometimes described as "dephlogisticated air" was regarded as a compound by Lavoisier. One of its components was the element or principle that he called "principe oxygine"; the other component was "the matter of fire and heat," which Lavoisier, along with most of his contemporaries, also called "caloric"!

65. For a similar view, see Papineau (forthcoming, sec. 4). Part of the relevant passage is quoted in section 12 of this chapter.

66. Luhrmann's book is an ethnographic study of witches in contemporary England. The views recounted in this quotation are widely shared in the groups she studied. I'm grateful to Philip Kitcher for drawing my attention to Luhrmann's work.

67. For some useful discussion, see Stein (1992a) and some of the other essays in Stein (1992b). For a detailed and fascinating discussion of the political negotiations involved in deciding whether or not a controversial psychiatric condition, Binge Eating Disorder, really exists, see McCarthy and Gerring (1994). And for a richly textured account of the social and political underpinnings of the debate about the existence of Multiple Personality Disorder, see Hacking (1995).

68. Though I do have lots of views about how they *can't* be defended. See Stich (1990, chaps. 2, 4, and 6).

69. I am grateful to Ted Warfield for bringing this passage to my attention.

70. I owe this observation to Warren Dow.

71. Those negotiations do not take place in isolation, of course. They are carried on at the same time as the empirical and philosophical debates, sketched in section 3, about the virtues and shortcomings of commonsense psychology. And it seems unlikely that any consensus will emerge on what ontological conclusion to draw if folk psychology were to turn out to be wrong in ways that few believe it will. To see the point, consider the analogy with phlogiston. Suppose that phlogiston theory had turned out to be wrong but that its defects were quite different from what we now take them to be. Should we conclude that phlogiston exists or not? Obviously, the answer depends on the details. But there are lots of imaginable cases in which we would have no idea what to say. The answer is just as indeterminate now as it was before Lavoisier. Since there is no need to decide what conclusion to accept in all possible cases, those engaged in the process typically don't even try.

72. For further discussion, see Laudan (1987; 1990) and Stich (1990, chap. 6; 1993b).

73. For the remainder of this section, I will follow Papineau in using "F," "F_1," "G," etc. as dummy names of words, and using underlining, as in "F," "G," etc. for dummy names of a theoretical property or other entity.

74. Though there are also some important differences. A detailed account of the analogies and disanalogies would be an intriguing project, but it's one that I'll have to save for another occasion. The central papers in the debate between Carnap and Quine are Carnap (1950; 1952; 1955) and Quine (1936; 1951; 1953b; 1963).

CHAPTER 2

Connectionism, Eliminativism, and the Future of Folk Psychology

With William Ramsey and Joseph Garon

1 Introduction

In the years since the publication of Thomas Kuhn's *Structure of Scientific Revolutions,* the term *scientific revolution* has been used with increasing frequency in discussions of scientific change, and the magnitude required of an innovation before someone or other is tempted to call it a revolution has diminished alarmingly. Our thesis in this chapter is that if a certain family of connectionist hypotheses turn out to be right, they will surely count as revolutionary, even on stringent pre-Kuhnian standards. There is no question that connectionism has already brought about major changes in the way many cognitive scientists conceive of cognition. However, as we see it, what makes certain kinds of connectionist models genuinely revolutionary is the support they lend to a thoroughgoing eliminativism about some of the central posits of commonsense (or "folk") psychology. Our focus here is on beliefs or propositional memories, though the argument generalizes straightforwardly to all the other propositional attitudes. If we are right, the consequences of this kind of connectionism extend well beyond the confines of cognitive science, since these models, if successful, will require a radical reorientation in the way we think about ourselves.

Here is a quick preview of what is to come. Section 2 gives a brief account of what eliminativism claims and sketches a pair of premises that eliminativist arguments typically require. Section 3 says a bit about how we conceive of commonsense psychology and the propositional attitudes that it posits. It also illustrates one sort of psychological model that exploits and builds on the posits of folk psychology. Section 4 is devoted to connectionism. Models that have been called *connectionist* form a fuzzy and heterogeneous set whose members often share little more than a vague family resemblance. However, our argument linking connectionism to eliminativism will work only for a restricted domain of connectionist models, interpreted in a particular way; the main job of section 4 is to say what that domain is and how the models in the domain are to be interpreted. In section 5, we illustrate what a connectionist model of belief that comports with our strictures might look like, and we go on to argue that if models of this sort are correct, then things look bad for commonsense psychology. Section 6 assembles some objections and replies. The final section is a brief conclusion.

Before plunging in, we should emphasize that the thesis we propose to defend is a *conditional* claim: *If* connectionist hypotheses of the sort we will sketch turn out to be right, so, too, will eliminativism about propositional attitudes. Since our goal is only to show how connectionism and eliminativism are related, we will make no effort to argue for the truth or falsity of either doctrine. In particular, we will offer no argument in favor of the version of connectionism required in the antecedent of our conditional. Indeed, our view is that it is early days yet— too early to tell with any assurance how well this family of connectionist hypotheses will fare. Those who are more confident of connectionism may, of course, invoke our conditional as part of a larger argument for doing away with the propositional attitudes.[1] But, as John Haugeland once remarked, one man's *ponens* is another man's *tollens*. And those who take eliminativism about propositional attitudes to be preposterous or unthinkable may well view our arguments as part of a larger case against connectionism. Thus, we'd not be at all surprised if trenchant critics of connectionism, like Fodor and Pylyshyn, found both our conditional and the argument for it to be quite congenial.[2]

2   Eliminativism and Folk Psychology

Eliminativism, as we shall use the term, is a fancy name for a simple thesis. It is the claim that some category of entities, processes, or properties exploited in a commonsense or scientific account of the world do not exist. So construed, we are all eliminativists about many sorts of things. In the domain of folk theory, witches are the standard example. Once upon a time, witches were widely believed to be responsible for various local calamities. But people gradually became convinced that there are better explanations for most of the events in which witches had been implicated. There being no explanatory work for witches to do, sensible people concluded that there were no such things. In the scientific domain, phlogiston, caloric fluid, and the luminiferous aether are the parade cases for eliminativism. Each was invoked by serious scientists pursuing sophisticated research programs. But in each case, the program ran aground in a major way, and the theories in which the entities were invoked were replaced by successor theories in which the entities played no role. The scientific community gradually came to recognize that phlogiston and the rest do not exist.

As these examples suggest, a central step in an eliminativist argument will typically be the demonstration that the theory in which certain putative entities or processes are invoked should be rejected and replaced by a better theory. And that raises the question of how we go about showing that one theory is better than another. Notoriously, this question is easier to ask than to answer. However, it would be pretty widely agreed that if a new theory provides more accurate predictions and better explanations than an old one, and does so over a broader range of phenomena, and if the new theory comports as well or better with well-established theories in neighboring domains, then there is good reason to think that the old theory is inferior and that the new one is to be preferred. This is hardly a complete account of the conditions under which one theory is to be preferred to another, though for our purposes it will suffice.

But merely showing that a theory in which a class of entities plays a role is inferior to a successor theory plainly is not sufficient to show that the entities do not exist. Often a more appropriate conclusion is that the rejected theory was wrong, perhaps seriously wrong, about some of the properties of the entities in its domain, or about the laws governing those entities, and that the new theory gives us a more accurate account *of those very same entities*. Thus, for example, pre-Copernican astronomy was very wrong about the nature of the planets and the laws governing their movement. But it would be something of a joke to suggest that Copernicus and Galileo showed that the planets Ptolemy spoke of do not exist.[3]

In other cases, the right thing to conclude is that the posits of the old theory are reducible to those of the new. Standard examples here include the reduction of temperature to mean molecular kinetic energy, the reduction of sound to wave motion in the medium, and the reduction of genes to sequences of polynucleotide bases.[4] Given our current concerns, the lesson to be learned from these cases is that even if the commonsense theory in which propositional attitudes find their home is replaced by a better theory, that would not be enough to show that the posits of the commonsense theory do not exist.

What more would be needed? What is it that distinguishes cases

like phlogiston and caloric, on the one hand, from cases like genes or
the planets on the other? Or, to ask the question in a rather different
way, what made phlogiston and caloric candidates for elimination? Why
wasn't it concluded that phlogiston is oxygen, that caloric is kinetic energy, and that the earlier theories had just been rather badly mistaken
about some of the properties of phlogiston and caloric?

Let us introduce a bit of terminology. We will call theory changes
in which the entities and processes of the old theory are retained or
reduced to those of the new one *ontologically conservative* theory changes.
Theory changes that are not ontologically conservative we will call *ontologically radical*. Given this terminology, the question we are asking is
how to distinguish ontologically conservative theory changes from ontologically radical ones.

Once again, this is a question that is easier to ask than to answer.
There is, in the philosophy-of-science literature, nothing that even
comes close to a plausible and fully general account of when theory
change sustains an eliminativist conclusion and when it does not. In the
absence of a principled way of deciding when ontological elimination is
in order, the best we can do is to look at the posits of the old theory—
the ones that are at risk of elimination—and ask whether there is anything in the new theory that they might be identified with or reduced
to. If the posits of the new theory strike us as deeply and fundamentally
different from those of the old theory, in the way that molecular motion seems deeply and fundamentally different from the "exquisitely
elastic" fluid posited by caloric theory, then it will be plausible to conclude that the theory change has been a radical one and that an eliminativist conclusion is in order. But since there is no easy measure of
how "deeply and fundamentally different" a pair of posits are, the conclusion we reach is bound to be a judgment call.[5]

To argue that certain sorts of connectionist models support eliminativism about the propositional attitudes, we must make it plausible
that these models are not ontologically conservative. Our strategy will
be to contrast these connectionist models, models like those set out in
section 5, with ontologically conservative models like the one sketched
at the end of section 3, in an effort to underscore just how ontologically
radical the connectionist models are. But here we are getting ahead of
ourselves. Before trying to persuade you that connectionist models are
ontologically radical, we need to take a look at the folk psychological
theory that the connectionist models threaten to replace.

3 *Propositional Attitudes and Commonsense Psychology*

For present purposes, we will assume that commonsense psychology
can plausibly be regarded as a theory and that beliefs, desires, and the
rest of the propositional attitudes are plausibly viewed as posits of that
theory. Though this is not an uncontroversial assumption, the case for

it has been well argued by others.[6] Once it is granted that commonsense psychology is indeed a theory, we expect it will be conceded by almost everyone that the theory is a likely candidate for replacement. In saying this, we do not intend to disparage folk psychology or to beg any questions about the status of the entities it posits. Our point is simply that folk wisdom on matters psychological is not likely to tell us all there is to know. Commonsense psychology, like other folk theories, is bound to be incomplete in many ways and very likely to be inaccurate in more than a few. If this were not the case, there would be no need for a careful, quantitative, experimental science of psychology. With the possible exception of a few diehard Wittgensteinians, just about everyone is prepared to grant that there are many psychological facts and principles beyond those embedded in common sense. If this is right, then we have the first premise needed in an eliminativist argument aimed at beliefs, propositional memories, and the rest of the propositional attitudes. The theory that posits the attitudes is indeed a prime candidate for replacement.

Though commonsense psychology contains a wealth of lore about beliefs, memories, desires, hopes, fears, and the other propositional attitudes, the crucial folk psychological tenets in forging the link between connectionism and eliminativism are the claims that propositional attitudes are *functionally discrete, semantically interpretable* states that play a *causal role* in the production of other propositional attitudes and ultimately in the production of behavior. Following the suggestion in Stich (1983), we'll call this cluster of claims *propositional modularity.*[7] (The reader is cautioned not to confuse this notion of propositional modularity with the very different notion of modularity defended in Fodor 1983.)

There is a great deal of evidence that might be cited in support of the thesis that folk psychology is committed to the tenets of propositional modularity. The fact that commonsense psychology takes beliefs and other propositional attitudes to have semantic properties deserves special emphasis. According to common sense:

1. when people see a dog nearby they typically come to believe *that there is a dog nearby;*
2. when people believe *that the train will be late if there is snow in the mountains,* and come to believe *that there is snow in the mountains,* they will typically come to believe *that the train will be late;*
3. when people who speak English say, "There is a cat in the yard," they typically believe *that there is a cat in the yard.*

And so on, for indefinitely many further examples. Note that these generalizations of commonsense psychology are couched in terms of the *semantic* properties of the attitudes. It is in virtue of being the belief *that p* that a given belief has a given effect or cause. Thus, commonsense psychology treats the predicates expressing these semantic prop-

erties, predicates such as 'believes *that the train is late*', as *projectable* predicates—the sort of predicates that are appropriately used in nomological
or law-like generalizations.

Perhaps the most obvious way to bring out folk psychology's com-
mitment to the thesis that propositional attitudes are *functionally discrete*
states is to note that it typically makes perfectly good sense to claim that
a person has acquired (or lost) a single memory or belief. Thus, for
example, on a given occasion it might plausibly be claimed that when
Henry awoke from his nap he had completely forgotten that the car
keys were hidden in the refrigerator, though he had forgotten nothing
else. In saying that folk psychology views beliefs as the sorts of things
that can be acquired or lost one at a time, we do not mean to be denying that having any particular belief may presuppose a substantial network of related beliefs. The belief that the car keys are in the refrigerator is not one that could be acquired by a primitive tribesman who knew
nothing about cars, keys, or refrigerators. But once the relevant background is in place, as we may suppose it is for us and for Henry, it
seems that folk psychology is entirely comfortable with the possibility
that a person may acquire (or lose) the belief that the car keys are in
the refrigerator while the remainder of his beliefs remain unchanged.
Propositional modularity does not, of course, deny that acquiring one
belief often leads to the acquisition of a cluster of related beliefs. When
Henry is told that the keys are in the refrigerator, he may come to
believe that they haven't been left in the ignition or in his jacket pocket.
But then again he may not. Indeed, on the folk psychological conception of belief, it is perfectly possible for a person to have a long-
standing belief that the keys are in the refrigerator and to continue
searching for them in the bedroom.[8]

To illustrate the way in which folk psychology takes propositional
attitudes to be functionally discrete, *causally active* states, let us sketch a
pair of more elaborate examples.

In commonsense psychology, behavior is often explained by appeal
to certain of the agent's beliefs and desires. Thus, to explain why Alice
went to her office, we might note that she wanted to send some e-mail
messages (and, of course, she believed she could do so from her office).
However, in some cases an agent will have several sets of beliefs and
desires, each of which *might* lead to the same behavior. Thus, we may
suppose that Alice also wanted to talk to her research assistant and that
she believed he would be at the office. In such cases, commonsense
psychology assumes that Alice's going to her office might have been
caused by either one of the belief/desire pairs, or by both, and that
determining which of these options obtains is an empirical matter. So,
it is entirely possible that on *this* occasion Alice's desire to send some e-
mail played no role in producing her behavior; it was the desire to talk
with her research assistant that actually caused her to go to the office.
However, had she not wanted to talk with her research assistant, she
might have gone to the office anyhow, because the desire to send some

e-mail, which was causally inert in her actual decision making, might then have become actively involved. Note that in this case common-sense psychology is prepared to recognize a pair of quite distinct, semantically characterized states, one of which may be causally active while the other is not.

Our second illustration is parallel to the first but focuses on beliefs and inference rather than desires and action. On the commonsense view, it may sometimes happen that a person has a number of belief clusters, any one of which might lead him to infer some further belief. When he actually does draw the inference, folk psychology assumes that it is an empirical question what he inferred it from and that this question typically has a determinate answer. Suppose, for example, that Inspector Clouseau believes that the butler said he spent the evening at the village hotel and that he said he arrived back on the morning train. Suppose Clouseau also believes that the village hotel is closed for the season and that the morning train has been taken out of service. Given these beliefs, along with some widely shared background beliefs, Clouseau might well infer that the butler is lying. If he does, folk psychology presumes that the inference might be based either on his beliefs about the hotel, or on his beliefs about the train, or both. It is entirely possible, from the perspective of commonsense psychology, that although Clouseau has long known that the hotel is closed for the season, this belief played no role in his inference on this particular occasion. Once again we see commonsense psychology invoking a pair of distinct propositional attitudes, one of which is causally active on a particular occasion while the other is causally inert.

In the psychological literature, there is no shortage of models for human belief or memory which follow the lead of commonsense psychology in supposing that propositional modularity is true. Indeed, prior to the emergence of connectionism, just about all psychological models of propositional memory, save for those urged by behaviorists, were comfortably compatible with propositional modularity. Typically, these models view a subject's store of beliefs or memories as an interconnected collection of functionally discrete, semantically interpretable states which interact in systematic ways. Some of these models represent individual beliefs as sentence-like structures—strings of symbols which can be individually activated by transferring them from long-term memory to the more limited memory of a central processing unit. Other models represent beliefs as a network of labeled nodes and labeled links through which patterns of activation may spread. Still other models represent beliefs as sets of production rules.[9] In all three sorts of models, it is generally the case that for any given cognitive episode, like performing a particular inference or answering a question, some of the memory states will be actively involved, and others will be dormant.

In figure 2-1 we have displayed a fragment of a "semantic network" representation of memory, in the style of Collins and Quillian (1972). In this model, each distinct proposition in memory is represented by an

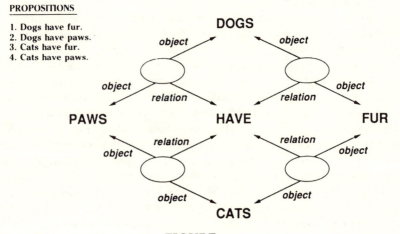

SEMANTIC NETWORK

PROPOSITIONS

1. Dogs have fur.
2. Dogs have paws.
3. Cats have fur.
4. Cats have paws.

FIGURE 2-1

oval node along with its labeled links to various concepts. By adding assumptions about the way in which questions or other sorts of memory probes lead to activation spreading through the network, the model enables us to make predictions about speed and accuracy in various experimental studies of memory. For our purposes, three facts about this model are of particular importance. First, since each proposition is encoded in a functionally discrete way, it is a straightforward matter to add or subtract a *single* proposition from memory while leaving the rest of the network unchanged. Thus, for example, figure 2-2 depicts the result of removing one proposition from the network in figure 2-1. Sec-

FIGURE 2-2

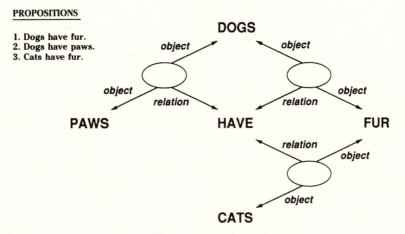

SEMANTIC NETWORK

PROPOSITIONS

1. Dogs have fur.
2. Dogs have paws.
3. Cats have fur.

ond, the model treats predicates expressing the semantic properties of beliefs or memories as *projectable*.[10] They are treated as the sorts of predicates that pick out scientifically genuine *kinds*, rather than mere accidental conglomerates, and thus are suitable for inclusion in the statement of law-like regularities. To see this, we need only consider the way in which such models are tested against empirical data about memory acquisition and forgetting. Typically, it will be assumed that if a subject is told (for example) that the policeman arrested the hippie, then the subject will (with a certain probability) remember *that the policeman arrested the hippie*.[11] And this assumption is taken to express a nomological generalization—it captures something law-like about the way in which the cognitive system works. So, while the class of people who *remember that the policeman arrested the hippie* may differ psychologically in all sorts of way, the theory treats them as a psychologically natural kind. Third, in any given memory search or inference task exploiting a semantic network model, it makes sense to ask which propositions were activated and which were not. Thus, a search in the network of figure 2-1 might terminate without ever activating the proposition that cats have paws.

4 A Family of Connectionist Hypotheses

Our theme in the previous section was that commonsense psychology is committed to propositional modularity and that many models of memory proposed in the cognitive psychology literature are comfortably compatible with this assumption. In the present section we want to describe a class of connectionist models which, we will argue, are *not* readily compatible with propositional modularity. The connectionist models we have in mind share three properties:

> **1.** their encoding of information in the connection weights and in the biases on units is *widely distributed* rather than being *localist;*
> **2.** individual hidden units in the network have no comfortable symbolic interpretation; they are *subsymbolic*, to use a term suggested by Paul Smolensky;
> **3.** the models are intended *as cognitive models*, not merely as *implementations* of cognitive models.

A bit later in this section we will elaborate further on each of these three features, and in the next section we will describe a simple example of a connectionist model that meets our three criteria. However, we are under no illusion that what we say will be sufficient to give a sharp-edged characterization of the class of connectionist models we have in mind. Nor is such a sharp-edged characterization essential for our argument. It will suffice if we can convince you that there is a significant class of connectionist models which are incompatible with the propositional modularity of folk psychology.

Before saying more about the three features on our list, we would do well to give a more general characterization of the sort of models we are calling "connectionist" and introduce some of the jargon that comes with the territory. To this end, let us quote at some length from Paul Smolensky's lucid overview;

> Connectionist models are large networks of simple, parallel computing elements, each of which carries a numerical *activation value* which it computes from neighboring elements in the network, using some simple numerical formula. The network elements or *units* influence each other's values through connections that carry a numerical strength or *weight.* . . .
>
> In a typical . . . model, input to the system is provided by imposing activation values on the *input units* of the network; these numerical values represent some encoding or *representation* of the input. The activation on the input units propagates along the connections until some set of activation values emerges on the *output units;* these activation values encode the output the system has computed from the input. In between the input and output units there may be other units, often called *hidden units,* that participate in representing neither the input nor the output.
>
> The computation performed by the network in transforming the input pattern of activity to the output pattern depends on the set of connection strengths; *these weights are usually regarded as encoding the system's knowledge* [emphasis added]. In this sense, the connection strengths play the role of the program in a conventional computer. Much of the allure of the connectionist approach is that many connectionist networks *program themselves,* that is, they have autonomous procedures for tuning their weights to eventually perform some specific computation. Such *learning procedures* often depend on training in which the network is presented with sample input/output pairs from the function it is supposed to compute. In learning networks with hidden units, the network itself "decides" what computations the hidden units will perform; because these units represent neither inputs nor outputs, they are never "told" what their values should be, even during training. (1988, 1)

One point must be added to Smolensky's portrait. In many connectionist models, the hidden units and the output units are assigned a numerical "bias," which is added into the calculation determining the unit's activation level. The learning procedures for such networks typically set both the connection strengths and the biases. Thus, in these networks the system's knowledge is usually regarded as encoded in *both* the connection strengths and the biases.

So much for a general overview. Let us now try to explain the three features that characterize those connectionist models we take to be incompatible with propositional modularity.

1. In many nonconnectionist cognitive models, like the one illustrated at the end of section 3, it is an easy matter to locate a functionally distinct part of the model encoding each proposition or state of affairs represented in the system. Indeed, according to Fodor and Pylyshyn

(1988, 57), "conventional [computational] architecture requires that there be distinct symbolic expressions for each state of affairs that it can represent." In some connectionist models, an analogous sort of functional localization is possible, not only for the input and output units but for the hidden units as well. Thus, for example, in certain connectionist models, various individual units or small clusters of units are themselves intended to represent specific properties or features of the environment. When the connection strength from one such unit to another is strongly positive, this might be construed as the system's representation of the proposition that if the first feature is present, so is the second. However, in many connectionist networks, it is not possible to localize propositional representation beyond the input layer: That is, there are no particular features or states of the system which lend themselves to a straightforward semantic evaluation. This can sometimes be a real inconvenience to the connectionist model builder when the system as a whole fails to achieve its goal because it has not represented the world the way it should. When this happens, as Smolensky notes, "it is not necessarily possible to localize a failure of veridical representation. Any particular state is part of a large causal system of states, and failures of the system to meet goal conditions cannot in general be localized to any particular state or state component" (1988, 15). It is connectionist networks of this sort, in which it is not possible to isolate the representation of particular propositions or states of affairs within the nodes, connection strengths, and biases, that we have in mind when we talk about the encoding of information in the biases, weights, and hidden nodes being *widely distributed* rather than *localist*.

2. As we've just noted, there are some connectionist models in which some or all of the units are intended to represent specific properties or features of the system's environment. These units may be viewed as the model's symbols for the properties or features in question. However, in models where the weights and biases have been tuned by learning algorithms, it is often not the case that any single unit or any small collection of units will end up representing a specific feature of the environment in any straightforward way. As we shall see in the next section, it is often plausible to view such networks as collectively or holistically encoding a set of propositions, although none of the hidden units, weights, or biases are comfortably viewed as *symbols*. When this is the case, we will call the strategy of representation invoked in the model *subsymbolic*. Typically (perhaps always?), networks exploiting subsymbolic strategies of representation will encode information in a widely distributed way.

3. The third item on our list is not a feature of connectionist models themselves but a point about how the models are to be interpreted. In making this point, we must presuppose a notion of theoretical or explanatory level which, despite much discussion in the recent literature, is far from being a paradigm of clarity.[12] Perhaps the clearest way

to introduce the notion of explanatory level is against the background of the familiar functionalist thesis that psychological theories are analogous to programs which can be implemented on a variety of very different sorts of computers.[13] If one accepts this analogy, then it makes sense to ask whether a particular connectionist model is intended as a model at the psychological level or at the level of underlying neural implementation. Because of their obvious, though in many ways very partial, similarity to real neural architectures, it is tempting to view connectionist models as models of the implementation of psychological processes. And some connectionist model builders endorse this view quite explicitly. So viewed, however, connectionist models are not *psychological* or *cognitive* models at all, any more than a story of how cognitive processes are implemented at the quantum mechanical level is a psychological story. A very different view that connectionist model builders can and often do take is that their models are at the psychological level, not at the level of implementation. So construed, the models are in competition with other psychological models of the same phenomena. Thus, a connectionist model of word recognition would be an alternative to—and not simply a possible implementation of—a nonconnectionist model of word recognition; a connectionist theory of memory would be a competitor to a semantic network theory, and so on. Connectionists who hold this view of their theories often illustrate the point by drawing analogies with other sciences. Smolensky, for example, suggests that connectionist models stand to traditional cognitive models (like semantic networks) in much the same way that quantum mechanics stands to classical mechanics. In each case, the newer theory is deeper, more general, and more accurate over a broader range of phenomena. But in each case, the new theory and the old are competing at the same explanatory level. If one is right, the other must be wrong.

In light of our concerns in this paper, there is one respect in which the analogy between connectionist models and quantum mechanics may be thought to beg an important question. For while quantum mechanics is conceded to be a *better* theory than classical mechanics, a plausible case could be made that the shift from classical to quantum mechanics was an ontologically *conservative* theory change. In any event, it is not clear that the change was ontologically *radical*. If our central thesis in this paper is correct, then the relation between connectionist models and more traditional cognitive models is more like the relation between the caloric theory of heat and the kinetic theory. The caloric and kinetic theories are at the same explanatory level, though the shift from one to the other was pretty clearly ontologically radical. In order to make the case that the caloric analogy is the more appropriate one, it will be useful to describe a concrete, though very simple, connectionist model of memory that meets the three criteria we have been trying to explicate.

5   A Connectionist Model of Memory

Our goal in constructing the model was to produce a connectionist network that would do at least some of the tasks done by more traditional cognitive models of memory and perspicuously exhibit the sort of distributed, subsymbolic encoding described in the previous section. We began by constructing a network, we'll call it network A, that would judge the truth or falsehood of the sixteen propositions displayed above the line in figure 2-3. The network was a typical three-tiered feed-forward network consisting of sixteen input units, four hidden units, and one output unit, as shown in figure 2-4. The input coding of each proposition is shown in the center column in figure 2-3. Outputs close to 1 were interpreted as true, and outputs close to zero were interpreted as false. Back propagation, a familiar connectionist learning algorithm, was used to "train up" the network, thereby setting the connection weights and biases. Training was terminated when the network consistently gave an output higher than 0.9 for each true proposition and lower than 0.1 for each false proposition. Figure 2-5 shows the connection weights between the input units and the leftmost hidden unit in the trained-up network, along with the bias on that unit. Figure 2-6 indicates the connection weights and biases further upstream. Fig-

FIGURE 2-3

	Proposition	Input	Output
1	Dogs have fur.	11000011 00001111	1 true
2	Dogs have paws.	11000011 00110011	1 true
3	Dogs have fleas.	11000011 00111111	1 true
4	Dogs have legs.	11000011 00111100	1 true
5	Cats have fur.	11001100 00001111	1 true
6	Cats have paws.	11001100 00110011	1 true
7	Cats have fleas.	11001100 00111111	1 true
8	Fish have scales.	11110000 00110000	1 true
9	Fish have fins.	11110000 00001100	1 true
10	Fish have gills.	11110000 00000011	1 true
11	Cats have gills.	11001100 00000011	0 false
12	Fish have legs.	11110000 00111100	0 false
13	Fish have fleas.	11110000 00111111	0 false
14	Dogs have scales.	11000011 00110000	0 false
15	Dogs have fins.	11000011 00001100	0 false
16	Cats have fins.	11001100 00001100	0 false

Added Proposition

17	Fish have eggs.	11110000 11001000	1 true

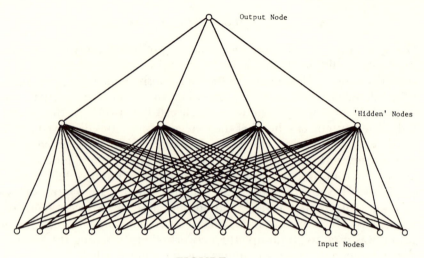

FIGURE 2-4

Network A

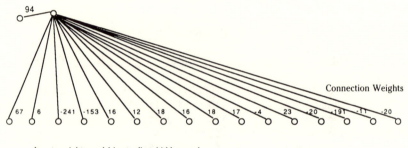

Input weights and bias to first hidden node
in network with 16 propositions.

FIGURE 2-5

ure 2-7 shows the way in which the network computes its response to the proposition *Dogs have fur* when that proposition is encoded in the input units.

There is a clear sense in which the trained-up network A may be said to have stored information about the truth or falsity of propositions 1–16 since when any one of these propositions is presented to the network it correctly judges whether the proposition is true or false. In this respect, it is similar to various semantic network models which can be constructed to perform much the same task. However, there is a striking difference between network A and a semantic network model like the one depicted in figure 2-1. For, as we noted earlier, in the semantic network there is a functionally distinct subpart associated with

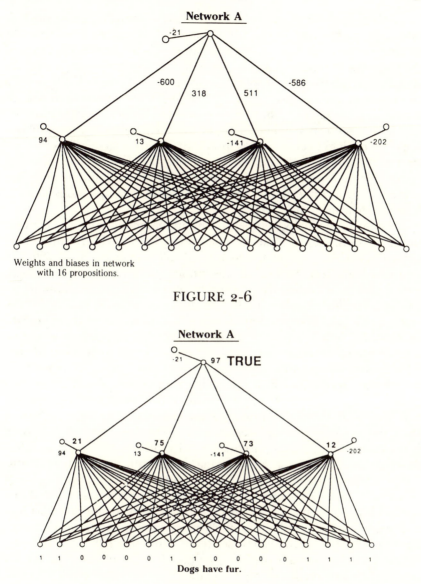

Weights and biases in network
with 16 propositions.

FIGURE 2-6

Dogs have fur.

FIGURE 2-7

each proposition, and thus it makes perfectly good sense to ask, for any probe of the network, whether or not the representation of a specific proposition played a causal role. In the connectionist network, by contrast, there is no distinct state or part of the network that serves to represent any particular proposition. The information encoded in network A is stored holistically and distributed throughout the network. Whenever information is extracted from network A, by giving it an input string and seeing whether it computes a high or a low value for the output unit, *many* connection strengths, *many* biases, and *many* hidden units play a role in the computation. And any particular weight or unit or bias will help to encode information about *many* different propositions. It simply makes no sense to ask whether or not the representation of a particular proposition plays a causal role in the network's computation. It is in just this respect that our connectionist model of memory seems radically incongruent with the propositional modularity of commonsense psychology. For, as we saw in section 2-3, commonsense psychology seems to presuppose that there is generally some answer to the question of whether a particular belief or memory played a causal role in a specific cognitive episode. But if belief and memory are subserved by a connectionist network like ours, such questions seem to have no clear meaning.

The incompatibility between propositional modularity and connectionist models like ours can be made even more vivid by contrasting network A with a second network, we'll call it network B, depicted in figures 2-8 and 2-9. Network B was trained up just as the first one was, except that one additional proposition was added to the training set (coded as indicated below the line in figure 2-3). Thus, network B encodes all the same propositions as network A plus one more. In semantic network models, and other traditional cognitive models, it would be an easy matter to say which states or features of the system encode the added proposition, and it would be a simple task to determine whether or not the representation of the added proposition played a role in a particular episode modeled by the system. But, plainly, in the connectionist network those questions are quite senseless. The point is not that there are no differences between the two networks. Quite the opposite is the case; the differences are many and widespread. But these differences do not correlate in any systematic way with the functionally discrete, semantically interpretable states posited by folk psychology and by more traditional cognitive models. Since information is encoded in a highly distributed manner, with each connection weight and bias embodying information salient to many propositions, and information regarding any given proposition scattered throughout the network, the system lacks functionally distinct, identifiable substructures that are semantically interpretable as representations of individual propositions.

The contrast between network A and network B enables us to make our point about the incompatibility between commonsense psychology and these sorts of connectionist models in a rather different way. We noted in section 2 that commonsense psychology treats predicates expressing the semantic properties of propositional attitudes as projectable. Thus 'believes that dogs have fur' or 'remembers that dogs have fur' will be projectable predicates in commonsense psychology. Now, both network A and network B might serve as models for a cognitive agent who believes that dogs have fur; both networks store or represent the information that dogs have fur. Nor are these the only two. If we

Network B

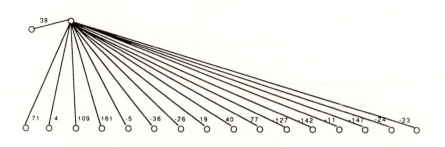

Input weights and bias to first hidden node
in network with 17 propositions.

FIGURE 2-8

Network B

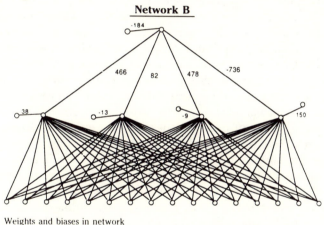

Weights and biases in network
with 17 propositions.

FIGURE 2-9

were to train up a network on the seventeen propositions in figure 2-3 plus a few (or minus a few), we would get yet another system, which is as different from networks A and B as these two are from each other. The moral here is that though there are *indefinitely* many connectionist networks that represent the information that dogs have fur just as well as network A does, these networks have no projectable features in common that are describable in the language of connectionist theory. From the point of view of the connectionist model builder, the class of networks that might model a cognitive agent who believes that dogs have fur is not a genuine kind at all but simply a chaotically disjunctive set.

Commonsense psychology treats the class of people who believe that dogs have fur as a psychologically natural kind; connectionist psychology does not.[14]

6   Objections and Replies

The argument we've set out in the previous sections has encountered no shortage of objections. In this section, we will try to reconstruct the most interesting of these and indicate how we would reply.

Objection 1: Models like A and B are not serious models for human belief or propositional memory.

Of course, the models we've constructed are tiny toys that were built to illustrate the features set out in section 3 in a perspicuous way. They were never intended to model any substantial part of human propositional memory. But various reasons have been offered for doubting that anything like these models could ever be taken seriously as psychological models of propositional memory. Some critics have claimed that the models simply will not scale up—that while teaching a network to recognize fifteen or twenty propositions may be easy enough, it is just not going to be possible to train up a network that can recognize a few thousand propositions, still less a few hundred thousand.[15] Others have objected that while more traditional models of memory, including those based on sentence-like storage, those using semantic networks, and those based on production systems, all provide some strategy for *inference* or *generalization* which enables the system to answer questions about propositions it was not explicitly taught, models like those we have constructed are incapable of inference and generalization. It has also been urged that these models fail as accounts of human memory because they provide no obvious way to account for the fact that suitably prepared humans can easily acquire propositional information one proposition at a time. Under ordinary circumstances, we can just *tell* Henry that the car keys are in the refrigerator, and he can readily record this fact in memory. He doesn't need anything like the sort of massive retraining that would be required to teach one of our connectionist networks a new proposition.

Reply 1: If this were a paper aimed at defending connectionist models of propositional memory, we would have to take on each of these putative shortcomings in some detail. And in each instance, there is at least something to be said on the connectionist side. Thus, for example, it just is not true that networks such as A and B don't generalize beyond the propositions on which they've been trained. In network A, for example, the training set included

Dogs have fur.   Cats have fur.
Dogs have paws.   Cats have paws.
Dogs have fleas.   Cats have fleas.

It also included
      Dogs have legs
but not
      Cats have legs.
When the network was given an encoding of this last proposition, however, it generalized correctly and responded affirmatively. Similarly, the
network responded negatively to an encoding of
      Cats have scales
though it had not previously been exposed to this proposition.

However, it is important to see that this sort of point-by-point-re-
sponse to the charge that networks like ours are inadequate models
for propositional memory is not really required, given the thesis we
are defending in this paper. For what we are trying to establish is a
conditional thesis: *If* connectionist models of memory of the sort we describe in section 3 are right, *then* propositional-attitude psychology is in
serious trouble. Since conditionals with false antecedents are true, we
win by default if it turns out that the antecedent of our conditional
is false.

> *Objection 2a:* Our models do not really violate the principle of
> propositional modularity, since the propositions the system has
> learned are coded in functionally discrete ways, though this may
> not be obvious.

We've heard this objection elaborated along three quite different
lines. The first line—let's call it objection 2a—notes that functionally
discrete coding may often be *very* hard to notice and cannot be expected
to be visible on casual inspection. Consider, for example, the way in
which sentences are stored in the memory of a typical von Neuman
architecture computer—for concreteness we might suppose that the
sentences are part of an English text and are being stored while the
computer is running a word-processing program. Parts of sentences
may be stored at physically scattered memory addresses linked together
in complex ways, and, given an account of the contents of all relevant
memory addresses, one would be hard put to say where a particular
sentence is stored. But, nonetheless, each sentence is stored in a *functionally discrete* way. Thus, if one knew enough about the system, it
would be possible to erase any particular sentence it is storing by tam-
pering with the contents of the appropriate memory addresses while
leaving the rest of the sentences the system is storing untouched. Similarly, it has been urged, connectionist networks may in fact encode
propositions in functionally discrete ways, though this may not be evi-
dent from a casual inspection of the trained-up network's biases and
connection strengths.

Reply 2a: It is a bit difficult to come to grips with this objection,
since what the critic is proposing is that in models like those we have
constructed there *might* be some covert functionally discrete system of

propositional encoding that has yet to be discovered. In response to this, we must concede that indeed there might. We certainly have no argument that even comes close to demonstrating that the discovery of such a covert functionally discrete encoding is impossible. Moreover, we concede that if such a covert system were discovered, then our argument would be seriously undermined. However, we're inclined to think that the burden of argument is on the critic to show that such a system is not merely possible but *likely;* in the absence of any serious reason to think that networks like ours do encode propositions in functionally discrete ways, the mere logical possibility that they might is hardly a serious threat.

The second version of objection 2—we'll call it *objection 2b*—makes a specific proposal about the way in which networks like A and B might be discretely, though covertly, encoding propositions. The encoding, it is urged, is to be found in the pattern of activation of the hidden nodes, when a given proposition is presented to the network. Since there are four hidden nodes in our networks, the activation pattern on presentation of any given input may be represented as an ordered 4-tuple. Thus, for example, when network A is presented with the encoded proposition *Dogs have fur,* the relevant 4-tuple would be (21, 75, 73, 12), as shown in Figure 2–7. Equivalently, we may think of each activation pattern as a point in a four-dimensional hyperspace. Since each proposition corresponds to a unique point in the hyperspace, that point may be viewed as the encoding of the proposition. Moreover, that point represents a functionally discrete state of the system.[16]

Reply 2b: What is being proposed is that the pattern of activation of the system on presentation of an encoding of the proposition *p* be identified with the belief that *p.* But this proposal is singularly implausible. Perhaps the best way to see this is to note that in commonsense psychology beliefs and propositional memories are typically of substantial duration; and they are the sorts of things that cognitive agents generally have lots of even when they are not using them. Consider an example. Are kangaroos marsupials? Surely you've believed for years that they are, though in all likelihood this is the first time today that your belief has been activated or used.[17] An activation pattern, however, is not an enduring state of a network; indeed, it is not a state of the network at all except when the network has had the relevant proposition as input. Moreover, there is an enormous number of other beliefs that you've had for years. But it makes no sense to suppose that a network could have many activation patterns continuously over a long period of time. At any given time, a network exhibits at most one pattern of activation. So, activation patterns are just not the sorts of things that can plausibly be identified with beliefs or their representations.

Objection 2c: At this juncture, a number of critics have suggested that long-standing beliefs might be identified not with activation patterns, which are transient states of networks, but with *dispositions to produce activation patterns.* Thus, in network A, the belief that dogs have fur would not be identified with a location in activation hyperspace but with the network's *disposition* to end up at that location when the proposition is presented. This *dispositional state* is an enduring state of the system; it is a state the network can be in no matter what its current state of activation may be, just as a sugar cube may have a disposition to dissolve in water even when there is no water nearby.[18] Some have gone on to suggest that the familiar philosophical distinction between dispositional and occurrent beliefs might be captured, in connectionist models, as the distinction between dispositions to produce activation patterns and activation patterns themselves.

Reply 2c: Our reply to this suggestion is that while dispositions to produce activation patterns are indeed *enduring* states of the system, they are not the right sort of enduring states—they are not the discrete, independently causally active states that folk psychology requires. Recall that on the folk psychological conception of belief and inference, there will often be a variety of quite different underlying causal patterns that may lead to the acquisition and avowal of a given belief. When Clouseau says that the butler did it, he may have just inferred this with the help of his long-standing belief that the train is out of service. Or he may have inferred it by using his belief that the hotel is closed. Or both long-standing beliefs may have played a role in the inference. Moreover, it is also possible that Clouseau drew this inference some time ago and is now reporting a relatively long-standing belief. But it is hard to see how anything like these distinctions can be captured by the dispositional account in question. In reacting to a given input, say *p,* a network takes on a specific activation value. It may also have dispositions to take on other activation values on other inputs, say *q* and *r.* But there is no obvious way to interpret the claim that these further dispositions play a causal role in the network's reaction to *p*— or, for that matter, that they do not play a role. Nor can we make any sense of the idea that on one occasion the encoding of *q* (say, the proposition that the train is out of service) played a role while the encoding of *r* (say, the proposition that the hotel is closed) did not and on another occasion things went the other way around. The propositional modularity presupposed by commonsense psychology requires that belief tokens be functionally discrete states capable of causally interacting with one another in some cognitive episodes and of remaining causally inert in other cognitive episodes. However, in a distributed connectionist system like network A, the dispositional state which produces one activation pattern is functionally inseparable from the dispositional state which produces another. Thus, it is impossible to isolate some propositions as causally active in certain cognitive episodes while others are not. We conclude that reaction pattern dispositions won't do as belief tokens. Nor, so far as we can see, are there any other states of networks like A and B that will fill the bill.

7 Conclusion

The thesis we have been defending in this paper is that connectionist models of a certain sort are incompatible with the propositional modularity embedded in commonsense psychology. The connectionist models in question are those which are offered as models at the *cognitive* level and in which the encoding of information is widely distributed and subsymbolic. In such models, we have argued, there are no *discrete, semantically interpretable* states that play a *causal* role in some cognitive episodes but not others. Thus, there is in these models nothing with which the propositional attitudes of commonsense psychology can plausibly be identified. If these models turn out to offer the best accounts of human belief and memory, we will be confronting an *ontologically radical* theory change—the sort of theory change that will sustain the conclusion that propositional attitudes, like caloric and phlogiston, do not exist.

Notes

Thanks are due to Ned Block, Paul Churchland, Gary Cottrell, Adrian Cussins, Jerry Fodor, John Heil, Frank Jackson, David Kirsh, Patricia Kitcher, and Philip Kitcher for useful feedback on earlier versions of this paper. Talks based on the paper have been presented at the UCSD Cognitive Science Seminar and at conferences sponsored by the Howard Hughes Medical Foundation and the University of North Carolina at Greensboro. Comments and questions from these audiences have proved helpful in many ways.

    1. See, for example, P. M. Churchland (1981; 1986), where explicitly eliminativist conclusions are drawn on the basis of speculations about the success of cognitive models similar to those we shall discuss.

    2. Fodor and Pylyshyn (1988).

    3. We are aware that certain philosophers and historians of science have actually entertained ideas similar to the suggestion that the planets spoken of by pre-Copernican astronomers do not exist. See, for example, Kuhn (1962, chap. 10), and Feyerabend (1981, chap. 4). However, we take this suggestion to be singularly implausible. Eliminativist arguments can't be that easy. Just what has gone wrong with the accounts of meaning and reference that lead to such claims is less clear. For further discussion on these matters, see Kuhn (1983) and Philip Kitcher (1978; 1983).

    4. For some detailed discussion of scientific reduction, see Nagel (1961), Schaffner (1967), Hooker (1981), and Philip Kitcher (1984). The genetics case is not without controversy. See Philip Kitcher (1982; 1984).

    5. It's worth noting that judgments on this matter can differ quite substantially. At one end of the spectrum are writers like Feyerabend (1981) and perhaps Kuhn (1962), for whom relatively small differences in theory are enough

to justify the suspicion that there has been an ontologically radical change. Toward the other end are writers like Lycan, who writes:

> I am at pains to advocate a very liberal view. . . . I am entirely willing to give up fairly large chunks of our commonsensical or platitudinous theory of belief or of desire (or of almost anything else) and decide that we were just wrong about a lot of things, without drawing the inference that we are no longer talking about belief or desire. . . . I think the ordinary word "belief" (qua theoretical term of folk psychology) points dimly toward a natural kind that we have not fully grasped and that only mature psychology will reveal. I expect that "belief" will turn out to refer to some kind of information bearing inner state of a sentient being, . . . but the kind of state it refers to may have only a few of the properties usually attributed to beliefs by common sense. (1988a, 31–32)

On our view, both extreme positions are implausible. As we noted earlier, the Copernican revolution did not show that the planets studied by Ptolemy do not exist. But Lavoisier's chemical revolution *did* show that phlogiston does not exist. Yet on Lycan's "very liberal view," it is hard to see why we should not conclude that phlogiston really does exist after all—it's really oxygen, and prior to Lavoisier "we were just very wrong about a lot of things."

6. For an early and influential statement of the view that commonsense psychology is a theory, see Sellars (1956). More recently, the view has been defended by P. M. Churchland (1970; 1979, chaps. 1 and 4) and by Fodor (1987, chap 1). For the opposite view, see Wilkes (1978), Madell (1986), and Sharpe (1987).

7. See Stich (1983, 237ff).

8. Cherniak (1986, chap. 3) notes that this sort of absentmindedness is commonplace in literature and in ordinary life and sometimes leads to disastrous consequences.

9. For sentential models, see McCarthy (1968; 1980; and 1986), and Kintsch (1974). For semantic networks, see Quillian (1966), Collins and Quillian (1972); Rumelhart, Lindsay, and Norman (1972), Anderson and Bower (1973), and Anderson (1976; 1980, chap. 4). For production systems, see Newell and Simon (1972), Newell (1973), Anderson (1983), and Holland et al. (1986).

10. For the classic discussion of the distinction between projectable and nonprojectable predicates, see Goodman (1965).

11. See, for example, Anderson and Bower (1973).

12. Broadbent (1985), Rumelhart and McClelland (1985), Rumelhart, McClelland, and PDP Research Group (1986, chap. 4), Smolensky (1988), Fodor and Pylyshyn (1988).

13. The notion of program being invoked here is itself open to a pair of quite different interpretations. For the right reading, see Ramsey (1989).

14. This way of making the point about the incompatibility between connectionist models and commonsense psychology was suggested to us by Jerry Fodor.

15. This point has been urged by Daniel Dennett, among others.

16. Quite a number of people have suggested this move, including Gary Cottrell and Adrian Cussins.

17. As Lycan notes, on the commonsense notion of belief, people have lots of them "even when they are asleep" (1988a, 57).

18. Something like this objection was suggested to us by Ned Block and by Frank Jackson.

CHAPTER 3

What *Is* Folk Psychology?

With Ian Ravenscroft

1   Introduction

For the last two decades, a doctrine called *eliminative materialism* (or sometimes just *eliminativism*) has been a major focus of discussion in the philosophy of mind. It is easy to understand why eliminativism has attracted so much attention, for it is hard to imagine a more radical and provocative doctrine. What eliminativism claims is that the intentional states and processes that are alluded to in our everyday descriptions and explanations of people's mental lives and their actions are *myths*. Like the gods that Homer invoked to explain the outcome of battles, or the witches that Inquisitors invoked to explain local catastrophes, they *do not exist*. According to eliminativists, there are no such things as beliefs or desires or hopes or fears or thoughts. These putative states and processes are the badly misguided posits of a seriously mistaken theory, just like phlogiston and caloric fluid and the luminiferous aether.[1]

If eliminativism is right, then as Jerry Fodor has suggested, it might well be "the greatest intellectual catastrophe in the history of our species" (1987, xii). To see why, we need only consider the consequences of the doctrine in various domains of intellectual activity. Let's start with history: Did Lincoln sign the Emancipation Proclamation because he wanted to abolish slavery? Or was it because he thought it would be a strategically useful move, helping to weaken the Confederacy? If eliminativism is right, then neither of these explanations could possibly be correct since there are no wants and there are no thoughts. Consider epistemology: From Descartes to the present, epistemologists have tried to construct a systematic theory that will tell us which of a person's beliefs are justified and which are not. But if eliminativism is right, there are no justified beliefs; there are no beliefs at all. Or consider anthropology: Some researchers have claimed that a variety of human emotions, like fear, surprise, and disgust, are cultural universals rooted in biology; others have urged that all emotions are "social constructions." But if eliminativism is right, then there is something profoundly misguided about this dispute. For fear, surprise, and disgust are intentional states, and eliminativism claims that there are no such things. Finally, consider psychology: If eliminativism is right, then much of what goes on in clinical psychology is bound to be useless. People's problems can't be remedied by removing irrational beliefs or making them aware of subconscious desires; there are no such things. And, obviously, if eliminativism is right, then as Fodor insists, many cognitive psychologists ought to "do [their] science in some other way." Or at least they "should stop spending the taxpayer's money" (1990b, 202–3).

Although advocates of eliminativism are not always as clear or careful as one might wish, they are typically inclined to make four distinct claims that might be formulated as follows:

> **1.** "Belief," "desire," and other familiar intentional-state expressions are among the theoretical terms of a commonsense theory of the mind. This theory is often called *folk psychology*.
> **2.** Folk psychology is a seriously mistaken theory. Many of the claims it makes about the states and processes that give rise to behavior, and many of the presuppositions of those claims, are false.
> **3.** A mature science that explains how the mind/brain works and how it produces the behavior we observe will not refer to the commonsense intentional states and processes invoked by folk psychology. Beliefs, desires, and the rest will not be part of the ontology of a mature scientific psychology.
> **4.** The intentional states of commonsense psychology do not exist.

It is clear that the first of these claims is a crucial presupposition of the second. After that, the putative relations among the claims get a bit murky. It sometimes appears that both friends and foes of eliminativism assume that (2) can be used to establish (4). And, of course, if (4) is right, then (3) comes pretty much for free. For if beliefs and desires don't exist, then surely a mature science has no business invoking them. In other places it seems that (2) is taken to support (3). If that's the way the argument is supposed to go, then presumably (3) will be taken to support (4), though explicit arguments from one to the other are not easy to find.

Most of the literature debating the plausibility of eliminativism has focused on the second of these claims.[2] In this chapter, however, our focus will be on the first. That premise of the eliminativist argument has already provoked a certain amount of debate, with some writers protesting that commonsense psychology cannot be regarded as a causal or explanatory theory because its principles are partly normative or largely analytic. Others maintain that the basic function of folk psychology is not to predict and explain but to warn, promise, congratulate, and do a thousand and one other jobs that are fundamental to the smooth workings of our interpersonal lives.[3] Eliminativists typically concede most of these points but argue that it makes little difference. Whatever other uses it may have, they insist, folk psychology is still a causal and explanatory theory, and a seriously mistaken one (see Stich 1983, chap. 10; P. M. Churchland 1989).

We propose to raise a rather different collection of concerns about the idea that ordinary intentional expressions are theoretical terms in a commonsense theory. Our central contention is that this idea can be unpacked (and, indeed, *has* been unpacked) in a variety of very different ways. Though many writers on both sides of the eliminativism debate take (1) to be unambiguous and unproblematic, there are actually *lots* of things that the label "folk psychology" might be (and *has* been) used to denote. Moreover, on *some* interpretations of (1), the remainder of the eliminativist argument will be in serious trouble. For on some readings, folk psychology is not the sort of thing that makes claims or expresses propositions. Thus, it is not the sort of thing that *can* be either true or false. And obviously, on those readings, the second step in the eliminativist argument couldn't possibly be right. For if folk psychology makes no claims, it makes no false claims. Our goal in this chapter is to pull apart these various readings of "folk psychology" and to get as clear as possible on which ones are and which are not compatible with the remainder of the eliminativsts' argument.

Before getting on to that, however, it will be useful to consider another issue. The idea that "belief," "desire," and other intentional locutions are terms embedded in a commonsense theory has become commonplace in the philosophy of mind. But though talk of a "folk theory" and its "posits" is all but ubiquitous in the recent literature, it is also rather puzzling. Ordinary folk certainly don't take themselves to be invoking a theory when they use intentional terms to explain other people's behavior. Still less do they think they are using a theory when they report their own beliefs and desires. So why is it that so many philosophers and cognitive scientists are convinced that our everyday predictions and explanations of behavior do involve some sort of theory? Why does this idea seem so plausible to many philosophers and psychologists and so implausible to almost everyone else? One good way to approach these questions is to track down the history of the idea. That is what we propose to do in the two sections to follow. While we do not pretend to be serious historical scholars, we think it is pretty clear that the view set out in (1) has two major historical roots. One of them is to be found in the work of Wilfrid Sellars, the other in the dominant explanatory strategy of contemporary cognitive science.

2   Folk Psychology's Sellarsian Roots

A major theme in Sellars's philosophy is a sustained attack on "the myth of the given"—the idea that some of our beliefs or claims have a privileged epistemic status because the facts that make them true are "given" to us by experience. One class of claims that has traditionally been accorded this special status are pronouncements about one's own "sense data" or the content of one's perceptual experience. On the traditional view, a person's sincere claim that she is now seeing a blue object might well turn out to be mistaken. But her sincere claim that she is now experiencing blue sense data (or that she is now having experiences "as if" she were seeing a blue object) could not turn out to be mistaken. Another class of claims that are immune from error, according to the traditional view, are claims about one's own apparent memories and beliefs. Stich can't be certain that he has in fact climbed Ayers Rock. But he can be certain that he now seems to remember climbing Ayers Rock. And while his belief itself might be false, his sincere claim that he believes he climbed Ayers Rock on his forty-second birthday can't be mistaken. Sellars was a trenchant critic of these claims to certainty and of the foundationalist epistemology that typically went along with them. And though his assault on the traditional notion of sense data is not directly relevant to the eliminativists' skepticism about intentional states, his attack on the idea that our claims about our own beliefs and memories could not be mistaken most emphatically is. For, of course, if Stich's sincere claim that he believes he climbed Ayers Rock is enough to guarantee that he *does* believe it, then, since we make such sincere claims all the time, beliefs must exist, and eliminativism is a nonstarter.

To counter the idea that our claims about our own beliefs and thoughts are underwritten by a special, introspective faculty that guarantees the truth of those claims, Sellars begins by "making a myth . . . or, to give it an air of up-to-date respectability, by writing a piece of science fiction—anthropological science fiction" (1956, 309). For our purposes, Sellars's myth can be viewed as having three stages. The first of these is "a stage in pre-history in which humans are limited to what I shall call a Rylean language, a language of which the fundamental descriptive vocabulary speaks of public properties of public objects located in Space and enduring through Time" (309). At this stage in the myth, our "Rylean ancestors" have no terms in their language for beliefs, thoughts, or other "inner mental episodes." The second stage in the myth begins with the appearance in this "Neo-Rylean culture" of "a genius—let us call him Jones" (314).

> In the attempt to account for the fact that his fellow men behave intelli-
> gently not only when their conduct is threaded on a string of overt verbal
> episodes—that is to say, as we would put it, when they "think out loud"—
> but also when no detectable verbal output is present, Jones develops a
> *theory* according to which overt utterances are but the culmination of a
> process which begins with certain inner episodes. *And let us suppose that his
> model for these episodes* which initiate the events which culminate in overt
> verbal behavior *is that of overt verbal behavior itself. In other words, using the
> language of the model, the theory is to the effect that overt verbal behavior is the
> culmination of a process which begins with "inner speech."* (317–18; emphasis
> in original)

At this stage of Sellars's myth, the theory is only applied to other
people. But in the third stage, Jones and his compatriots learn to apply
the theory to themselves. At first, they apply it to themselves in much
the same way that they apply it to others. They infer various theoretical
claims by attending to their own behavior. A bit later, they discover a
new way of applying the language of the theory to themselves. Here is
how Sellars tells the tale:

> Once our fictitious ancestor, Jones has developed the theory that overt
> verbal behavior is the expression of thoughts, and taught his compatriots
> to make use of the theory in interpreting each other's behavior, it is but
> a short step to the use of this language in self-description. Thus, when
> Tom, watching Dick, has behavioral evidence which warrants the use of
> the sentence (in the language of the theory) "Dick is thinking 'p' " . . .
> Dick, using the same behavioral evidence, can say, in the language of the
> theory, "I am thinking 'p' ". . . . And it now turns out—need it have?—
> that Dick can be trained to give reasonably reliable self-descriptions, using
> the language of the theory, without having to observe his overt behavior.
> Jones brings this about, roughly, by applauding utterances by Dick of "I
> am thinking that p" when the behavioral evidence strongly supports the
> theoretical statement "Dick is thinking that p"; and by frowning on utter-
> ances of "I am thinking that p," when the evidence does not support this
> theoretical statement. Our ancestors begin to speak of the privileged ac-
> cess each of us has to his own thoughts. *What began as a language with a
> purely theoretical use has gained a reporting role.* (320; emphasis in original)

So, in Sellars's myth, expressions of the form "I am thinking that p" are
theoretical expressions which have acquired "a reporting use in which
one is not drawing inferences from behavioral evidence" (321).

Now if, like Sellars, one is concerned to rebut the claim that our
reports of our own thoughts are beyond challenge, the myth of Jones
suggests how the argument might run. For suppose the myth were
true. The inner episodes that Jones hypothesizes in stage two are supposed to be real events that are causally linked with behavioral episodes.
Positing them to account for certain aspects of the observable behavior
of people is, as Sellars stresses, on all fours with positing molecules to

account for certain aspects of the observable behavior of gases. Thus, for mental states as for molecules, there will be some occasions on which the inference from the observed behavior to the theoretical claim may be mistaken. Occasionally, an anomalous event may cause the observed behavior in the absence of the hypothesized internal state. Similarly, when we have been trained to give "reasonably reliable self-descriptions, using the language of the theory, without having to observe [our own] overt behavior" it may occasionally happen that this process misfires and that we describe ourselves as thinking that *p*, in the absence of the hypothesized internal state. Moreover, though Sellars himself did not stress the point, there is a more pervasive way in which our self-descriptions might turn out to be wrong. For it might turn out that Jones was less of a genius than we had thought—more of a Velikovsky, perhaps, than a Newton. His entire theory might turn out to be a bad idea. Other thinkers might discover better ways to explain the behavior that Jones's theory was designed to explain—ways that don't posit internal states modeled on observable verbal behavior. If that's the way the myth unfolds, then it may not be just the occasional theoretical self-description that turns out to be false. They may *all* be false.

Before we take these possibilities seriously, however, there is a pair of problems that must be confronted. The first of these focuses on the status of the myth itself. The possibilities set out in the previous paragraph were preceded by the *supposition* that the myth is true. But surely that's just silly. There was no historical Jones or anyone much like him, and there is no reason at all to suppose that talk about thoughts and other inner mental events was introduced as an explicit theoretical posit. Presumably, what Sellars would say here is that the myth is a bit like Wittgenstein's ladder, which we kick away after we have climbed it. The reason for telling the myth about Jones is to loosen the grip of another myth, this one the Cartesian "myth" in which introspection gives rise to infallible knowledge about our own mental states. If the Sellarsian myth were true, then we would talk *just as we now do* about inner mental states. But this talk would be both theoretical and fallible. Once we appreciate the point, the myth is irrelevant. It doesn't much matter what the actual history of our language is. What matters is that people could talk about inner mental states just the way we do, and their sincere self reports could be mistaken.

A second problem in assessing the significance of Sellars's myth focuses not on the truth of the myth but on the nature of the theory that the myth describes. As Sellars tells the story, Jones actually set out a theory and taught it to his compatriots. But nothing much like that seems to go on in our current practice. We don't explicitly teach our children a theory that enables them to apply mental terms to other people. Indeed, unlike Jones and his friends, we are not even able to *state* the theory, let alone teach it. If you ask your neighbor to set out the principles of the theory of the mind that she has taught her children, she won't have the foggiest idea what you're talking about. An essential step in Sellars's argument is the claim that, if the myth were true, we would talk just as we now do about mental states. But isn't this rather implausible? Surely, if each of us had been taught an explicit theory of the mind, and if we invoke this theory in applying mental-state terms to others, then both our developmental history and our adult linguistic practice would be rather different from what they actually are. At a minimum, there would be more awareness and discussion of the theory and more explicit appeal to its principles than we find in current linguistic practice. Rather than tackling this problem head-on, we think the best strategy, at this point, is to break off our discussion of Sellars and attend to the other major source of the idea that mental states are the posits of a folk theory. As we noted earlier, that source is to be found in the dominant explanatory strategy of contemporary cognitive science. As our discussion of that strategy proceeds, we will find an obvious way in which a neo-Sellarsian might respond to the objection that none of *us* can even state Jones's theory, let alone teach it.

3 Cognitive Science and the Appeal to Tacit Theory

From its earliest days, a central concern of cognitive science has been the explanation of various cognitive or behavioral capacities. The capacity of speakers to recognize and make various judgments about sentences of their language was among the first to be studied in detail. Other pioneering studies attempted to explain the capacity to solve various sorts of problems including problems in logic, chess problems, cryptarithmetic problems, and a variety of others. During the last three decades, many additional capacities have been explored. In all of this work, the most common explanatory strategy is to suppose that people's performance in executing these various capacities is guided by an internalized "knowledge base" or "knowledge structure." Typically, a knowledge structure will be a set of principles or rules that constitute a recipe or program enabling people to carry out the activity in question by exploiting more basic capacities in a systematic way. Those more basic capacities can themselves be explained by reiterating the strategy at a lower level. They are decomposed into still more basic ones, which are systematically marshaled under the guidance of another recipe or program.

The first philosophical account of this approach to psychological explanation that we know of was provided in Jerry Fodor's paper "The Appeal to Tacit Knowledge in Psychological Explanation" (1968). And, though the picture has become a fairly familiar one, we think it is worth quoting Fodor's vivid exposition at some length:

Here is the way we tie our shoes:

There is a little man who lives in one's head. The little man keeps a library. When one acts upon the intention to tie one's shoes, the little man fetches down a volume entitled *Tying One's Shoes*. The volume says such things as: "Take the left free end of the shoelace in the left hand. Cross the left free end of the shoelace over the right free end of the shoelace . . .", etc.

When the little man reads the instruction "take the left free end of the shoelace in the left hand", he pushes a button on a control panel. The button is marked "take the left free end of a shoelace in the left hand." When depressed, it activates a series of wheels, cogs, levers, and hydraulic mechanisms. As a causal consequence of the functioning of these mechanisms, one's left hand comes to seize the appropriate end of the shoelace. Similarly, *mutatis mutandis,* for the rest of the instructions.

The instructions end with the word "end". When the little man reads the word "end", he returns the book of instructions to his library.

That is the way we tie our shoes. (63–64)

Now, as Fodor goes on to note, there are some obvious things wrong with this story. First, of course, the whimsical bit about the cogs and wheels will have to be replaced by a more biological story. Second, and more seriously,

some of the behaviors . . . involved in shoe tying are of considerable complexity. . . . A serious theory of the behavioral integrations involved in tying one's shoes must explicate this complexity. . . . Prima facie . . . grasping a shoelace should be considered complex behavior, because doing so involves motions that also play a role in other actions.

We might thus consider expanding the population in one's head to include subordinate little men who superintend the execution of the "elementary" behaviors involved in complex sequences like grasping a shoelace. When the little man reads "take the left free end of the shoelace in the left hand", we imagine him ringing up the shop foreman in charge of grasping shoelaces. The shop foreman goes about supervising that activity in a way that is, in essence, a microcosm of supervising tying one's shoe. Indeed the shop foreman might be imagined to superintend a detail of wage slaves, whose functions include: searching inputs for traces of shoelace, flexing and contracting fingers on the left hand, etc. (64–65)

A bit later, Fodor explains how this process ultimately comes to an end:

We refine a psychological theory by replacing global little men by less global little men, each of whom has fewer unanalyzed behaviors to perform than did his predecessors. . . .

A completed psychological theory must provide systems of instructions to account for the forms of behavior available to an organism, and it must do so in a way that makes reference to no unanalyzed psychological processes. One way of clarifying the latter requirement is the following. Assume that there exists a class of *elementary* instructions which the nervous system is specifically wired to execute. Each elementary instruction specifies an *elementary operation,* and an elementary operation is one which the normal nervous system can perform but of which it cannot perform a proper part. Intuitively speaking the elementary operations are those which have no theoretically relevant internal structure. (65–66)

There are three additional points that need to be made before asking how this explanatory strategy links up with our concerns about folk psychology. The first is that the strategy does not require that bosses have any conscious access to the information their underlings are using. In some cases, a person may be able to tell us a great deal about the principles that guide his activity; in other cases, he may be able to report some of the principles but not others; and in still other cases, he may not have a clue about how he accomplishes the task. In those cases where the person can't recount or even recognize the principles he (or one of his subsystems) is using, it is often said that the principles are "tacit" or "unconscious." The second point is that it is often natural enough to describe the principles being used as a "theory" of the task domain or of how to accomplish the task in question. So, putting this point together with the previous one, it will sometimes be the case that the principles specified in an explanation of the sort Fodor envisions will constitute a "tacit or unconscious theory" of the domain or task in question. Here, of course, we have an obvious way to address the problem that we left unresolved in our discussion of Sellars's myth. If people regularly exploit *tacit* theories of the sort that Fodor describes, then we should not expect them to be aware of the principles of the theory or to appeal to those principles in discussion.

The third point is a bit more subtle. In Fodor's account, the little man inside the head has a single book specifying a set of rules for accomplishing the task at hand. But we might also imagine that in some instances the little man has *two* books for a given ability. One of the books contains declarative sentences rather than rules. These might, for example, be a set of axioms for some branch of mathematics or science. Or they might be a set of principles detailing generalizations and more idiosyncratic facts in some other domain. Now, of course, axioms or generalizations or statements of fact cannot, by themselves, tell us how to do anything. That's the job of the second book, which is much the same as the book imagined in Fodor's shoe-tying example. It provides rules for using the information in the first book to accomplish some task. So, for example, if the first book contains statements of the laws in some branch of physics, the second book might contain rules which specify how to use these laws to solve physics problems. Or perhaps the first book contains an axiomatic specification of all the sentences in a given language, and the second book contains a set of rules for using this specification efficiently in determining whether or not a given sentence is in the language. If one thinks of theories as the sorts of things that make claims, and thus as the sorts of things that can be true or false, then one might be inclined to say that only the books containing declarative sentences count as theories. The books that contain programs or recipes can do a good job or a bad job at accomplishing their task. But since they don't make any claims, they don't count as theories. We don't think that anything much turns on this terminological issue. What is important is the point about truth. If the little man accomplishes his task using only a recipe or a program, we may, if we wish, choose to describe that program as a theory. But it makes no obvious sense to say that the "theory" he is exploiting is either true or false.

4 *Interpreting Folk Psychology*

The central goal of this paper, it will be recalled, is to explore various possible interpretations of the assumption that beliefs, desires, and other commonsense mental states are posits of a folk theory of the mind. We are now in a position to tackle that project head-on.

Cognitive science, as we have just seen, typically attempts to explain cognitive and behavioral capacities by positing an internalized and often tacit theory. Among the various capacities that normal adults display, there is a fascinating cluster in which talk of mental states looms large. It is hardly surprising that many people have been tempted by the idea that this cluster of capacities might be explained by appeal to a tacit theory. Before considering the various ways in which such an explanation might work, we would do well to assemble at least a partial list of the "folk psychological" capacities or abilities that need explaining.

1. Perhaps the most obvious of these is the one that was center stage in Sellars's myth of Jones. We use terms like 'believe', 'think', 'want,' and 'desire' to *describe* ourselves and each other. We say things like the following all the time:

> Columbus believed that the earth was round.
> Henry VIII wanted a male heir.
> Anna thinks there is someone knocking at the door.

And, while we occasionally dispute such claims, in the overwhelming majority of cases they are readily accepted and strike us as completely unproblematic. This widespread agreement is a manifestation of a widely shared capacity to describe—or as philosophers sometimes like to say, to *interpret*—people using intentional idioms.[4]

2. We not only describe people using these folk psychological idioms, we also use the descriptions to construct *explanations* of people's behavior. We say things like "Henry VIII divorced Catherine of Aragon because he wanted a male heir" and "Anna is looking through the peep-hole because she thinks that there is someone knocking at the

door." And here, too, in the vast majority of cases these explanations are widely accepted and strike us as entirely unproblematic. Within our culture, a capacity to construct this sort of explanation seems to be universal among normal adults.

3. In addition to offering explanations of behavior, we are also quite adept at producing *predictions* of how people will behave. Sometimes these predictions are embedded in a discourse that also mentions the beliefs, desires, and other mental states of the person whose behavior is being predicted. But on other occasions, we predict someone's behavior without saying anything about her mental states. In one respect, our ability to produce predictions is rather similar to the previous two abilities on our list. For in this case, too, there is remarkably widespread interpersonal agreement. Asked to predict what the motorist will do as she approaches the red light, almost everyone says that she will stop. But there is another respect in which the ability to predict is much more impressive than the ability to offer descriptions and explanations. For in the case of predictions, there is often an independent and readily available check on their accuracy. And, as many philosophers have noted, it is a striking fact that in the vast majority of cases our predictions turn out to be *correct*. Though we are certainly not infallible, it is very often the case that people do what we predict they are going to do.

4. The ability to produce predictions of people's behavior is one which manifests itself in our *linguistic* behavior. But we also have a capacity to *anticipate* other people's behavior without saying anything at all. In watching a baseball game, our eyes immediately jump to the hot-tempered manager when the umpire throws his star player out of the game. We anticipate that he will come storming out of the dugout. Seeing the furious manager approaching, the umpire may anticipate what is to come and beat a hasty, though silent, retreat. Now it might be thought that these cases are just like the ones in which people make verbal predictions, except that they don't actually utter the prediction. They just say it silently to themselves. But there is also a *prima facie* similarity between our ability to anticipate people's behavior and the ability that animals have to anticipate the behavior of other organisms. The family cat is very good at anticipating which way mice will run and at anticipating which way the neighbor's dog will run. In both cases, he reacts appropriately, though we rather doubt that he is saying anything to himself as he does it.

5. The final entry on our list is the only one that overtly involves what might be thought of as *principles* or *generalizations* of a folk psychological theory. There is a wide range of generalizations about the interactions among stimuli, mental states, and behavior that people in our culture occasionally utter and are generally quite willing to endorse when asked. To give you a feel for the sort of ability we have in mind, consider whether or not you agree with the following claims:

5a. When a normal person is looking at a traffic light which changes from red to green, she usually comes to believe that it has changed from red to green.

5b. If a person believes that all scorpions are poisonous, and if she comes to believe that Henry's pet is a scorpion, then she will typically come to believe that Henry's pet is poisonous.

5c. If a person sitting at a bar wants to order a beer, and if she has no stronger desire to do something that is incompatible with ordering a beer, then typically she will order a beer.

We trust you agreed with all of them. In so doing, you were manifesting the widely shared ability to recognize folk psychological generalizations.

That's the end of our list of capacities. It is, as we noted earlier, only a partial list. Normal adults in our society have lots of other abilities in which talk of mental states plays a central role. In the absence of a theory about the mechanisms underlying these abilities, there is no obvious or natural way of drawing a boundary and saying exactly which capacities do and do not count as folk psychological capacities. That vagueness will make for problems as we proceed. But for the moment, we propose to ignore it and focus on the five capacities we have listed.

Let's begin by assuming that something like Fodor's story provides the correct explanation for those abilities, and let's consider some of the ways in which this story might be developed. To start us off, let's ask how the explicit generalizations mentioned in (5) are related to the underlying knowledge structure—the book that the little man in the head consults. Perhaps the simplest answer is that *these very generalizations* are encoded in the underlying knowledge structure. Indeed, to tell a really simple story, we might suppose that the underlying knowledge structure consists of *nothing but* these explicit generalizations. If this simple story were right, then all the principles we use in employing our various folk psychological abilities would be readily recognizable. But, for two very different reasons, we think this is an unlikely option. First, there are just too many generalizations. People who find (5a)–(5c) to be intuitively obvious will find an all but infinite class of similar generalizations to be equally obvious. And it seems absurd to suppose that all of those generalizations are internally represented. A natural suggestion here is that what we have internally represented is a set of more abstract generalizations—we might think of them as "axioms" of folk psychology—which in conjunction with other internalized information entail (5a)–(5c) and all the other more concrete generalizations that we recognize as intuitively obvious. The second problem with our simple story is just the opposite of the first. If we restrict ourselves to the generalizations that people are prepared to endorse, then in all likelihood there are too few of them to do the job required. A serious and fully explicit account of how we accomplish the feats recounted in (1)–(5) will almost certainly require more rules and principles than people can state or recognize as intuitively obvious. It is to be expected that in this area, as in every other area that cognitive scientists have explored, there is a great deal of information being used that is simply not accessible to introspection. If this is right, then at least part of what is written in the little man's book will be "tacit" or "unconscious." Moreover, some of the information that is not available to introspection may not even be statable in terms that the agent can understand. Linguistic ability provides a valuable analogy here. If Chomsky and his followers are even close to being right about the "tacit knowledge" that subserves a speaker's ability to judge whether or not a given sentence is grammatical, then most people would require a crash course in generative linguistics before they could begin to understand an explicit statement of what they "tacitly know."

We can now begin to pull apart some of the very different ways in which the label "folk psychology" might be used. In a series of influential papers, David Lewis (1970, 1972) drew attention to what he called the "platitudes" of commonsense psychology. These are generalizations that are "common knowledge" among ordinary folk. Almost everyone assents to them, and almost everyone knows that almost everyone else assents to them. These platitudes are, near enough, the intuitively obvious generalizations discussed in the previous paragraph. On Lewis's view, these platitudes constitute an implicit definition of the terms of commonsense psychology. But suppose that the speculations in the last paragraph are correct, and that platitudes like (5a)–(5c) are the consciously accessible consequences of a substantially richer set of mostly tacit or unconscious psychological rules and generalizations that people in our culture share. Suppose, further, that these tacit rules and generalizations also play a central role in explaining folk psychological capacities like (1)–(4).[5] If these suppositions are correct, then we might well be tempted to reserve the term "folk psychology" for the *underlying, internally represented* rules and generalizations. Moreover, a neo-Lewisian might well propose that it is these internal generalizations that fix the meaning or reference of the terms of commonsense psychology.

There is, however, nothing mandatory about this terminology. We might equally well elect to use the term "folk psychology" in a way that is more akin to Lewis's usage—as a label for the collection of folk psychological "platitudes" that people in our culture readily recognize and assent to.[6] Or, since the collection of "platitudes" is likely to be large and ungainly, we might reserve the label "folk psychology" for a set of more abstract generalizations—a "theory" if you will—that systematizes the platitudes in a perspicuous way and that (perhaps in conjunction with some other commonly known information) entails them. That systematization might well invoke terms and concepts that are quite unfamiliar to ordinary folk, in the same way that an attempt to systematize our linguistic intuitions probably would. What makes the proposals set out in this paragraph fundamentally different from the various possibilities considered in the previous paragraph is that on these readings, *"folk psychology" is not claimed to be an internally represented knowledge structure or body of information; it is not part of the mechanism that subserves the abilities recounted in (1)–(5).* On these readings, folk psychology "ain't in the head." To mark this distinction, we propose to call these accounts of folk psychology *external* accounts. Accounts on which folk psychology *is* part of the mechanism subserving (1)–(5) we call *internal.*

The distinction between internal and external accounts of folk psychology is at least roughly parallel to a distinction between two different ways of interpreting the sorts of generative grammars produced by linguists. Linguistic intuitions are a principal source of data for generative grammar. These intuitions are spontaneous judgments about the grammaticality and other grammatical features of sentences presented to a speaker. And it is generally agreed that a correct grammar is a theory which entails most of those judgments. On the analogy we are urging, linguistic intuitions are analogous to people's spontaneous judgments about the correctness or incorrectness of proposed folk psychological platitudes. Some theorists (e.g., Stich 1972 and perhaps Soames 1984) claim that capturing the intuitions (along with "simplicity") is all that is expected of a grammar; a correct grammar, on this view, is nothing more than a useful systematization or axiomatization of linguistic intuitions. Other theorists (e.g., Chomsky and Katz 1974, Fodor 1981c) have higher aspirations for grammar. On their view, a grammar should not only capture (or entail) most linguistic intuitions, it should also be part of the mechanism that is causally responsible for the production of those intuitions and for a variety of other linguistic capacities. On this view, people are assumed to have an internally represented body of linguistic rules or principles that is brought into play in producing linguistic intuitions and in processing and producing speech. A correct grammar is one that specifies the internally represented rules. Understood in this way, grammar is analogous to folk psychology construed *internally.* On the other view, grammar is analogous to folk psychology construed *externally.*

It has often been noted that when grammars are construed externally, they may be seriously underdetermined both by the data of linguistic intuition and by considerations of simplicity. There may be a number of quite different, though comparably simple, ways to construct a theory that entails most of a speaker's linguistic intuitions. So, on an external view of grammar, there may be several quite different grammars of a language or a dialect, all of which are equally correct. Much the same is true for external accounts of folk psychology. For even if we find some principled way of saying which "platitudes" or folk psychological intuitions a theory must systematize, there may be very different, though comparably simple, ways in which this can be done.

This point is particularly important if, as we speculated earlier, a good systematization of folk psychological intuitions may invoke terms or concepts that are unfamiliar to the people whose intuitions are being systematized. For these concepts might well be viewed as among the deeper "theoretical" notions of folk psychology. They are thus prime candidates for the eliminativist critique. But if there is no unique external systematization of folk psychology, then *the eliminativist who adopts an external account of folk psychology will have no determinate target.*

Let us return, now, to internal accounts of folk psychology. For the remainder of this section, we propose to explore various ways in which attempts to construct internal accounts might turn out and to consider the implications of these various possibilities for the eliminativist's argument.

At the end of section 3, we noted that for any given capacity the little man in the head may have *two* books rather than one. The information guiding the exercise of various cognitive capacities may divide into two parts: one consisting of declarative sentences or some similar notation for encoding propositions about the relevant domain and the other consisting of rules or procedures which specify what to do with these declarative sentences—how to use them to accomplish the task at hand. Applying this distinction to the case of commonsense psychology, we might conjecture that the knowledge structure underlying the skills in (1)–(5) divides into two parts. One of these is a set of (putative) laws and/or generalizations and/or facts about the ways in which the states of commonsense psychology interact with each other, with environmental stimuli, with behavior, and with other relevant aspects of an agent's situation. The other part is a program—a set of rules for extracting predictions, explanations, etc. from these laws, generalizations, and facts. If this is how the system works, it suggests two quite distinct ways in which the term "folk psychology" might be employed. It might be used as a label for the entire knowledge structure (the program plus the propositional information), or it might be reserved just for the part that contains the propositional information. On that latter usage, it makes perfectly good sense to ask whether folk psychology is true or false. On the former usage, however, only part of folk psychology is the sort of thing that can be true or false.

There is, however, another possibility to reckon with here, one that is much less congenial to the eliminativist's argument. It might turn out that the system subserving folk psychological skills contains only one book, not two, because the system is all rules and no propositions. If that's how the system works, and if we adopt the internal reading according to which "folk psychology" is used as a label for this system, then it will make no clear sense to say that folk psychology is either true or false. So if, as is entirely possible, folk psychology (construed internally) is all rules and no propositions, then the second step of the eliminativist's argument cannot possibly be correct. The upshot of all this is that eliminativists who adopt an internal view of folk psychology are committed to an empirical speculation—the speculation that folk psychology *isn't* all rules and no propositions—and this speculation might well turn out to be mistaken.[7]

There is also quite a different way in which it might turn out that folk psychology, construed internally, is not the sort of thing that can possibly be either true or false. Thus far we have been following Fodor in assuming that the "knowledge structure" underlying our folk psychological abilities is encoded in something akin to a language. But during the last decade, there has been a growing tendency in cognitive science to propose theories in which the information subserving various abilities is not encoded in anything like linguistic form. Perhaps the most widely discussed theories of this type are those that propose to account for certain cognitive capacities by positing one or another sort of connectionist device. Quite a different idea for the nonlinguistic encoding of information is the hypothesis that mental models of various sorts underlie our cognitive capacities (Johnson-Laird 1983). Both the connectionist approach and the mental models approach are very controversial, of course. Moreover, to draw the conclusions we want to draw from them, we have to proceed rather carefully. It is perfectly possible to view certain sorts of connectionist models and certain sorts of mental model theories as storing information that can be straightforwardly captured by a set of propositions or a set of sentences (McGinn 1989, chap. 3). Indeed, in some cases mental models and connectionist networks can actually be used to encode declarative sentences, or something very much like them. Thus, it is not the case that connectionist or mental model approaches are inevitably in conflict with propositional or even linguistic accounts of information storage. However, in other connectionist and mental model theories, there may be no unique and well-motivated way to map or translate the information stored into a set of propositions or declarative sentences. If a theory of this sort should prove to provide the best account of folk psychological skills like those sketched in (1)–(5), then we might well use the label "folk psychology" for the connectionist network or mental model posited by the theory. But since *ex hypothesis* there is no well-motivated mapping from the network or model to a set of declarative sentences or propositions, it would make no obvious sense to say that folk psychology is either true or false. So in this case, too, eliminativists who adopt an internal view of folk psychology are buying into a controversial empirical assumption. They are assuming that folk psychological skills are *not* subserved by connectionist networks or mental models of the sort lately considered. Without this assumption, the eliminativist's argument couldn't get started.

It's time to sum up. A central theme in this section has been that there are various quite different ways in which we might choose to use the term "folk psychology." A first choice turns on the distinction between external and internal readings. External accounts either collect or systematize the intuitively recognizable generalizations of commonsense psychology, while internal accounts focus on the cognitive mechanism that underlies our ability to have those intuitions, to predict behavior, etc. If we opt for an external reading of "folk psychology", then folk psychology is clearly the sort of thing that makes claims, and some of those claims might turn out to be false. So, on external readings, the eliminativist is guaranteed a target. But since there may be many quite different, comparably simple ways to systematize the intuitively recognized generalizations, that target may be far from unique. Also, the target may not be all that interesting, since on external accounts the principles of folk psychology may have little or nothing to do with the impressive range of commonsense psychological skills that people possess. They may have nothing to do with the processes by which we actually produce intentional descriptions, predictions, and explanations of behavior.

Internal accounts use the label "folk psychology" for the knowledge structures that actually underlie skills like those recounted in (1)–(5). So, on internal accounts, folk psychology plays a major role in the explanation of our ability to predict and explain each other's behavior. But on internal construals of folk psychology, the eliminativists' argument *may* turn out to be incoherent, for it is entirely possible that the knowledge structure underlying our commonsense psychological skills consists *entirely* of instructions, or it may be a connectionist device or mental model that does not map comfortably on to a set of sentences or propositions. The eliminativist who adopts an internal reading of "folk psychology" must make the risky bet that none of these options will turn out to be correct. For if one of them is correct, then premise 2 in the eliminativists' argument can't be right, since folk psychology is not the sort of thing that can be either true or false.

We're afraid that all of this has turned out to be rather complicated. Perhaps figure 3-1 will be of some help in seeing how the various possible interpretations of 'folk psychology' that we have been pulling apart are related to each other.[8] The options that are compatible with step 2 in the eliminativist argument are on the left; those that are not are on the right. There is, however, one increasingly important view of folk psychology that does not fit comfortably anywhere in figure 3-1. To conclude this chapter, we propose to take a brief look at this view and its implications for eliminativism.

5 *Eliminativism and Simulation Theory*

As we noted in section 3, the most common explanatory strategy in cognitive science posits internalized bodies of information, or "knowledge structures", that are brought into play when people exercise cognitive capacities. Language processing, various sorts of problem solving, visual recognition, and a host of other abilities have been studied from

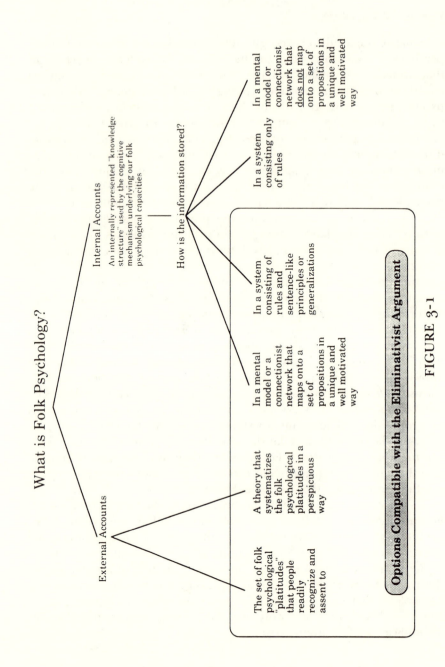

What is Folk Psychology?

External Accounts

The set of folk psychological "platitudes" that people readily recognize and assent to

A theory that systematizes the folk psychological platitudes in a perspicuous way

In a mental model or a connectionist network that maps onto a set of propositions in a unique and well motivated way

In a system consisting of rules and sentence-like principles or generalizations

Internal Accounts

An internally represented "knowledge structure" used by the cognitive mechanism underlying our folk psychological capacities.

How is the information stored?

In a system consisting only of rules

In a mental model or connectionist network that does not map onto a set of propositions in a unique and well motivated way

Options Compatible with the Eliminativist Argument

FIGURE 3-1

within this explanatory paradigm. To many people, it seems inevitable that an explanation of folk psychological capacities like those recounted in (1)–(5) will also posit some sort of internally represented information store. But in recent years, a number of philosophers and psychologists, most prominently Robert Gordon (1986, 1992), Alvin Goldman (1989, 1992), and Paul Harris (1992), have suggested a way in which some of the capacities on our list might be explained without using anything much like the internalized knowledge structures that are omnipresent in contemporary cognitive science. Their central idea is that we might predict other people's behavior by using our own decision-making system to stimulate someone else's decision making. To make this strategy work, we must first (consciously or unconsciously) imagine ourselves in the situation of the "target"—the person whose behavior we are trying to predict. We imagine what his beliefs are and what his desires are (to the extent that these are relevantly different from our own). We then feed these imagined (or "pretend") beliefs and desires into our decision-making system and allow it to decide what to do. But rather than acting on that decision, we use it as a basis for predicting what the target person will do. If we have done a good job in imagining the target's beliefs and desires, and if his decision-making system works in much the same way that ours does, then our decision will be the same as his, and our prediction will be correct.[9]

Some critics of this proposal have suggested that it could not possibly work or that it must *covertly* appeal to internalized rules or knowledge structures. We think both of these contentions are mistaken. The simulation theory provides a real alternative to the prevailing explanatory strategy in cognitive science for explaining our capacity to predict and explain other people's behavior. We are far from being advocates of the simulation theory, however, because we don't think it does a very good job of explaining the experimental data on the acquisition and deployment of folk psychological skills. The details of this critique make for a long story, which one of us has tried to tell elsewhere (see chapter 4 and Stich and Nichols, 1995).

Our present concern is not to renew the debate over the correctness of simulation theory but rather to ask what happens to the eliminativist argument if it should turn out (contrary to our expectations) that simulation theory is correct. A number of authors on both sides of the debate have maintained that if simulation theory is right, eliminativism will be undermined. Here is how Stich and Nichols (1992) argue for this conclusion:

> *Eliminativists* maintain that there really are no . . . [intentional states]. Beliefs and desires are like phlogiston, caloric and witches; they are the mistaken posits of a radically false theory. The theory in question is "folk psychology"—the collection of psychological principles and generalizations which, according to eliminativists (and most of their opponents),

underlies our everyday explanations of behavior. The central premise in the eliminativist's argument is that neuroscience (or connectionism or cognitive science) is on the verge of demonstrating persuasively that folk psychology is false. But if Gordon and Goldman are right, they will have pulled the rug out from under the eliminativists. For if what underlies our ordinary explanatory practice is not a theory at all, then obviously it cannot be a radically false theory. There is a certain delightful irony in the Gordon/Goldman attack on eliminativism. Indeed, one might almost view it as attempting a bit of philosophical jujitsu. The eliminativists claim that there are no such things as beliefs and desires because the folk psychology that posits them is a radically false theory. Gordon and Goldman claim that the theory which posits a tacitly known folk psychology is *itself* radically false, since there are much better ways of explaining people's abilities to interpret and predict behavior. Thus, if Gordon and Goldman are right, *there is no such thing as folk psychology!* [10]

Now, it's our contention that Stich and Nichols (and Gordon and Goldman) were being much too hasty in concluding that simulation theory puts eliminativism out of business.[11] And, in light of the distinctions we drew in the previous section, the reason should be obvious. Simulation theory suggests an account of the mechanisms underlying our capacity to predict and explain people's behavior, and that explanation makes no appeal to an internalized theory or knowledge structure. So, if simulation theory is correct, then *on the internal reading* there is no such thing as folk psychology. But simulation theorists do not deny the obvious fact that people have intuitions about folk psychological platitudes; nor do they deny that it might be possible to systematize those intuitions by constructing a theory that entails them. That theory would be a folk psychology *on the external reading,* and it might well turn out to be a seriously mistaken theory. So, the right conclusion to draw from the assumption that simulation theory is correct is not the jazzy claim that eliminativism has been undermined but only the much more modest claim that eliminativists must opt for an external account of folk psychology.

Notes

1. Another species of eliminativism claims that conscious states do not exist. In this chapter, however, our focus will be on the version of eliminativism that takes intentional states as its target.

2. See, for example, P. M. Churchland (1981), P. S. Churchland (1986), Fodor (1987), Horgan and Woodward (1985), Jackson and Pettit (1990), Patricia Kitcher (1984), Ramsey, et al. (1990), Sterelny (1990), Stich (1983), and Von Eckardt (1993).

3. See, for example, Sharpe (1987) and Wilkes (1981; 1984; 1991).

4. It is often claimed that at least some of those intentional idioms, and the capacity to apply them, vary markedly from culture to culture (see, for example, Hacking 1982; Needham 1972; and the essays collected in Harré

1986). That sort of cultural relativism, if it turns out to be correct, is entirely compatible with the various accounts of folk psychology to be set out in this section. If people in different cultures use different intentional categories, and if their use of these categories is guided by a tacit theory, then the tacit theories will also differ from culture to culture.

5. As we noted earlier, there is no obvious way of deciding which capacities to count as folk psychological capacities. Thus, the current supposition is itself a bit vague. It might turn out that the rules and generalizations subserving (1)–(5) are a tightly integrated set, perhaps even a "module" in something like the sense set out in Fodor (1983). If that is the case, then we would do well to let these integrated rules and generalizations determine which capacities to count as folk psychological—the folk psychological capacities are the capacities that these rules and generalizations explain. But it might also turn out that the rules and generalizations we use are not modular or even tightly integrated—that different subsets of rules and generalizations explain different capacities. If that's how things work, then the only way to eliminate the vagueness is by stipulation. Folk psychological capacities will not be a psychologically natural kind.

6. Here again the proposal is a bit vague, since there is no obvious well-motivated way to determine which platitudes count as "folk psychological". Nor is it clear how widely accepted a claim must be in order to count as a "plat-itude".

7. A caveat: even if folk psychology (construed internally) is all rules and no propositions, it may be the case that the rules of this folk psychological program, or the concepts they invoke, presuppose various claims that could turn out to be false. The notion of presupposition being relied on here could do with considerable clarification. But assuming that adequate clarification can be provided, the presuppositions of folk psychology might be a suitable target for the eliminativist's critique.

8. Thanks are due to Christopher O'Brien for help in preparing figure 3-1.

9. Advocates of simulation theory have also proposed ways in which this process might be used to generate intentional descriptions and explanations (see chapter 4, sec. 3).

10. For similar arguments, see Gordon (1986, 170) and Goldman (1989, 182).

11. This constitutes a change in view for one of us (S.S.), prompted, in large measure, by the arguments urged by the other (I.R.). The argument set out in this paragraph was first proposed by Ravenscroft. At about the same time, much the same argument was proposed by Gerard O'Brien (1993), Ian Hunt, and Kenneth Taylor (1993). Stich wishes to thank all of these philoso-phers for convincing him that his previous view was mistaken.

CHAPTER 4

How Do Minds Understand Minds? Mental Simulation versus Tacit Theory

With Shaun Nichols

1   Introduction

A central goal of contemporary cognitive science is the explanation of cognitive abilities or capacities (Cummins 1983). During the last three decades, a wide range of cognitive capacities has been subjected to careful empirical scrutiny. The adult's ability to produce and comprehend natural-language sentences and the child's capacity to acquire a natural language were among the first to be explored (Chomsky 1965; Fodor et al. 1974; Pinker 1989). There is also a rich literature on the ability to solve mathematical problems (Greeno 1983), the ability to recognize objects visually (Rock 1983; Gregory 1970; Marr 1982), the ability to manipulate and predict the behavior of middle-sized physical objects (McCloskey 1983a, 1983b; Hayes 1985), and a host of others.

In all of this work, the dominant explanatory strategy proceeds by positing an internally represented *knowledge structure*—typically a body of rules or principles or propositions—which serves to guide the execution of the capacity to be explained. These rules or principles or propositions are often described as the agent's "theory" of the domain in question. In some cases, the theory may be partly accessible to consciousness; the agent can tell us some of the rules or principles he is using. More often, however, the agent has no conscious access to the knowledge guiding his behavior. The theory is "tacit" (Chomsky 1965) or "subdoxastic" (Stich 1978b). Perhaps the earliest philosophical account of this explanatory strategy is set out in Jerry Fodor's paper "The Appeal to Tacit Knowledge in Psychological Explanations" (1968). Since then, the idea has been elaborated by Dennett (1978a), Lycan (1981, 1988b), and a host of others.

Among the many cognitive capacities that people manifest, there is one cluster that holds a particular fascination for philosophers. Included in this cluster is the ability to describe people and their behavior (including their linguistic behavior) in intentional terms—or to "interpret" them, as philosophers sometimes say. We exercise this ability when we describe John as *believing that the mail has come* or when we say that Anna *wants to go to the library*. By exploiting these intentional descriptions, people are able to offer explanations of each other's behavior (Susan left the building *because* she believed that it was on fire) and to predict each other's behavior, often with impressive accuracy. Since the dominant strategy for explaining any cognitive capacity is to posit an internally represented theory, it is not surprising that in this area, too, it is generally assumed that a theory is being invoked (P. M. Churchland 1981, 1989; Fodor 1987; Olson et al. 1988; Sellars 1956). The term "folk psychology" has been widely used as a label for the largely tacit psychological theory that underlies these abilities, though as noted in the previous chapter, there are a number of other things for which the label might also be used. During the last decade or so there has been a fair amount of empirical work aimed at describing or modeling folk psychology and tracking its emergence and development in the child (D'Andrade 1987; Leslie 1987; Astington et al. 1988; Wellman 1990; Perner 1991; Gopnik 1993; Baron-Cohen 1995).

Recently, however, Robert Gordon, Alvin Goldman, Paul Harris, Gregory Currie, and a number of other writers have offered a bold challenge to the received view about the cognitive mechanisms underlying our ability to describe, predict, and explain people's behavior (Currie 1995a; Goldman 1989, 1992; Gordon 1986, 1991, 1992; Harris 1992; Montgomery 1987; Ripstein 1987; Heal 1986).[1] Though they differ on the details, these philosophers agree in denying that an internally represented folk psychological theory plays a central role when we exercise our ability to predict, explain, and interpret other people. They also agree that a special sort of mental simulation in which we use ourselves as a model for the person we are describing or predicting will play an important role in the correct account of the mechanisms subserving these abilities. In this chapter, although we will occasionally mention the views of other advocates of simulation, our principal focus will be on Gordon and Goldman. If these philosophers are right then the dominant explanatory strategy in cognitive science, the strategy that appeals to internally represented knowledge structures, will be shown to be mistaken in at least one crucial corner of our mental lives. And if it is mistaken there, then perhaps theorists exploring other cognitive capacities can no longer simply take the strategy for granted.[2]

There can be no doubt that if Gordon and Goldman are right, then the impact on both cognitive science and the philosophy of mind will be considerable. But it is a lot easier to doubt that their views about mental simulation are defensible. The remainder of this chapter will be devoted to developing these doubts. Here's the game plan for the pages to follow. In sections 2 and 3, we will try to get as clear as we can on what the simulation theorists claim. We'll begin, in Section 2, with an account of the special sort of simulation that lies at the heart of the Gordon/Goldman proposal. In that section, our focus will be on the way that simulation might be used in the *prediction* of behavior. In section 3, we'll explore the ways in which mental simulation might be used to explain two other cognitive capacities that have been of special interest to philosophers: *explaining* behavior and producing *intentional descriptions* or *interpretations*. We'll also consider the possibility that simulation might be used in explaining the *meaning* of intentional terms like 'believes' and 'desires'. Since the accounts of simulation that Gordon and Goldman have offered have been a bit sketchy, there will be a lot of filling in to do in sections 2 and 3. But throughout both sections, our goal will be sympathetic interpretation; we've tried hard not to build straw men. In the following two sections, our stance turns critical. In section 4, we will do our best to assemble all the arguments offered by Gordon and Goldman in support of their simulation theory and to explain why none of them are convincing. In section 5 we will offer an argument of our own, aimed at showing why, in light of currently available evidence, the simulation theory is very implausible indeed. Section 6 is a brief conclusion.

2   Predicting Behavior: Theory, Simulation, and Imagination

Suppose you are an aeronautical engineer and that you want to predict how a newly built plane will behave at a certain speed. There are two rather different ways in which you might proceed. One way is to sit down with pencil and paper, a detailed set of specifications of the plane, and a state-of-the-art textbook on aerodynamic theory and try to calculate what the theory entails about the behavior of the plane. Alternatively, you could build a model of the plane, put it in a wind tunnel, and observe how it behaves. You have to use a bit of theory in this second strategy, of course, since you have to have some idea which properties of the plane you want to duplicate in your model. But there is a clear sense in which a theory is playing the central role in the first prediction and a model or simulation is playing a central role in the second.[3]

Much the same story could be told if what you want to do is predict the behavior of a person. Suppose, for example, you want to predict what a certain rising young political figure would do if someone in authority tells him to administer painful electric shocks to a person strapped in a chair in the next room. One approach is to gather as much data as you can about the history and personality of the politician and then consult the best theory available on the determinants of behavior under such circumstances. Another approach is to set up a Milgram-style experiment and observe how some other people behave.[4] Naturally, it would be a good idea to find experimental subjects who are psychologically similar to the political figure whose behavior you are trying to predict. Here, as before, theory plays a central role in the first prediction, while a simulation plays a central role in the second.

In both the aeronautical case and the psychological case, we have been supposing that much of the predicting process is carried on outside the predictor. You do your calculations on a piece of paper; your simulations are done in wind tunnels or laboratories. But, of course, it will often be possible to internalize this process. The case is clearest when a theory is being used. Rather than looking in a textbook, you could memorize the theory, and rather than doing the calculations on a piece of paper, you could do them in your head. Moreover, it seems entirely possible that you could learn the theory so well that you are hardly conscious of using it or of doing any explicit calculation or reasoning. Indeed, this, near enough, is the standard story about a wide variety of cognitive capacities.

A parallel story might be told for predictions using simulations. Rather than building a model and putting it in a wind tunnel, you could imagine the model in the wind tunnel and see how your imaginary model behaves. Similarly, you could imagine putting someone in a Milgram-style laboratory and see how your imaginary subject behaves. But obviously, there is a problem lurking here. For while it is certainly possible to imagine a plane in a wind tunnel, it is not at all clear how you could successfully imagine the behavior of the plane unless you had a fair amount of detailed information about the behavior of planes in situations like this one. When the simulation uses a real model plane, the world tells you how the model will behave. You just have to look and see. But when you are only imagining the simulation, there is no real model for you to look at. So, it seems that you must have an internalized knowledge structure, to guide your imagination. The theory, or knowledge structure, that you are exploiting may, of course, be a tacit one, and you may be quite unaware that you are using it. But unless we suppose your imagination is guided by some systematic body of information about the behavior of planes in situations like this one, the success of your prediction would be magic.

When you are imagining the behavior of a person, however, there are various ways in which the underlying system might work. One possibility is that imagining the behavior of a person is entirely parallel to imagining the behavior of a plane. In both cases, your imagination is guided by a largely tacit theory or knowledge structure. But there is also a very different mechanism that might be used. In the plane case, you don't have a real plane to observe, so you have to rely on some stored information about planes. You do, however, have a real, human cognitive system to observe—your own. Here's a plausible, though obviously oversimplified, story about how that system normally works. At any given time you have a large store of beliefs and desires. Some of the beliefs are derived from perception, others from inference. Some of the desires (like the desire to get a drink) arise from systems monitoring bodily states, others (like the desire to go into the kitchen) are "subgoals" generated by the decision-making (or "practical reasoning") system. The decision-making system, which takes your beliefs and desires as input, does more than generate subgoals, it also somehow or other comes up with a decision about what to do. That decision is then passed on to the "action controllers"—the mental mechanisms responsible for sequencing and coordinating the behavior necessary to carry out the decision. Rendered boxologically, the account just sketched appears in figure 4-1.

Now suppose that it is possible to take the decision making system "off-line" by disengaging the connection between the system and the action controllers. You might then use it to generate decisions that you are not about to act on. Suppose further that in this off-line mode you can feed the decision-making system some hypothetical or "pretend" beliefs and desires—beliefs and desires that you do not actually have but that the person whose behavior you're trying to predict does. If all this were possible, you could then sit back and let the system generate a decision. Moreover, if your decision-making system is similar to the one in the person whose behavior you're trying to predict, and if the hypothetical beliefs and desires you've fed into your system off-line are close to the ones that he has, then the decision that your system generates will often be similar to the one that his system generates. There is no need for a special internalized knowledge structure here; no tacit folk psychological theory is being used. Rather, you are using (part of) your own cognitive mechanism as a model for (part of) his. Moreover, just as in the case where the prediction exploits a theory, this whole process may be largely unconscious. It may be that all you are aware of is the prediction itself. Alternatively, if you consciously imagine what the target of your prediction will do, it could well be the case that your imagination is guided by this simulation rather than by some internally represented psychological theory.

We now have at least the outline of an account of how mental simulation might be used in predicting another person's behavior. An entirely parallel story can be told about predicting our own behavior under counterfactual circumstances. If, for example, I want to know what

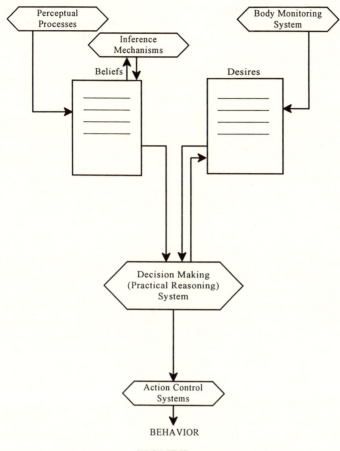

Perceptual
Processes

Body Monitoring
System

Inference
Mechanisms

Beliefs

Desires

Decision Making
(Practical Reasoning)
System

Action Control
Systems

BEHAVIOR

FIGURE 4-1

I would do if I believed that there was a burglar in the basement, I can simply take my decision making system off-line and provide it with the pretend belief that there is a burglar in the basement.[5]

In the next section, we'll try to get clear on how this process of simulation might be used in explaining various other cognitive capacities. But before attending to that task, we would do well to assemble a few quotations to confirm our claim that the story we've told is very close to the one that those we'll be criticizing have in mind. Gordon is much more explicit than Goldman on the use of simulation in prediction. Here's a passage from his 1986 paper:

> Our decision-making or practical reasoning system gets partially disengaged from its 'natural' inputs and fed instead with suppositions and images (or their 'subpersonal' or 'subdoxastic' counterparts). Given these artificial pretend inputs the system then 'makes up its mind' what to do.

> Since the system is being run off-line, as it were, disengaged also from its natural output systems, its 'decision' isn't actually executed but rather ends up as an anticipation . . . of the other's behavior. (Gordon 1986, 170)

And another, this time from an unpublished manuscript contrasting his view to Fodor's:

> The Simulation Theory as I present it holds that we explain and predict behavior not by applying a theory but simply by exercising a skill that has two components: the capacity for practical reasoning—roughly, for making decisions on the basis of facts and values—and the capacity to introduce "pretend" facts and values into one's decision-making typically to adjust for relevant differences in situation and past behavior. One predicts what the other will decide to do by making a decision oneself—a "pretend" decision, of course, made only in imagination—after making such adjustments. (1990, 3)

Gordon later suggests that the capacity to simulate in this way may be largely innate:

> [Evidence] suggests that the readiness for simulation is a prepackaged "module" called upon automatically in the perception of other human beings.[6] It suggests also that supporting and complementing the conscious, reportable procedure we call putting ourselves in the other's place, those neural systems that are responsible for the formation of emotions and intentions are, often without our knowledge, allowed to run off-line: They are partially disengaged from their "natural" inputs from perception and memory and fed artificial pretend inputs; uncoupled also from their natural output systems, they terminate not as intentions and emotions but as anticipations of, or perhaps just unconscious motor adjustments to, the other's intentions, emotions, behavior. (5)

3   Other Uses for Simulation: Explanation, Interpretation, and the Meaning of Intentional Terms

Let's turn now to people's ability to offer intentional explanations of other people's actions. How might mental simulation be used to account for that ability? Consider, for example, a case similar to one proposed by Gordon (1986, 163ff.). We are seated at a restaurant and someone comes up to us and starts speaking to us in a foreign language. How might simulation be exploited in producing an intentional explanation for that behavior?

One proposal, endorsed by both Gordon and Goldman, begins with the fact that simulations can be used in predictions and goes on to suggest that intentional explanations can be generated by invoking something akin to the strategy of analysis-by-synthesis. In using simulations to predict behavior, hypothetical beliefs and desires are fed into our own decision-making system (being used off-line of course), and we predict that the agent would do what we would decide to do, given those beliefs and desires. A first step in explaining a behavioral episode that has already occurred is to see if we can find some hypothetical beliefs and desires which, when fed into our decision mechanism, will produce a decision to perform the behavior we want to explain.

Generally, of course, there will be *lots* of hypothetical beliefs and desires that might lead us to the behavior in question. Here are just a few:

> **1.** If we believe someone only speaks a certain foreign language and we want to ask him something, then we would decide to speak to him in that language.
> **2.** If we want to impress someone and we believe that speaking in a foreign language will impress him, then we will decide to speak to him in that language.
> **3.** If we believe that speaking to someone in a foreign language will make him laugh, and if we want to make him laugh, then we will decide to speak to him in that language.

And so on. Each of these simulation-based predictions provides the kernel for a possible explanation of the behavior we are trying to explain. To decide among these alternative explanations, we must determine which of the input belief/desire pairs is most plausibly attributed to the agent. Some belief/desire pairs will be easy to exclude. Perhaps the agent is a dour fellow; he never wants to make anyone laugh. If we believe this to be the case, then (3) won't be very plausible. In other cases, we can use information about the agent's perceptual situation to assess the likelihood of various beliefs. If Mary has just made a rude gesture directly in front of the agent, then it is likely the agent will believe that Mary has insulted him. If the rude gesture was made behind the agent's back, then it is not likely he will believe that she has insulted him. In still other cases, we may have some preexisting knowledge of the agent's beliefs and desires. But, as both Goldman and Gordon note, it will often be the case that there are lots of alternative explanations that can't be excluded on the basis of evidence about the agent's circumstances or his history. In these cases, Goldman maintains, we simply assume that the agent is psychologically similar to us—we attribute beliefs that are "natural for us" (Goldman 1989, 178) and reject (or perhaps do not even consider) hypotheses attributing beliefs that we consider to be less natural (178–79). Gordon tells much the same story:

> No matter how long I go on testing hypotheses, I will not have tried out *all* candidate explanations of the [agent's] behavior. Perhaps some of the unexamined candidates would have done at least as well as the one I settle for, if I settle: perhaps indefinitely many of them would have. But these would be 'far fetched', I say intuitively. Therein I exhibit my inertial bias. The less 'fetching' (or 'stretching', as actors say) I have to do to track the other's behavior, the better. I tend to *feign* only when necessary, only

when something in the other's behavior doesn't fit. This inertial bias may be thought of as a 'least effort' principle: the 'principle of least pretending'. It explains why, other things being equal, I will prefer the less radical departure from the 'real' world—i.e. from what I myself take to be the world. (1986, 164)[7]

Though the views endorsed by Gordon and Goldman are generally very similar, the two writers do differ in their emphasis. For Gordon, prediction and explanation loom large, while for Goldman, the capacity to interpret people, or to describe them in intentional terms, is given pride of place. Part of the story Goldman tells about simulation-based intentional description relies on the account of simulation-based explanation that we have just sketched. One of the ways we determine which beliefs and desires to attribute to people is by observing their behavior and then attributing the intentional states that best explain their behavior. A second simulation-based strategy for determining which beliefs and desires to attribute focuses on the agent's perceptual situation and on his or her "basic likings or cravings":

> From your perceptual situation, I infer that you have certain perceptual experiences or beliefs, the same ones I would have in your situation. I may also assume (pending information to the contrary) that you have the same basic likings that I have: for food, love, warmth, and so on. (Goldman 1989, 170).

As we read them, there is only one important point on which Gordon and Goldman actually disagree. The accounts of simulation-based prediction, explanation, and interpretation that we have sketched all seem to require that the person doing the simulating must already understand intentional notions like belief and desire. A person can't pretend he believes that the cookies are in the cookie jar unless he understands what it is to believe that the cookies are in the cookie jar; nor can a person imagine that she wants to make her friend laugh unless she understands what it is to want to make someone laugh. Moreover, as Goldman notes, when simulation is used to attribute intentional states to agents, it "assumes a prior understanding of what state it is that the interpreter attributes to [the agent]" (1989, 182). Can the process of simulation somehow be used to explain the meaning or truth conditions of locutions like 'S believes that p' and 'S desires that q'? Goldman is skeptical and tells us that "the simulation theory looks distinctly unpromising on this score" (182). But Gordon is much more sanguine. Building on earlier suggestions by Quine, Davidson, and Stich, he proposes the following account:

> My suggestion is that
> (2) [*Smith believes that* Dewey won the election.]
> be read as saying the same thing as
> (1) [Let's do a Smith simulation. Ready? *Dewey won the election.*]
> though less explicitly. (Gordon 1986, 167)

We are not at all sure we understand this proposal, and Gordon himself concedes that "the exposition and defense of this account of belief are much in need of further development" (167). But no matter. We think we do understand the simulation-based accounts of prediction, explanation, and interpretation that Gordon and Goldman both endorse. We're also pretty certain that none of these accounts is correct. In the sections that follow, we will try to say why.

4   Arguments in Support of Simulation-Based Accounts

In this section, we propose to assemble all the arguments we've been able to find in favor of simulation-based accounts and say why we don't think any of them is persuasive. Then, in the following section, we will go on to offer an argument of our own aimed at showing that there is a fair amount of evidence that simulation-based accounts cannot easily accommodate, though more traditional theory-based accounts can. Before turning to the arguments, however, we would do well to get a bit clearer about the questions that the arguments are (and are not) intended to answer.

The central idea in the accounts offered by Gordon and Goldman is that in predicting, explaining, or interpreting other people we simulate them by using part of *our own* cognitive systems "off-line". There might, of course, be other kinds of simulation in which we do not exploit our own decision-making system in order to model the person we are simulating. But these other sorts of simulation are not our current concern. To avoid confusion, we will henceforth use the term *off-line simulation* for the sort of simulation that Gordon and Goldman propose. The question in dispute, then, is whether off-line simulation plays a central role in predicting, explaining, or interpreting other people. Gordon and Goldman say yes; we say no.

It would appear that the only serious alternatives to the off-line simulation story are various versions of the "theory-theory" which maintain that prediction, explanation, and interpretation exploit an internally represented theory or knowledge structure—a tacitly known "folk psychology." So, if an advocate of off-line simulation can mount convincing arguments against the theory-theory, then he can reasonably claim to have made his case. The theory-theory is not the only game in town, but it is the only *other* game in town. It is not surprising, then, that in defending off-line simulation, advocates of the view spend a fair amount of time raising objections to the theory-theory. There are, however, a number of quite different ways in which the theory-theory may be elaborated. Failing to keep these differences in mind has led some writers to argue against one type of theory-theory and to conclude that because that type of theory-theory is wrong, simulation theory must be right. To help avoid this sort of muddle, we'll spend a few pages setting out some of the different ways in which the theory-theory can be developed and explaining how failing to keep track of them can lead to mischief.

1. In the early days of cognitive science, during the 1960s and 1970s, most models aimed at explaining cognitive capacities posited internally represented knowledge structures that invoked explicit rules or explicit sentence-like principles. But during the last fifteen years, there has been a growing dissatisfaction with sentence-based and rule-based knowledge structures, and a variety of alternatives have been explored. Perhaps the most widely discussed alternatives are connectionist models in which the knowledge used in making predictions is stored in the connection strengths between the nodes of a network. In many of these systems, it is difficult or impossible to view the network as encoding a set of sentences or rules.[8] Other theorists have proposed quite different ways in which nonsentential and nonrule-like strategies could be used to encode information (see, for example, Johnson-Laird 1983). Against the background of this controversy, it is not surprising that some theory-theorists (e.g., Fodor 1987) maintain that our commonsense folk psychological knowledge is represented in a sentence-like format, while others (e.g., P. M. Churchland 1989) maintain that it is stored in a non-sentential connectionist format.

2. A number of authors, including Fodor (1987) and Wellman (1990), contend that folk psychology invokes "theoretical" entities or processes that are quite distinct from the more readily observable events and processes that folk psychology will be called on to predict and explain. They also maintain that folk psychology includes a significant number of law-like or nomological generalizations and that the theoretical constructs of folk psychology will be "closely or 'lawfully' interrelated with one another" (Gopnik and Wellman 1992, 147). If this is correct, then folk psychology will bear a strong resemblance to the standard philosophical portrait of scientific theories in domains like physics and chemistry. But, of course, there are lots of domains of commonsense knowledge in which it is rather implausible to suppose that the mentally represented "knowledge structure" includes theoretical constructs linked together in law-like ways. Knowledge of cooking or of current affairs are likely candidates here, as is the knowledge that underlies our judgments about what is polite and impolite in our culture. And it is entirely possible that folk psychological knowledge will turn out to resemble the knowledge structures underlying cooking or politeness judgments rather than the knowledge structures that underlie the scientific predictions and explanations produced by a competent physicist or chemist.

Unfortunately, there is no terminological consensus in these debates. Some writers prefer to reserve the term 'theory' for sentence-like or rule-based systems. For these writers, most connectionist models do not invoke what they would call an internally represented theory. Other writers are more liberal in their use of 'theory,' and are prepared to count just about any internally stored body of information about a given domain as an internally represented theory of that domain. For these writers, connectionist models and other nonsentential models do encode a tacit theory. Also, there are some authors who would decline to use the term 'theory' even for a sententially stored body of folk psychological knowledge if it did not posit "theoretical" entities and nomological generalizations that tie them together.

We don't think there is any substantive issue at stake here. But the terminological disagreements can generate considerable confusion. Thus, for example, someone who used 'theory' in a restrictive way might well conclude that if a connectionist (or some other nonsentence-based) account of our ability to predict other people's behavior turns out to be the right one, then the theory-theory is mistaken. So far, so good. But it is important to see that the falsity of the theory-theory (narrowly construed) is no comfort at all to the off-line simulation theorist. The choice between off-line simulation theories and theory-theories is plausibly viewed as exhaustive only when 'theory' is used in the inclusive rather than the restrictive way. Similarly, someone who declined to use the term 'theory' for a body of information that included no lawlike generalizations might conclude that the theory-theory is false if there are no law-like generalizations to be found. But once again, the discovery that the theory-theory (narrowly construed) is false would lend no support at all to the off-line simulation theory. On the inclusive reading of 'theory,' any mentally represented body of information about a domain counts as a theory, regardless of how the information is encoded or whether it includes theoretical constructs or nomological generalizations. For the remainder of this chapter, we propose to adopt the inclusive interpretation of 'theory'. On this interpretation, and only on this interpretation, reasons to think that the theory-theory is mistaken will be reasons to think that the off-line simulation theory is correct. In the pages that follow, we will be defending the claim that our capacity to predict, explain, and interpret people is subserved by a tacit theory (where 'theory' is interpreted inclusively) and that this capacity does not rely on off-line simulation. We take no stand at all on the question of how this theory is stored in the mind or on the question of whether or not the theory includes law-like generalizations. Let's turn now to the arguments that have been offered in favor of simulation theory.

> *Argument 1:* No one has been able to state the principles of the internally represented folk psychological theory posited by the theory-theory.

Both Goldman and Gordon go on at some length about the fact that it has proven very difficult to state the principles or laws of the folk psychological theory that, according to the theory-theorist, guide our interpretations and predictions:

Attempts by philosophers to articulate the putative laws or 'platitudes' that comprise our folk theory have been notably weak. Actual illustrations of such laws are sparse in number; and when examples are adduced, they commonly suffer from one of two defects: vagueness and inaccuracy. . . . But why, one wonders, should it be so difficult to articulate laws if we appeal to them all the time in our interpretative practice? (Goldman 1989, 167; see also Gordon 1986, 166, and Gordon 1990, 7)

Reply: Goldman is certainly right about one thing. It is indeed very difficult to articulate the principles of folk psychology precisely and accurately. But it is hard to see why this fact should be of any comfort to advocates of the off-line simulation theory. For much the same could be said about the knowledge structures underlying all sorts of cognitive capacities. It has proven enormously difficult to state the principles underlying a speaker's capacity to judge the grammaticality of sentences in her language. Indeed, after three decades of sustained effort, we don't have a good grammar for even a single natural language. Nor do we have a good account of the principles underlying people's everyday judgments about the behavior of middle-sized physical objects, or about their ability to solve mathematical problems, or about their ability to play chess, etc. But, of course, in all of these domains, the theory-theory really is the only game in town. The off-line simulation story makes no sense as an account of our ability to judge grammaticality or of our ability to predict the behavior of projectiles.

The difficulties encountered by those who have sought to describe the rules or principles underlying our grammatical (or mathematical or physical) abilities have convinced a growing number of theorists that our knowledge in these domains is not stored in the form of rules or principles. That conviction has been an important motive for the development of connectionist and other sorts of nonsentential and nonrule-based models. But none of this should encourage an advocate of the off-line simulation theory, since the dispute between connectionist models and rule-based models is a dispute *among theory-theorists.* Of course, on a narrow interpretation of 'theory,' on which only rule-based and sentence-based models count as theories, the success of connectionism would indeed show that the "theory-theory" is mistaken. But, as we have taken pains to note, a refutation of the theory-theory will support the off-line simulation account only when 'theory' is interpreted broadly.

Argument 2: Mental simulation models have been used with some success by a number of cognitive scientists.

Here's how Goldman makes the point:

Several cognitive scientists have recently endorsed the idea of mental simulation as one cognitive heuristic, although these researchers stress its use for knowledge in general, not specifically knowledge of others' mental states. Kahneman and Tversky (1982) propose that people often try to answer questions about the world by an operation that resembles the running of a simulation model. The starting conditions for a 'run', they say, can either be left at realistic default values or modified to assume some special contingency. Similarly, Rumelhart [et al. 1972] describe the importance of 'mental models' of the world, in particular, models that simulate how the world would respond to one's hypothetical actions. (1989, 174)

Reply: It is our contention that this argument rests on the failure to distinguish two fundamentally different sorts of models. While the term 'simulation model' may be appropriate for models of both sorts, the models Goldman mentions are not examples of *off-line simulation* at all. Indeed, quite the opposite is the case. They are paradigm cases of the use of a rich body of mentally represented information about the domain in question; thus, they are clear cases of models that exploit the strategy of the theory-theory.

The "simulation models" that Goldman cites work in much the same way as the computer models often constructed by researchers trying to predict the behavior of complex systems. Such models typically rely on mathematical equations and other sorts of information about the principles governing the behavior of the system to be predicted. For example, suppose we wanted to determine how long it would take a forest fire in Yellowstone Park to reach surrounding towns under prevailing conditions and what path the fire would take. The speed at which the fire will progress depends partly on the moisture conditions, the wind conditions, and the density of the forest. As a result, a good computer model will include equations that capture the impact of these variable conditions as well as information about the size of the forest and the location of the towns. A "run" of such a model might proceed by calculating the progress of the fire at various moments from its inception onward, and it is quite natural to call such a run a simulation. However, this sort of simulation obviously relies on a complex, informationally rich *theory*. It bears next to no similarity to the sort of off-line simulation that we are criticizing here.

Perhaps this point will be clearer if we consider how a simulation model of the sort Goldman describes might be used in predicting someone's behavior. The model, like the simulation model of the forest fire, would have to include lots of rules or principles about how people behave (that is, it would have to include a substantial body of psychological theory). To get our prediction, we would provide the model with "the starting conditions for a 'run'," which would presumably include information about the current mental states and environment of the person whose behavior we wish to predict. The model would then calculate or infer the behavior of the person at various times in the future. Though this process might well be described as a simulation of the person's behavior, it is obviously a theory-driven process. Goldman seems to be claiming that if people actually predict other people's behavior by running a simulation model of this sort in their heads, it would vindicate the off-line simulation theory. But obviously, this is exactly the wrong conclusion to draw. If people use *this* sort of simulation model, then they are using an informationally rich *theory* (a folk psychology) to make their predictions.

Argument 3: "To apply the alleged commonsense theory would demand anomalous precocity."

What we've just quoted is a section heading in one of Gordon's unpublished papers (Gordon 1990, sec. 3.5). He goes on to note that recent studies have shown children as young as two and a half "already see behavior as dependent on belief and desire." It is, he suggests, more than a bit implausible that children this young could acquire and use "a theory as complex and sophisticated" as the one that the theory-theory attributes to them. Goldman elaborates the argument as follows:

> Children seem to display interpretive skills by the age of four, five or six. If interpretation is indeed guided by laws of folk psychology, the latter must be known (or believed) by this age. Are such children sophisticated enough to represent such principles? And how, exactly, would they acquire them? One possible mode of acquisition is cultural transmission (e.g. being taught them explicitly by their elders). This is clearly out of the question, though, since only philosophers have even tried to articulate the laws, and most children have no exposure to philosophers. Another possible mode of acquisition is private construction. Each child constructs the generalizations for herself, perhaps taking clues from verbal explanations of behavior which she hears. But if this construction is supposed to occur along the lines of familiar modes of scientific theory construction, some anomalous things must take place. For one thing, all children miraculously construct the same nomological principles. This is what the (folk-)theory theory ostensibly implies, since it imputes a single folk psychology to everyone. In normal cases of hypothesis construction, however, different scientists come up with different theories. (1989, 167–68)

Reply: There is no doubt that if the theory-theory is right, then the child's feat is indeed an impressive one. Moreover, it is implausible to suppose that the swift acquisition of folk psychology is subserved by the same learning mechanism that the child uses to learn history or chemistry or astronomy. But, once again, we find it hard to see how this can be taken as an argument against the theory-theory and in favor of the off-line simulation theory. For there are other cases in which the child's accomplishment is comparably impressive and comparably swift. If contemporary generative grammar is even close to being right, the knowledge structures that underlie a child's linguistic ability are enormously complex. Yet children seem to acquire the relevant knowledge structures even more quickly than they acquire their knowledge of folk psychology. Moreover, children in the same linguistic community all acquire much the same grammar, despite being exposed to significantly different samples of what will become their native language. Less is known about the knowledge structures underlying children's abilities to anticipate the behavior of middle-sized physical objects. But there is every reason to suppose that this "folk physics" is at least as complex as folk psychology and that it is acquired with comparable speed. Given the importance of all three knowledge domains, it is plausible to suppose that natural selection has provided the child with lots of help—either in the form of innate knowledge structures or in the form of special purpose learning mechanisms. But whatever the right story about acquisition turns out to be, it is perfectly clear that in the case of grammar, and in the case of folk physics, what is acquired must be some sort of internally represented theory. Off-line simulation could not possibly account for our skills in those domains. Since the speed of language acquisition and the complexity of the knowledge acquired do not (indeed, could not) support an off-line simulation account of linguistic ability, we fail to see why Gordon and Goldman think that considerations of speed and complexity lend any support at all to the off-line simulation account of our skills in predicting, explaining, and interpreting behavior.

Argument 4: The off-line simulation theory is much simpler than the theory-theory.

Other things being equal, we should surely prefer a simpler theory to a more complex one. And on Gordon's view,

> the simulation alternative makes [the theory-theory] strikingly unparsimonious. Insofar as the store of causal generalizations posited by [the theory-theory] mirrors the set of rules *our own* thinking typically conforms to, the Simulation Theory renders it altogether otiose. For whatever rules our own thinking typically conforms to, our thinking continues to conform to them within the context of simulation. . . . In the light of this far simpler alternative, the hypothesis that people must be endowed with a special stock of laws corresponding to rules of logic and reasoning is unmotivated and unparsimonious. (1990, 7)

Reply: When comparing the simplicity of a pair of theories, it is important to look at the whole theory in both cases, not just at isolated parts. It is our contention that if one takes this broader perspective, the greater parsimony of the simulation theory simply disappears. To see the point, note that for both the theory-theory and the simulation theory the mechanism subserving our predictions of other people's behavior must have two components. One of these may be thought of as a database that somehow stores or embodies information about how people behave. The other component is a mechanism which applies that information to the case at hand—it extracts the relevant facts from the database. Now, if we look only at the database, it does indeed seem that the theory-theory is "strikingly unparsimonious," since it must posit an elaborate system of internally represented generalizations or rules—or perhaps some other format for encoding the regularities of folk psychology. The simulation theory, by contrast, uses the mind's decision making system as its database, and that decision-making system would have to be there on any theory, because it explains how we make real, "on-line" decisions. So the off-line simulation theory gets its database for free.

But now let's consider the other component of the competing theories. Merely *having* a decision-making system will not enable us to make predictions about other people's behavior. We also need the capacity to take that system off-line, feed it pretend inputs, and interpret its outputs as predictions about how someone else would behave. When we add the required cognitive apparatus, the picture of the mind that emerges is sketched in figure 4-2. Getting this "control mechanism" to work smoothly is sure to be a *very* nontrivial task. How do things look in the case of the theory-theory? Well, no matter how we go about making predictions about other people, it is clear that in making predictions about physical systems we can't use the off-line simulation strat-

FIGURE 4-2

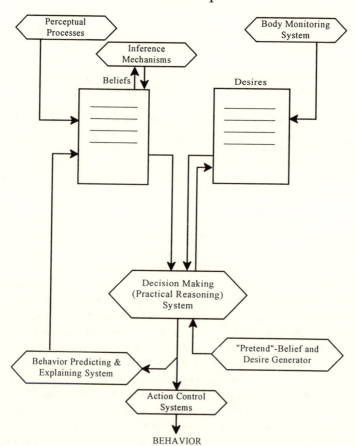

egy; we have to use some sort of internalized theory (though, of course, it need not be a sentence-like or rule-based theory). Thus, we know that the mind is going to have to have some mechanism for extracting information from internalized theories and applying it to particular cases. (In figure 4-1 we assumed that this mechanism is housed along with the other "inference mechanisms" that are used to extract information from preexisting beliefs.) If such a mechanism will work for an internally represented folk physics, it is plausible to suppose that, with minor modifications, it will also work for an internally represented folk psychology. So, while the simulation theorist gets the database for free, it looks like the theory-theorist gets the "control mechanism" for free. All of this is a bit fast and loose, of course. But we don't think either side of this argument can get much more precise until we are presented with up-and-running models to compare. Until then, neither side can gain much advantage by appealing to simplicity.

Argument 5: When we introspect about our predictions of other people's behavior, it sometimes seems that we proceed by imagining how we would behave in their situation.

Here is how Goldman makes the point:

> The simulation idea has obvious initial attractions. Introspectively, it seems as if we often try to predict others' behavior—or predict their (mental) choices—by imagining ourselves in their shoes and determining what we would choose to do. (1989, 169)

And here is Gordon:

> [C]hess players report that, playing against a human opponent or even against a computer, they visualize the board from the other side, taking the opposing pieces for their own and vice versa. Further, they pretend that their reasons for action have shifted accordingly. . . . Thus transported in imagination, they 'make up their mind what to do.' (1986, 161–62)

Both authors are aware that appeal to introspection can be a two-edged sword, since it also often happens that we predict other people's behavior *without* introspecting any imaginary behavior:

> There is a straightforward challenge to the psychological plausibility of the simulation approach. It is far from obvious, introspectively, that we regularly place ourselves in another person's shoes, and vividly envision what we would do in his circumstances. (Goldman 1989, 176)

> Imagery is not always needed in such simulations. For example, I need no imagery to simulate having a million dollars in the bank. (Gordon 1986, 161)

To deal with this "challenge," Goldman proposes a pair of replies. First, simulation need not always be introspectively vivid—it can often be "semi-automatic, with relatively little salient phenomenology" (1989, 176). Second, not all interpretations rely on simulation—in many cases, interpreters rely solely on "inductively acquired information," though the information is "historically derived from earlier simulations" (Goldman 1989, 176).

Reply: We don't propose to make any fuss at all about the frequent absence of "salient phenomenology." For it is our contention that when the issue at hand is the nature of the cognitive mechanism subserving our capacity to interpret and predict other people's behavior, the entire issue of introspective imagination is a red herring. Indeed, it is two red herrings. To see the first of them, consider one of the standard examples used to illustrate the role of imagery in thought. Suppose we ask you, "How many windows are there in your house?" How do you go about answering? Almost everyone reports that they imagine themselves walking from room to room, counting the windows as they go. What follows from this about the cognitive mechanism that they are exploiting? Well, one thing that surely does not follow is that off-line simulation is involved. The only way that people could possibly answer the question accurately is to tap into some internally represented store of knowledge about their house; it simply makes no sense to suppose that off-line simulation is being used here. So, even if a cognitive process is always accompanied by vivid imagery, that is no reason at all to suppose that the process exploits off-line simulation. From this we draw the obvious conclusion. The fact that prediction and interpretation sometimes involve imagining oneself in the other person's shoes is less than no reason at all to suppose that off-line simulation is involved.

It might be suggested that, though imagery provides no support for the off-line simulation hypothesis, it does challenge the theory-theory when 'theory' is interpreted narrowly. For it shows that some of the information we are exploiting in interpretation and prediction is not stored in the form of sentences or rules. But even this is far from obvious. There is a lively debate in the imagery literature in which "descriptionalists" like Pylyshyn (1981) and Dennett (1969; 1978c) maintain that the mechanisms underlying mental imagery exploit language-like representations, while "pictorialists" like Kosslyn (1981, 1994) and Fodor (1975) argue that images are subserved by a separate, nonlinguistic sort of representation. We don't propose to take sides in this dispute. For present purposes, it is sufficient to note that, unless it is supplemented by a persuasive argument in favor of pictorialism and against descriptionism, the introspective evidence does not even challenge the theory-theory construed narrowly.

> *Argument 6:* The off-line simulation account is supported by recent experimental studies focusing on children's acquisition of the ability to interpret and predict other people.

On our view, this is far and away the most interesting argument that has been offered in favor of the off-line simulation theory. To see exactly what the experimental studies do, and do not, support, we'll have to look at both the evidence and the argument with considerable care. Gordon does a good job of describing one important set of experiments.

> Very young children give verbal expression to predictions and explanations of the behavior of others. Yet up to about the age of four they evidently lack the concept of belief, or at least the capacity to make allowances for false or differing beliefs. Evidence of this can be teased out by presenting children with stories and dramatizations that involve dramatic irony: where we the audience know something important the protagonist doesn't know. . . .
>
> In one such story (illustrated with puppets) the puppet-child Maxi puts his chocolate in the box and goes out to play. While he is out, his mother transfers the chocolate to the cupboard. Where will Maxi look for the chocolate when he comes back? In the box, says the five year old, pointing to the miniature box on the puppet stage: a good prediction of a sort we ordinarily take for granted. . . . But the child of three to four years has a different response: verbally or by pointing, the child indicates the cupboard. (That is, after all, where the chocolate is to be found, isn't it?) Suppose Maxi wants to mislead his gluttonous big brother to the *wrong* place, where will he lead him? The five year old indicates the cupboard, where (unbeknownst to Maxi) the chocolate actually is. . . . The *younger* child indicates, incorrectly, the box. (1986, 168)

These results, Gordon maintains, are hard to square with the theory-theory. For if the theory-theory is correct, then

> before internalizing [the laws and generalizations of folk psychology] the child would simply be unable to predict or explain human action. And *after* internalizing the system, the child could deal indifferently with actions caused by *true* beliefs and actions caused by *false* beliefs. It is hard to see how the semantical question could be relevant. (169)

But, according to Gordon, these data are just what we should expect, if the off-line simulation theory is correct.

> The Simulation Theory [predicts that] prior to developing the capacity to simulate others for purposes of prediction and explanation, a child will make *egocentric errors* in predicting and explaining the actions of others. She will predict and explain as if whatever she herself counts as "fact" were also fact to the other; which is to say, she fails to make allowances in her predictions and explanations for false beliefs or for what the other isn't in a position to know. (1990, sec. 3.6, p. 11)

Reply: According to Gordon, the theory-theory can't easily explain the results of the "Maxi" experiment, though the off-line simulation theory predicts those results. We're not convinced on either score. Let's look first at just what the off-line simulation story would lead us to expect.

Presumably, by the time any of these experiments can be conducted, the child has developed a more or less intact decision-making system like the one depicted in figure 4-1. That system makes on-line decisions and thus determines the child's actions on the basis of her actual beliefs and desires. But by itself it provides the child with no way of predicting Maxi's behavior or anyone else's. If the off-line simulation theory is right, then in order to make predictions about other people's behavior two things must happen. First, the child must acquire the ability to take the output of the decision-making system off-line—treating its decisions as predictions or expectations rather than simply feeding them into the action-controlling system. Second, the child must acquire the ability to provide the system with input other than her own actual beliefs and desires. She must be able to supply the system with "pretend" input so that she can predict the behavior of someone whose beliefs and desires are different from her own. (These are the two capacities that are represented in figure 4-2 and absent in figure 4-1.) There is, of course, no a priori reason to suppose that these two steps happen at different times or that the one we've listed first will occur first. But if they do occur in that order, then we might expect there to be a period when the child could predict her own behavior (or the behavior of someone whose beliefs and desires are the same as hers) though she could not predict the behavior of people whose beliefs or desires are different from hers. It is less clear what to expect if the steps occur in the opposite order. Perhaps the result would be some sort of pretending or play-acting—behaving in a way that someone with different beliefs or desires would behave. Though until the child develops the capacity to take output of the decision-making system offline, she will not be able to predict other people's behavior or her own. So it looks like the off-line simulation story makes room for three possible developmental scenarios:

> **1.** The child acquires both abilities at the same time. In this case, we would expect to see two developmental stages. In the first, the child can make no predictions. In the second, she can make a full range of predictions about people whose beliefs and desires are different from her own.
> **2.** The child first acquires the ability to take the output offline and then acquires the ability to provide the system with pretend input. In this case, we would expect three developmental stages. In the first, the child can make no predictions. In the second, she can only make predictions about her own behavior or about the behavior of people whose beliefs and desires are identical to hers. In the third, she can make the full range of predictions.
> **3.** The child first acquires the ability to provide the system with pretend inputs and then acquires the ability to take the output offline. In this case, too, we would expect three developmental stages. The first and last stages are the same as those in (2), but in the middle stage the child can play-act but not make predictions.

Now let's return to the Maxi experiment. Which of these developmental scenarios do the children in these experiments exhibit? At first blush, it might be thought that the pattern Gordon reports is much the same as the one set out in scenario 2. But that would be a mistake. The younger children—those who are giving the wrong answers—are not predicting that Maxi would do what someone with their own beliefs and desires would do—for they have no desire to get the chocolate or to deceive the gluttonous brother. Those are Maxi's desires, not theirs. If anything, it would appear that these children are half way between the second and third stages of scenario 2: They can feed pretend desires into the decision-making system but not pretend beliefs. Of course, none of this shows that the off-line simulation theory is false. It is perfectly compatible with the theory to suppose that development proceeds as in 2, *and* that the transition from the second to the third stage proceeds in two substages—desires first, then beliefs. (This pattern is sketched in figure 4-3.) But it is, to say the least, something of an exaggeration to say that the off-line simulation theory "predicts" the experimental results. The most that can be said is that the theory is compati-

FIGURE 4-3

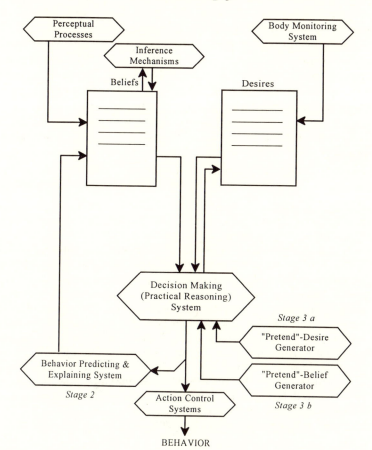

ble with the observed developmental pattern and with lots of other patterns as well.[9]

For the results that Gordon describes to be at all relevant to the dispute between the off-line simulation theory and the theory-theory, it would have to be the case that the latter theory is incompatible with the reported developmental pattern. But that is patently not the case. To see why, we should first note that the theory-theory is not committed to the claim that folk psychology is acquired all in one fell swoop. Indeed, one would expect just the opposite. If children really are acquiring a tacit theory of the mind, they probably acquire it a bit at a time. Thus, it might be the case that at a given stage in development children have mastered the part of the theory that specifies how beliefs and desires lead to behavior, though they have not mastered the entire story about how beliefs are caused. At this stage, they might simply assume that beliefs are caused by the way the world is; they might adopt the strategy of attributing to everyone the very same beliefs that they have. A child who has acquired this much of folk psychology would (incorrectly) attribute to Maxi the belief that the chocolate is in the cupboard. She would then go on to make just the predictions that Gordon reports. Of course, the theory-theory is also compatible with lots of other hypotheses about which bits of folk psychology are acquired first. Thus, like the off-line simulation theory, it is compatible with (but does not entail) lots of possible developmental patterns. So, it looks like the developmental studies that Gordon and Goldman cite can't be used to support one theory over the other.

> *Argument 7:* Autistic children are highly deficient in their ability to engage in pretend play. These children are also frequently unable to impute beliefs to others or to predict other people's behavior correctly.

Here's how Gordon sets out the argument:

> Practical simulation involves the capacity for a certain kind of systematic pretending. It is well known that *autistic* children suffer a striking deficit in the capacity for pretend-play. In addition, they are often said to 'treat people and objects alike'; they fail to treat others as subjects, as having 'points of view' distinct from their own. This failure is confirmed by their performance in prediction tests like the [Wimmer-Perner "Maxi" experiment] I have just described. A version of the Wimmer-Perner test was administered to autistic children of ages *six to sixteen* by a team of psychologists. . . . *Almost all* these children gave the wrong answer, the 3-year-old's answer. This indicates a highly specific deficit, not one in general intelligence. Although many autistic children are also mentally retarded, those tested were mostly in the average or borderline IQ range. Yet children with Down's syndrome, with IQ levels substantially below that range, suffered no deficit: almost all gave the right answer. My account of belief would predict that only those children who can engage in pretend-play can master the concept of belief. (1986, 196)

Goldman is rather more tentative. He claims only that the inability of autistic children "to impute beliefs to others and therefore predict their behavior correctly . . . might . . . be related to their lack of pretend play" (1989, 175).

Reply: The fact that autistic children are both incapable of pretend play and unable to predict the behavior of other people in Wimmer-Perner tests is very intriguing. Moreover, Gordon is certainly right in suggesting that the off-line simulation theory provides a possible explanation for these facts. If the off-line simulation theory is right, predicting the behavior of people whose beliefs differ from our own requires an ability to provide our own decision-making system with pretend input. And it is plausible to assume that this ability would also play a central role in pretend play. So, if we hypothesize that autistic children lack the ability to provide the decision-making system with pretend input, we could explain both their performance on the Wimmer-Perner test and their failure to engage in pretend play. But, of course, this will not count as an argument for the off-line simulation theory and against the theory-theory if the latter theory can offer an equally plausible explanation, of the facts. And it will require no creativity on our part to produce such an alternative explanation since one of the investigators who discovered the fact that autistic children do poorly in Wimmer-Perner tests has offered one himself.

Leslie takes as an assumption "the hypothesis that human cognition involves *symbolic computations* in the sense discussed . . . by Newell (1980) and particularly by Fodor" (1988, 21). He also assumes that an internalized theory of mind underlies the normal adult's ability to predict other people's behavior. An important theme in Leslie's work is that developmental studies with both normal and autistic children can help to illuminate the expressive resources of the "language of thought" in which our theory of mind is encoded. According to Leslie, the notion of a *metarepresentation* is central in understanding how our theory of mind develops. Roughly speaking, a metarepresentation is a mental representation about some other representational state or process. We exploit metarepresentations when we think that

Maxi believes that the chocolate is in the box

or that

Maxi's brother wants the chocolate

or that

Mommy is pretending that the banana is a telephone.

On Leslie's view, "autistic children do not develop a theory of mind normally" (39). And while "it is far too soon to say with any confidence what *is* wrong" with these children, he speculates that at the root of the problem may be an inability to use metarepresentations. If this were true, it would explain both their difficulty with pretend play and their failure on the Wimmer-Perner test.

Though we find Leslie's speculation interesting and important, it is no part of our current project to defend it. To make our case, we need only insist that, on currently available evidence, Leslie's hypothesis is no less plausible than Gordon's. Since Leslie's speculation presupposes that normal children acquire and exploit a theory of mind that is encoded in a language of thought, the evidence from studies of autistic children gives us no reason to prefer the off-line simulation account over the theory-theory.[10]

Our theme in this reply and in the previous one has been that the empirical evidence cited by Gordon and Goldman, while compatible with the off-line simulation theory, is also compatible with the theory-theory and thus does not support one theory over the other. But there are several studies in the recent literature that *can* be used to support one theory over the other. These studies report results that are comfortably compatible with the theory-theory though not with the off-line simulation account. Before we sketch those results, however, it is time to start a new section. In this section we've tried to show that none of the arguments in favor of the off-line simulation theory are persuasive. In the next one, we'll set out a positive case for the theory-theory.

5   In Defense of the Theory-Theory

When subjects do a good job at predicting the behavior of other people, it is often difficult to determine whether they are relying on off-line simulation or on an internalized theory. If they are relying on a theory, the details of the theory may not be readily available to conscious access. Thus, the mere fact that subjects can't report much about folk psychology or even recognize various characterizations of the information such a theory might contain provides no reason to conclude that they are not invoking a tacit theory. When subjects do a poor job of predicting the behavior of other people, however, the situation is quite different. In these cases, the explanatory resources of the theory-theory are considerably greater than those of the off-line simulation theory. On a simulation account like the one portrayed in figure 4-2, mistaken predictions can arise in one of two ways:

> **1.** The predictor's decision-making (or practical reasoning) mechanism is different from the target's.
> **2.** The pretend belief and desire generator has not provided the decision-making system with the right pretend beliefs and desires—i.e., with the ones that actually motivate the target person whose behavior is to be predicted.

If an experimental situation can be designed in which subjects systematically mispredict the behavior of targets, and in which it is unlikely that either (1) or (2) is the source of the problem, then the off-line simulation account will be seriously challenged. Often, however, these cases will be easily accommodated by the theory-theory, which can attribute the error to the fact that the internalized information on which the subject relies is mistaken or incomplete. If there is some psychological process that is unknown to folk psychology, and if this process affects people's behavior in a given sort of situation, then it is not surprising that subjects who rely on folk psychology to predict how others will behave in that situation will be mistaken in their predictions.

In an earlier publication (Stich and Nichols 1992), we reported an informal experiment that turned on just such an unsuspected psychological phenomenon. The phenomenon in question was first reported by Ellen Langer (1975). She called it "the illusion of control," but we prefer a less theory-laden label; we'll call it the Langer effect. In one of her experiments, Langer organized a football pool in the office of an insurance agency a few days prior to the Superbowl, selling tickets at $1 each. Some subjects were offered a choice of tickets; others were offered only one. The day before the big game, Langer said she would be willing to buy the tickets back from the subjects and asked how much they wanted for them. The surprising result was that subjects who had no choice of tickets sold them back for an average price of $1.96, while subjects who had a choice sold theirs back for an average price of $8.67.

In our informal experiment we read a description of Langer's experiment to a group of undergraduates and asked them to predict what Langer's subjects would do. Not surprisingly, the students got it wrong. They predicted no significant difference between the price asked by the no-choice subjects and the price asked by the subjects who were given a choice. We tried to use this result as an argument against simulation accounts of behavior prediction. But advocates of the off-line simulation theory were not convinced. Both Harris (1992) and Goldman (1992) complained that the way in which the facts were presented to the students made it very unlikely that they would use the right pretend beliefs and desires in generating their predictions. Each participant in Langer's experiment was exposed to only one condition—either choice or no-choice. And there was a delay of several days between buying the ticket and being asked to sell it back. In contrast, the students who were asked to predict how Langer's subjects would behave were told about both conditions, and the time delay between being told about the purchase and being asked to predict the sell-back price was only a minute or two. Given these differences, Harris and Goldman protested, it would hardly be surprising if the students used the wrong pretend inputs in making their prediction. In a later article (Stich and Nichols 1995), we concede that the criticism is a fair one. However, Nichols et al. (1996) then designed an experiment that tried to sidestep the shortcomings of the informal experiment.

The first issue that needed to be addressed was the importance of the time lag in Langer's original experiment. Was this an essential factor in producing Langer's effect? To answer this question, Nichols et al. conducted an experiment similar to Langer's but with no significant time lag. Subjects, who met one-on-one with the experimenter, were told that they would be asked to judge the grammaticality or ungrammaticality of fifteen sentences to be read by the experimenter. Before reading them the sentences, the experimenter explained that to reward the subjects for their participation, a lottery had been arranged. The prize was $30. At this point, some of the subjects were given a numbered lottery ticket by the experimenter. Other subjects were invited to select one of three lottery tickets that were offered. The experimenter then read the fifteen sentences and had subjects record their judgments on an answer sheet. The grammar-judgment task lasted about five minutes. When it was complete, the subjects were told that it might be necessary to run more subjects than planned. And since the experimenter wanted to give all subjects a reasonable chance at winning the lottery, he might want to buy back some of the lottery tickets. Subjects were asked to set a price at which they would be prepared to sell the lottery ticket back to the experimenter and to record that price on their answer sheet. There were a total of thirty subjects, fifteen in each condition. The mean price set by subjects in the no-choice condition was $1.60; the mean price set by subjects in the choice condition was $6.29 ($p < .05$). These results clearly indicate that the Langer effect can be obtained without any significant delay between the time the subjects receive the lottery tickets and the time they are asked for a price at which they will sell them back.

The next question to be addressed was whether observers can accurately predict the decision-making process that leads subjects in Langer-style experiments to set the prices they do. In order to assist observer-subjects in generating the best possible pretend inputs (if that is indeed what they do) Nichols et al. produced a pair of videotape recordings of a subject (actually a confederate) participating in the experimental procedures just described. The two tapes were identical except for the first two minutes in which the grammatical judgment task was explained and the lottery ticket was given (on one tape) or chosen (on the other tape). Each tape was shown to a separate group of observer-subjects. The observer-subjects were provided with answer sheets identical to the one provided to the subjects in the Langer-style experiment. Observer-subjects were asked to predict what the experimental subject on the tape would say about the grammaticality or ungrammaticality of each of the fifteen sentences. They were also asked to predict the price the subject on the tape would set for selling back his lottery ticket. There were thirty-eight observer-subjects in the choice condition and thirty-nine in the no-choice condition. The mean predicted buy-back price was $7.82 in the choice condition and $9.37 in the no-choice condition. (The difference is not statistically significant.) These results are summarized in figure 4-4. For completeness, Nichols et al. also calculated the success rate of observer-subjects on the grammatical-judgment prediction task. All four authors judged all of the sentences used to be

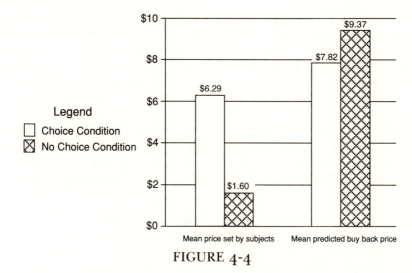

FIGURE 4-4

clearly grammatical or clearly ungrammatical. Using their judgments as a criterion of correctness, the observers predicted correctly 84 percent of the time, with no significant variation between the two conditions.

It is our contention that these experimental results pose a serious problem for those who think that behavior prediction relies on the sort of simulation sketched in figure 4-2. For, as we noted earlier, this sort of simulation has only two straightforward ways of accounting for systematically mistaken predictions. Either the predictors' decision-making systems differ from the targets' decision-making systems or the predictors are providing their decision-making systems with the wrong pretend inputs. In the Nichols et al. experiment, the first option is very implausible, since the predictors and the subjects in the Langer-style experiment were drawn from the same population. There is every reason to believe that if the predictors had been subjects in the Langer-style experiment, they would have behaved in much the same way that the actual subjects did. Moreover, the conditions for producing pretend inputs were about as good as they could possibly be, since predictors observed the target on videotape as he was making his decision, and postexperiment interviews with a number of subjects indicated that all of them correctly remembered whether or not the target they observed had been given a choice of lottery tickets. On the theory-theory account of how behavioral predictions work, these results are easy enough to explain. Folk psychology includes no information about the Langer effect, so predictors get it wrong. Perhaps advocates of the off-line simulation theory can produce a plausible alternative explanation of these results, one which is not uncomfortably ad hoc. But we haven't a clue what it might be.

The experiment done by Nichols et al. focused on the prediction of other people's behavior, when that behavior is strongly influenced by an "effect" whose existence comes as a surprise to most people. In another recent study, Lowenstein and Adler (forthcoming) looked at the ability of subjects to predict their own behavior, when that behavior is influenced by a little-known effect. What they found was that, in this case, too, people make the wrong predictions. Lowenstein and Adler exploited the recently discovered "endowment effect" (Thaler 1980)—a robust and rapidly appearing tendency for people to set a significantly higher value for an object if they actually own it than they would if they do not own it. Here is how Lowenstein and Adler describe the phenomenon:

> In the typical demonstration of the endowment effect (see, e.g., Kahneman, Knetsch and Thaler 1990), one group of subjects (sellers) are endowed with an object and are given the option of trading it for various amounts of cash; another group (choosers) are not given the object but are given a series of choices between getting the object or getting various amounts of cash. Although the objective wealth position of the two groups is identical, as are the choices they face, endowed subjects hold out for significantly more money than those who are not endowed. (2)

In an experiment designed to test whether "unendowed" subjects could predict the value they would set if they were actually to own the object in question, the experimenter first allowed subjects (who were members of a university class) to examine a mug engraved with the school logo. A form was then distributed to approximately half of the subjects, chosen at random, on which they were asked "to imagine that they possessed the mug on display and to predict whether they would be willing to exchange the mug for various amounts of money."[11] When all the subjects who received the form were finished filling it out, all the subjects were presented with a mug and given a second form with instructions analogous to those on the prediction form. But on the second form, it was made clear that they actually could exchange the mug for cash and that the choices they made on this second form would determine how much money they might get. "Subjects were told that they would receive the option that they had circled on one of the lines—which line had been determined in advance by the experimenter" (Lowenstein and Adler, forthcoming, 6). The results showed that subjects who had completed the first form substantially underpredicted the amount of money for which they would be willing to exchange the mug. In one group of subjects, the mean predicted exchange price was $3.73, while the mean actual exchange price for subjects asked to predict was $5.40. Moreover, there is reason to suppose that an "anchoring effect" led the actual exchange price for these subjects to be lower than it might otherwise have been, since the mean actual exchange price for subjects who did not make a prediction about their own selling price was $6.46.

In this experiment, as in the Nichols et al. experiment, it is hard to see how an advocate of simulation theory can offer a non—ad hoc explanation of the results. Obviously, the mistaken prediction cannot be the result of a difference between the decision-making mechanism of the predictor and the target since in this experiment the subjects are predicting their own decisions. Nor is it plausible for the simulation theorist to suppose that the pretend belief and desire generator would have a problem generating the pretend beliefs and desires that result from being told that one now actually owns the mug. For, if the pretense mechanism that the simulation theorist posits can't handle simple cases like pretending that one has been given a mug one has had ample opportunity to examine, then the pretense mechanism must be very fallible indeed. And if that is the case, then it is a mystery why our predictions turn out to be correct as often as they do. For the theory-theorist, by contrast, there is no puzzle about how the results are to be explained. Folk psychology just doesn't include any information about the endowment effect. So when the effect plays a major role in determining behavior, predictions based on folk psychology get it wrong.

6   Conclusion

This essay has been long, but the conclusion will be brief. The off-line simulation theory poses an intriguing challenge to the dominant paradigm in contemporary cognitive science. But it is our contention that the prospects for the off-line simulation theory are not very bright. None of the arguments offered in defense of the theory is at all persuasive, and there is a growing body of experimental evidence that would be very hard to explain if the off-line simulation account were correct. We don't claim to have provided a knock-down refutation of the off-line simulation theory. Knock-down arguments are hard to come by in cognitive science. But we do claim to have assembled a pretty serious case against the simulation theory. There may be cognitive capacities for which something akin to off-line simulation provides a plausible explanation, but the capacity to predict, explain, and describe people's behavior in intentional terms do not seem to be among them.[12]

Notes

This chapter contains material from three previous publications—Stich and Nichols (1992); Stich and Nichols (1995); and Nichols et al. (1996)—along with some new material that has not been previously published.

1. We are grateful to Robert Gordon for providing us with copies of several of his unpublished papers and for allowing us to quote from them at some length.

2. Indeed, in the recent literature, simulation theories have been offered for a wide variety of cognitive capacities including empathy (Goldman 1993),

aesthetic understanding (Currie 1995a), conditional planning (Harris 1992), and imagery (Currie, 1995b). For a critical discussion of some of these proposals, see Nichols et al. (1996).

3. The wind tunnel analogy is suggested by Ripstein (1987, 475ff.). Gordon also mentions the analogy (1991, 8), but he puts it to a rather different use.

4. For details of the Milgram experiments, see Milgram (1963).

5. The burglar-in-the-basement example is borrowed from Gordon (1986, 161).

6. The evidence Gordon cites includes the tendency to mimic other people's facial expressions and overt bodily movements and the tendency in both humans and other animals to direct one's eyes to the target of a conspecific's gaze.

7. Ripstein's account of the role of simulation in intentional explanation is quite similar.

> I wish to defend the claim that imagining what it would be like to be in "someone else's shoes" can serve to explain that person's actions. . . . I shall argue that imagining oneself in someone else's situation . . . allows actions to be explained without recourse to a theory of human behavior. . . .
>
> The same sort of modeling [that engineers use when they study bridges in wind tunnels] is important to commonsense psychology. I can use my personality to model yours by "trying on" various combinations of beliefs, desires and character traits. In following an explanation of what you do, I use my personality to determine that the factors mentioned would produce the result in question. . . . I do not need to know how you work because I can rely on the fact that I work in a similar way. My model . . . underwrites the explanation by demonstrating that particular beliefs and character traits would lead to particular actions under normal circumstances. (1987, 465, 476–77)

8. For more on connectionist models of this type, see chapter 2 in this volume.

9. Actually, the developmental facts are rather more complicated than Gordon suggests. For, as Leslie (1988) emphasizes, children are typically able to appreciate and engage in pretend play by the time they are two and a half years old—long before they can handle questions about Maxi and his false beliefs. It is not at all clear how the off-line simulation theory can explain both the early appearance of the ability to pretend and the relatively late appearance of the ability to predict the behavior of people whose beliefs and desires differ from one's own.

10. It's worth noting that both Gordon's account and Leslie's "predict that only those children who can engage in pretend play can master the concept of belief" (Gordon 1986, 169). This may prove a troublesome implication for both theorists, however, for it is not the case that *all* autistic children do poorly on the Wimmer-Perner test. In the original study reported by Baron-Cohen et al. (1985), only sixteen out of twenty autistic subjects failed the Wimmer-Perner test; the other four answered correctly. The investigators predicted that these four children "would also show evidence of an ability to pretend play" (43) Unfortunately, no data were reported on the pretend-play ability of these subjects. If it should turn out that some autistic children do well on the Wimmer-

Perner test and lack the ability for pretend play, both Gordon's explanation and Leslie's would be in trouble. If the facts do turn out this way, advocates of the theory-theory will have a variety of other explanations available. But it is much less clear that the off-line simulation account could explain the data, if some autistic children can't pretend but can predict the behavior of people with false beliefs.

11. Lowenstein and Adler (forthcoming, 5–6). The exact wording of the form was as follows:

> We are interested in your opinion about the mug displayed at the front of the room. Imagine that we gave you a mug exactly like the one you can see, and that we gave you the opportunity to keep it or trade it for some money. Below are a series of lines marked "Keep mug _____ Trade it for $amount _____." On each line check whether you would think that you would prefer to keep the mug or to trade it in for the amount of money written on the line. Check one or the other on every line.

The remainder of the page consisted of forty lines in which the amount of money for which the mug might be traded increased, from 25 cents to $10, in 25-cent increments.

12. For some discussion of other capacities whose explanation may require appeal to simulation, see Nichols et al. (1996).

CHAPTER 5

Intentionality and Naturalism

With Stephen Laurence

The deepest motivation for intentional irrealism derives not from such relatively technical worries about individualism and holism as we've been considering, but rather from a certain ontological intuition: that there is no place for intentional categories in a physicalistic view of the world; that the intentional can't be naturalized.

—Fodor (1987, 97)

1 Catastrophe Theory

Intentional irrealism is the doctrine that meaning is a myth. A bit more precisely, it is the claim that nothing in the world instantiates intentional properties—that intentional predicates are true of nothing. If intentional irrealism is correct, then it is not the case that

(1) 'Snow is white' means that snow is white

or that

(2) George Bush often thinks about winning the next election

or that

(3) Lincoln wanted to free the slaves.

Nor is it the case that

(4) Thinking about winning the election sometimes causes Bush to smile

or that

(5) Lincoln's desire to free the slaves caused him to sign the Emancipation Proclamation.

Obviously, intentional irrealism has some very startling consequences. If it is true, then a very substantial part of what we read in our textbooks, teach our children, and say to each other is mistaken. Indeed, as Fodor has remarked, with only a bit of hyperbole,

> if it isn't literally true that my wanting is causally responsible for my reaching, and my itching is causally responsible for my scratching, and my believing is causally responsible for my saying . . . if none of that is literally true, then practically everything I believe about anything is false and it's the end of the world. (1990c, 156)

Though we rather doubt that the world would come to an end, perhaps Fodor is closer to the mark in claiming that if intentional irrealism is correct and "commonsense intentional psychology really were to collapse, that would be, beyond comparison, the greatest intellectual catastrophe in the history of our species. . . . The collapse of the supernatural didn't compare" (1987, xii).

Very well, then, let's agree that intentional irrealism is a very radical doctrine. But why on earth should anyone *worry* about it? Why does anyone think it is even remotely plausible? In the quotation with which we began this chapter, Fodor maintains that the "deepest motivation for intentional irrealism" is the suspicion "that the intentional can't be naturalized." Viewed as a bit of sociology, it is our guess that Fodor is right. In recent years, many philosophers have put a very high priority on providing a "naturalistic" account of intentional categories.[1] Moreover, there is an unmistakable tone of urgency in much of this literature. Naturalizing the intentional isn't just an interesting project, it is vitally important. *Something dreadful* will follow if it doesn't succeed. And for many writers, we suspect, that dreadful consequence is intentional irrealism.[2] But this sociological fact raises a philosophical puzzle. *Why* would irrealism (or some comparably unsettling conclusion) follow if "the intentional can't be naturalized?" What is the connection between the existence or nonexistence of a naturalistic account of intentional categories and the truth or falsehood of claims like (1)–(5)? These are the questions that motivate this essay.

To answer them, of course, it will be necessary to say just what is involved in "naturalizing" the intentional. And, as we shall see, there is no shortage of answers to choose from. But not just any answer will do. A satisfactory account of what it is to "naturalize the intentional"—an account that makes sense of what Fodor sees as "the deepest motivation for intentional irrealism"—will have to satisfy a pair of constraints. First, it will have to sustain an argument from the premise that intentional notions can't be naturalized to the conclusion that intentional irrealism or some other deeply troubling doctrine is true. Second, there must be some reason to think that, when "naturalizing" is unpacked along the lines proposed, it is in fact the case that the intentional can't be naturalized. For even if nonnaturalizability entails irrealism, this is surely nothing to worry about if the claim that the intentional can't be naturalized is neither intuitively plausible nor supported by a convincing argument.

It is our contention that, while various accounts will satisfy one or the other of these constraints, there is no account of what it is to naturalize the intentional that will satisfy *both* of them. To support our contention, we will survey a number of proposals on what "naturalization" comes to, and we will go on to argue that none of these candidates will satisfy both of the constraints. Obviously, this strategy won't provide a conclusive case for our conclusion, since there may be some quite different account of naturalizing that does satisfy both constraints. But if so, we haven't a clue about what it might be.

If we are right, if there is no account that satisfies both constraints, then there is something deeply misguided about the urgency that imbues so much of the recent literature in this area. It may, of course, be perfectly reasonable to adopt one or another account of what it would be to naturalize the intentional, and to explore the possibility of bringing it off. A successful naturalization might well be an impressive and valuable accomplishment. But if it should turn out that intentional notions can't be naturalized, *no dire consequences will follow.* We will not have to rewrite history, or renounce intentional psychology, or revise the way we describe and explain people's behavior. It will not be the end of the world. It won't even be the beginning of the end.

Before launching into our survey of accounts of "naturalizing," a few words are in order on some of the other troubling consequences that might be thought to follow if naturalization does not succeed. In Fodor's writing, and elsewhere in the literature, the dominant worry is the one that has been center stage in this section: If the intentional can't be naturalized, then intentional irrealism will have won the day. But often enough, one finds suggestions of other calamities that may ensue if naturalization fails. One of these is that intentional states might turn out to be causally impotent. In the passage quoted earlier, for example, Fodor frets that it's the end of the world if it isn't literally true that his wanting is causally responsible for his reaching and his believing is causally responsible for his saying. In Fred Dretske's writing, the worry that intentional states might turn out to be causally inert is frequently cited as a motive for seeking a naturalized account of these states. Indeed, Dretske sometimes suggests that if intentional states are causally impotent, then perhaps we should not include them in our ontology at all: "If beliefs and desires are not causally relevant to behavior, I, for one, fail to see why it would be worth having them. . . . If reasons aren't causes, one of the chief—indeed (for certain people) the *only*—motive for including them in one's inventory of the mind, vanishes" (1989, 1).[3] Another, rather different concern is that if naturalization fails, then there could be no serious *science* of intentional psychology because there could be no *laws* that invoke intentional terms or intentional properties. We are no more impressed by these worries than we are about the concern over irrealism. For, as we shall argue in the sections that follow, on any reading of the claim that the intentional can't be naturalized which is even remotely likely to be true, neither of these calamitous consequences would follow.

2 Naturalizing and Conceptual Analysis

Once upon a time, something called *conceptual analysis* was all the rage in philosophy. The journals back then were filled with attempts to provide necessary and sufficient conditions for the application of a term or a concept. And, more often than not, when one philosopher published such an "analysis" another philosopher would describe a hypothetical situation in which we would intuitively say that the analysans applied and the analysandum did not, or vice versa. For people who remember those bygone days (only one of us does), much of the literature on naturalizing the intentional provokes a strong sense of deja vu. Consider, for example, the following quotation:

> The worry about representation is above all that the semantic (and/or the intentional) will prove permanently recalcitrant to integration in the natural order. . . . What is required to relieve the worry is therefore, at a minimum, the framing of *naturalistic* conditions for representation. That is, what we want at a minimum is something of the form 'R *represents* S' *is true iff* C where the vocabulary in which condition C is couched contains neither intentional nor semantic expressions. (Fodor 1984, 32)

Of course, an interest in providing necessary and sufficient conditions is not, by itself, enough to convict a philosopher of engaging in conceptual analysis. For typically, a conceptual analyst will not be happy with just any set of conditions that happen to be coextensive with the predicate being analyzed. If a proposed analysis is to be acceptable, it has to be the case that the coextension obtains not only in all actual cases but in imaginary or hypothetical cases as well. The biconditional specifying the analysis must not only be true, it must be *necessary*. Moreover, the alleged coextension in all possible worlds is supposed to be testable by consulting our linguistic intuition and determining what we would say about hypothetical cases. This method would seem to make the most sense if we suppose that the coextension derives from the meaning of the concepts that underlie our predicates—the analysans (the right-hand side of the biconditional) unpacks the meaning of the concept expressed by the analysandum.

Is it the case that Fodor and others who worry about the possibility that the intentional can't be naturalized are actually worried about the possibility that the meaning of intentional predicates or intentional concepts can't be set out as a set of necessary and sufficient conditions which do not themselves invoke intentional terms? We're not at all sure.

Indeed, it is our suspicion that these philosophers have *no* clear idea of what "naturalizing" amounts to and that much of their anxiety can be traced to this confusion. But if it is not clear that these philosophers really want a conceptual analysis, it is clear that if "naturalizing" is understood in this way, it will not satisfy the first of our two constraints.

Indeed, it is rather ironic that Fodor often seems to be troubled by the fact that our intentional concepts can't be analyzed in nonintentional terms. For among contemporary philosophers, no one has been more adamant than Fodor in insisting that we should not expect our terms or concepts to be analyzable *at all*. Here is an example of the sorts of things he says when this mood is upon him:

> It seems to me to be among the most important findings of philosophical and psychological research over the last several hundred years (say, since Locke first made the reductionist program explicit) that attempts at conceptual analysis practically always fail.
>
> Consider, for example, the failure of the reductionist program within the study of language. . . . What I'll call the *Definition Hypothesis* [is the claim that] (a, weak version) . . . many de facto lexical concepts are definable; and (b, strong version) that they are definable in a vocabulary of sensory-terms-plus-logical-syntax.
>
> It's simply notorious that the stronger version of this claim has proved to be untenable. . . . But what's equally true, and considerably more striking, is that the evidence seems to bear against the definition hypothesis even in the weak version; if there are no plausible cases of definition in a sensory vocabulary, there are also remarkably few plausible examples of definition in a *non*-sensory vocabulary, one indication of which is the striking paucity of working examples in the standard literature. There is 'bachelor', which is supposed to mean 'unmarried man'; . . . there are jargon terms, which are explicitly and stipulatively defined; . . . there is a handful of terms which belong to real, honest-to-God axiomatic systems; . . . and then there are the other half million or so items that the OED lists. About these last apparently nothing much can be done. (1981a, 283–84)

On our view, there can be no serious quarrel with Fodor's assessment of the track record of conceptual analysis. Though lots of very clever people have tried very hard to produce them over the centuries, we still have no plausible definitions for 'knowledge' or 'cause' or 'law' or 'freedom,' or for any of the other terms that loom large in philosophical discussion. Moreover, as Fodor goes on to illustrate, it is no easier to provide definitions for more mundane terms like 'paint' or 'parent' or 'pig'. The more one plays the game of trying to provide exceptionless, intuitively acceptable necessary and sufficient conditions, the more one is inclined to accept Fodor's conclusion: "When it comes to definitions, the examples almost always don't work" (1981a, 288).

What are we to make of this situation? Well, of course, it might be that conceptual analysis is just *hard* and that if we keep at it we will ultimately succeed in producing a significant number of intuitively acceptable definitions. However, it is also entirely possible that we will never succeed—that the project of defining most common predicates is simply impossible.

If it *is* impossible, this will have important consequences for those parts of philosophy and psychology that deal with the structure of human concepts. There is a venerable tradition in this area which assumes that the concept or mental structure underlying the use of most predicates is actually a mentally represented definition—a set of necessary and sufficient conditions. In deciding whether or not a term applies to a given case, this "classical view" maintains, we are either consciously or (more typically) unconsciously determining whether the case at hand satisfies the conditions of the definition. If it turns out that there just are no definitions for most terms, then obviously the classical account of the structure and use of concepts will have to go.[4]

In recent years, there has been a growing realization that the classical account of concepts is in deep trouble, and a number of interesting alternatives have been proposed. Perhaps the best known of these are the prototype and exemplar accounts of concepts developed by Eleanor Rosch and her associates. On the prototype theory, concepts are weighted lists of features that are characteristic of the most typical members of the category that the concept picks out. The list will generally include lots of features that are not necessary for category membership. On the exemplar story, concepts are, in effect, detailed mental descriptions of particular members of the category. Thus, for example, the concept underlying your use of the word 'dog' might include detailed descriptions of Lassie and Rin Tin Tin. In determining whether to categorize something as a dog, this theory maintains, you assess the similarity between the target and the various exemplars stored in semantic memory (see Smith and Medin 1981, chaps. 4–6). Fodor has proposed a very different alternative to the classical account of concepts. On his view, the concepts that underlie most of our one-word predicates have no structure at all—or at least none that is relevant to the semantic properties of the concept. Of course, if this is right it is very hard to see how these concepts might be learned. And that's just fine with Fodor, since he thinks they are all innate (see Fodor 1981a).

This is not the place to elaborate the details of these various "nonclassical" theories of concepts or to debate their virtues and shortcomings. Our reason for mentioning them was simply to make clear that there are lots of interesting theories about concepts on the market which are compatible with (and which might well explain) the finding that most of our concepts appear to have no intuitively acceptable definitions. So, if it is indeed the case that most concepts have no definitions, there is nothing much to worry about. Rather, the appropriate response is to get busy and try to determine which of the various nonclassical theories of concepts is correct. It would, by contrast, be simply *mad* to think that if most of our concepts can't be defined, then the terms that express those concepts are not true of anything. The inference from *The predicate '_____ is a pig' cannot be defined* to *There are no such things as pigs* is simply perverse. Concern about porcine irrealism is not even a remotely appropriate reaction to the collapse of the classical theory of concepts. But, of course, exactly the same can be said about intentional predicates. Perhaps there are good reasons to worry about intentional irrealism being true, but the fact that '*R* represents *C*' can't be defined surely isn't one of them.[5]

What about the other two concerns that we sketched at the end of section 1? If intentional terms can't be defined, does it follow that intentional states are causally impotent or that there are no laws invoking intentional properties? In both cases, we maintain, the answer is clearly *no*. To see why, consider a few analogies. If the classical theory of concepts is wrong, then there will be no way to provide necessary and sufficient conditions for predicates like '*x* shot *y*' or '*z* died'. But from this, surely, it does not even begin to follow that it is not literally true that being shot by John Wilkes Booth caused Lincoln to die. And, of course, if the classical theory is wrong, then terms like 'force', 'mass', and 'gravity' won't be definable, either. But it would be at best a bad joke to conclude from this that there are no laws that invoke these terms. If the classical view of concepts collapses, it will not take all of physics with it. The situation seems entirely parallel for intentional terms. If it turns out that they can't be analyzed or defined, this would provide no reason at all to conclude that intentional states are causally impotent or that there are no laws invoking them. So if "naturalizing the intentional" requires providing a classical analysis of intentional concepts, then if the intentional can't be naturalized, we have found no reason to think that anything at all troublesome will follow.

3 *Naturalizing, Natural Kinds, and Essential Properties*

To set the stage for our second account of what it might be to naturalize the intentional, we'll begin with a brief reminder of some very influential doctrines in the philosophy of language. Consider so-called natural kind predicates like 'water' or 'gold'. What is it that determines which parts of the world are in the extension of such predicates? According to the widely discussed causal-historical account of reference, the answer to this question must invoke the notion of "essential properties" of natural kinds—properties that everything in the extension of a natural-kind term must have. A bit fancifully, the causal-historical story might be sketched as follows:

> A kind term first acquires its referent when it is used to "baptize" or "dub" some newly noted samples of the stuff to which the term will refer. This process is sometimes described as "grounding" the predicate. Once the predicate has been grounded, it can be transmitted from one speaker

to another in appropriate communicative settings. And those to whom the predicate is passed can pass it on again. The speakers who originally ground the predicate need have no deep understanding of the nature of the stuff they are dubbing; indeed, they may have all sorts of wildly mistaken beliefs about it. The speakers who acquire the predicate via reference-preserving transmissions need never have come in contact with anything in the extension of the predicate. They, too, can harbor many false beliefs about the nature of the stuff to which the term refers.

Now obviously, there is something missing in this tale. For a predicate like 'gold' gets grounded on just a few samples of gold. And yet the extension of the predicate must include *all* the gold that ever has or ever will exist in the universe. What is the relation between the dubbed samples and the rest of the gold in the universe, in virtue of which the dubbing succeeds in attaching the term to all gold, wherever it may be? It is here that the doctrine of *essential properties* is typically brought into play. The basic idea is that individual items are grouped into natural kinds in virtue of the possession of certain essential properties, and it is the job of science to discover what these properties are. Thus, for example, science tells us that having atomic number 79 is the essential property of gold, that being H_2O is the essential property of water, and so on. When a natural-kind term gets grounded, the term comes to apply not only to the samples present at the dubbing but also to everything else in the universe that has the same essential properties.

How does all of this relate to the project of naturalizing the intentional? To see the answer, let's go back to the quotation from Fodor near the beginning of the previous section. What was worrying Fodor was that intentional categories might "prove permanently recalcitrant to integration in the natural order." And what was required to relieve the worry was "a framing of naturalistic conditions for representation . . . something of the form '*R* represents *S*' *is true iff C* where the vocabulary in which condition *C* is couched contains neither intentional nor semantic expressions." Our first pass at unpacking this requirement was to view it as a demand for a conceptual analysis. But it could equally well be viewed as asking for a specification of an underlying essential property—the property in virtue of which the predicate '*R* represents *S*' applies to all and only those pairs of things in the universe such that the first represents the second. On this interpretation, the biconditional needed to naturalize the representation relation would have a status akin to the one Putnam and others have attributed to biconditionals like:

(6) (x) x is water iff x is H_2O.

It is a necessary truth, but its necessity has nothing to do with the structure of the concepts that speakers invoke when they use the terms involved. It isn't known a priori, and it can't be discovered by probing intuitions or by doing psycholinguistics. The only way to discover it is to do the appropriate sort of science.

How likely is it that *this* is what philosophers want when they set

about trying to naturalize the intentional? Well, there are some practitioners of the craft who offer accounts of representation that rely
heavily on notions borrowed from science (typically evolutionary biology). Some of these writers go out of their way to explain that they are
not trying to capture our intuitions about representation and thus are
not worried by the fact that their analyses have counterintuitive consequences.[6] All of this is compatible with the interpretation that these
philosophers are seeking an account of the essential properties of representation. But we don't propose to press the point, since, as we noted
earlier, we rather suspect that most of the writers who worry about
naturalizing the intentional have no clear idea of what naturalizing
amounts to. What is clear is that if 'naturalizing' is interpreted in this
way, then once again it will not satisfy our first constraint.

One way of arguing for this claim would be to mount a head-on
assault on the whole idea of scientifically discoverable essential properties and on the account of the reference of natural-kind terms that goes
along with it. There is already a substantial literature pointing out the
shortcomings of this rather trendy package of ideas, and we have considerable sympathy with the emerging critique.[7] But all that would
make a very long argument, and we have a much shorter one to offer.

Suppose it is the case that the doctrine of essential properties and
the associated story about reference can survive serious scrutiny. Suppose further that when 'naturalizing' is interpreted in the way we've
just sketched, it turns out that '*R* represents *S*' and other intentional
predicates cannot be naturalized. Would this be enough to make intentional irrealism plausible? Surely, the answer is *no*. To see the point, we
need only note that there are endlessly many predicates for which no
one would even dream of seeking scientifically discoverable essential
properties. Yet it would be simply perverse to claim that these predicates can't be truly applied to anything. Nobody seriously thinks that
anything remotely analogous to (6) would be available for such one-
place predicates as 'couch', 'car', 'war', 'famine', or 'die', nor for two-
place predicates like 'owns', 'kills', 'throws', 'mates with', 'fixes', or
'crushes'. But it would be preposterous to suggest that this entails there
is no killing or war or famine and that no one ever owns anything
or dies. If natural-kind terms are defined as those whose extension is
determined by scientifically discoverable essential properties, then one
way of putting our point is that there are many, many predicates that
are not natural-kind terms, and the fact that they are not natural-kind
terms is no reason at all to suppose that they cannot be truly predicated
of anything. So, if it turns out that nothing analogous to (6) is forthcoming for intentional predicates, the right conclusion is not that those
predicates are true of nothing but simply that, in the sense lately defined, they are not natural-kind terms. And that would hardly be the
end of the world.

Could it be that while intentional irrealism doesn't follow from the
fact that intentional predicates aren't natural-kind terms, something

comparably unsettling does follow? Let's take a brief look at the pair of possibilities suggested at the end of section 1. The first of them focuses on the causal efficacy of intentional states. Might it be the case that if intentional predicates aren't natural-kind terms in the sense we've defined, then they can't be used to make causal claims that are literally true? This strikes us as a singularly implausible suggestion. For, as we noted earlier, it is literally true that being shot by John Wilkes Booth caused Abraham Lincoln to die, though neither 'shoots' nor 'dies' is likely to be the sort of term whose extension is determined by scientifically discoverable essential properties. So, even if it turns out that intentional predicates are not natural-kind terms in the sense we've defined, the causal efficacy of intentional states and processes might still be on a par with the causal efficacy of shooting, crushing, eating, or mating. And that should be efficacy enough for anyone.

A second possibility is that if intentional predicates aren't natural-kind terms, then perhaps there could be no science of intentional psychology. For, it might be argued, such a science would have to include intentional laws, and laws can only be stated with natural-kind terms. No kind terms, no laws; no laws, no science. Now as we see it, the problem here comes with the link between kind terms and laws. *Why* can laws only be stated with natural-kind terms? One might view it as simply a stipulative definition: natural-kind terms just are the sorts of terms that can occur in law-like statements. But now we have a potential equivocation on our hands. For we have been assuming that natural-kind terms are defined as those whose extension is determined by scientifically discoverable essential properties, and the current argument proposes a very different definition. Of course, it might be claimed that these two definitions pick out the same class of terms—that all and only terms whose extension is determined by scientifically discoverable essential properties can be used in law-like statements. But we find this a singularly implausible proposal. For in sciences far removed from psychology, there appears to be lots of terms invoked in laws for which nothing much like (6) is in the offing. We see no reason at all to suppose there are scientifically discoverable essential properties that fix the reference of terms like 'inflation', 'fitness', 'mass', 'gravity', or 'electric charge', for example. If this is right—if there are lots of terms invoked in scientific laws whose extensions are not fixed in the way that the causal-historical theory claims the extensions of terms like 'gold' are fixed—then the putative threat to intentional psychology disappears.

Thus far we have been arguing that an account of naturalizing the intentional which requires producing something akin to (6) will not satisfy the first of our two constraints. Neither intentional irrealism nor any other catastrophic consequence follows if the intentional can't be naturalized, when 'naturalizing' is interpreted in this way. But we are also inclined to think that if we take seriously the story about reference that serves as a backdrop for the current proposal on naturalizing, then our second constraint will not be satisfied, either. For if that story is correct, then the usual arguments aimed at showing that the intentional can't be naturalized just don't go through.

Those arguments typically begin by describing some feature or cluster of features that are important or essential for intentional states, *on the commonsense account of these states.* The arguments then try to show that respectable scientific theories cannot accommodate states with the features in question. The conclusions the arguments draw are just the ones that Fodor feared: that the intentional "will prove permanently recalcitrant to integration in the natural order" and that "there is no place for intentional categories in a physicalistic view of the world." However, if the causal-historical account of reference is correct, then the conclusions of these arguments do not follow from the premises. For on the causal-historical account, the essential properties that determine the extension of natural-kind terms are to be discovered by science, and our commonsense views about the things we are referring to with natural-kind terms may be wildly, hopelessly wrong. Indeed, the fact that ignorance and error do not undermine reference is taken to be a major selling point of the causal-historical theory.[8] But if our commonsense views about the things we are referring to may be seriously mistaken, then the (alleged) fact that common sense imbues intentional states with scientifically unacceptable features entails nothing at all about the scientific respectability of intentional states. For common sense may just be *wrong;* our intentional terms may actually refer to states that do not have these scientifically unacceptable features. So if the causal-historical theory of reference is correct, there can be no serious argument from premises about the commonsense characterization of intentional states to conclusions about the role that the intentional states referred to by commonsense psychology might play in scientifically acceptable theories. Without some argument along those lines, however, it is hard to see why we would have any reason to believe that the intentional can't be naturalized.[9]

4 *Naturalizing and Supervenience*

> It's hard to see . . . how one can be a Realist about intentionality without also being, to some extent or other, a Reductionist. If the semantic and the intentional are real properties of things, it must be in virtue of their identity with (or maybe of their supervenience on?) properties that are themselves *neither* intentional *nor* semantic. If aboutness is real, it must be really something else. (Fodor 1987, 98)

4.1 *The Game Plan*

Thus far we haven't done very well in finding interpretations of 'naturalizing' that satisfy our two constraints. But in the passage just quoted,

Fodor seems to be making a pair of suggestions that we haven't yet explored. To avoid irrealism, intentional properties must be *identical with* or *supervene upon* nonintentional properties. So, perhaps naturalization should be explained in terms of property identity or supervenience. In the current section, we'll consider whether either of *these* proposals satisfies our two constraints. Actually, we will focus almost entirely on supervenience, since on all plausible accounts of that notion, it is a weaker relation than identity. Indeed, on most accounts, property identity entails supervenience, and thus nonsupervenience entails nonidentity. So, if nothing nasty follows from the fact that the intentional doesn't supervene on the nonintentional, then the fact that intentional properties are not identical with nonintentional ones will be no cause for worry.

In restricting our attention to supervenience, we are not exactly making things easy for ourselves, however. For the literature on supervenience has blossomed profusely during the last few years, and this literature suggests a variety of different ways in which the idea that the intentional supervenes on the nonintentional may be spelled out.[10] These alternatives differ on a pair of dimensions. First, the notion of one class of properties supervening on another can be explicated in two different ways, one of which (so-called *strong supervenience*) entails the other *(weak supervenience)*. Second, there are various options that might be proposed as the "supervenience base" for intentional properties— the class of properties on which intentional properties are expected to supervene. In the arguments that follow, we will restrict our attention to weak supervenience. For, since strong supervenience entails weak supervenience, the failure of weak supervenience entails the failure of strong. Thus, if we can show that no untoward consequences follow when weak supervenience does not obtain, the same conclusion will follow if strong supervenience fails.

Here's the game plan. We'll begin with a brief explanation of the two notions of supervenience. We'll then attend to three different candidates that might be proposed as the supervenience base for intentional properties. In each of these three cases, we will argue that the constraints set out in section 1 are not met. In the first two cases, it is the first constraint that isn't satisfied: Neither irrealism nor the other unwelcome consequences follow if supervenience fails. In the third case, it is the second constraint that isn't satisfied. For in this case, it is wildly implausible that supervenience fails. We will follow all of this with a brief discussion of another notion of supervenience, so-called *global supervenience*, whose precise relation to the other two notions is a matter of some dispute. Here again, we will argue, nothing catastrophic follows if intentional properties fail to supervene on the various bases that have been proposed. End of game plan. It's time to get to work.

4.2   Two Notions of Supervenience

Supervenience is usually construed as a relation between two classes of properties. So to begin, let us adopt the following convention. Let B and S be two classes of properties (think of them as the base class and the supervenient class) whose members are $b_1, b_2, \ldots, b_i, \ldots$ and $s_1, s_2, \ldots s_i, \ldots$ respectively. Now, the basic idea is that one class of properties, S, supervenes on a second, B, if the presence or absence of properties in the first class is completely determined by the presence or absence of properties in the second class. There are various ways in which this basic idea can be made more precise.

Perhaps the most intuitive way to proceed is to exploit the notion of a B,- or S-doppelganger. A B-doppelganger of an object is an object that has exactly the same B properties as the original. An S-doppelganger is one which has exactly the same S properties. Thus, for example, if B includes only two sorts of properties, height and weight, then your B-doppelgangers are all and only those things that have the same height and weight that you do. One vivid way to explicate the various versions of the idea that B properties determine S properties is to use the picturesque language of possible worlds. If in all possible worlds, every pair of B-doppelgangers that exist in that world are also S-doppelgangers, then we will say that *S weakly supervenes on B*. So, if S weakly supervenes on B, then in any possible world we select, if we know that a pair of objects in that world share the same B properties, we know they share the same S properties as well. And if a pair of objects in that world do not share the same S properties, we know that there must be at least one B property that one has and the other doesn't. We can build a stronger notion of supervenience if we relax the restriction that the B-doppelgangers are in the same world. We will say that *S strongly supervenes on B* if all B-doppelgangers of an object, no matter what possible world they inhabit, are also S-doppelgangers. Obviously, strong supervenience entails weak supervenience. Plainly, there are lots of other distinctions that might be drawn by restricting attention to one or another special class of possible worlds. But we will leave all of that to the aficionados. Henceforth, when we use 'supervenience' we will mean weak supervenience, as characterized above, unless otherwise specified.

4.3   The Supervenience Base: Three Proposals

On what sorts of properties might it be thought (or hoped) that intentional properties should supervene? As we read the literature, there are at least three proposals for the base class on which intentional properties must supervene if nasty consequences are to be avoided. We propose to consider each of these proposals, proceeding from the most restrictive to the least.

4.3.1 Current, Internal, Physical Properties

The first idea is that something untoward will follow if the intentional properties of an organism do not supervene on the *current, internal, physical properties* of the organism. These are the properties that organisms share with their Putnamian doppelgangers—the hypothetical particle for particle replicas that exist in some far corner of space-time.[11] And if intentional properties supervene on current, internal, physical properties, then in any given world, organisms must have the same intentional properties as their Putnamian doppelgangers. What makes this proposal particularly interesting is that it is widely agreed that there are possible worlds in which organisms and their Putnamian doppelgangers *do not* share all of their intentional properties. Indeed, that's the main point that Putnam's famous thought experiment was supposed to establish. George Bush has many beliefs *about* Michail Gorbachev; he has no beliefs at all about Twin Gorbachev, the atom-for-atom replica in some far-off corner of the universe. The situation is just the opposite for George Bush's doppelganger. Twin Bush has lots of beliefs about Twin Gorbachev and none about the Gorbachev who leads his life in our part of the universe. But while there is considerable agreement about the fact that at least some intentional properties don't supervene on current, internal, physical properties, there is much less agreement on what unwelcome consequences this failure of supervenience is supposed to entail. Let's consider the options.

First on our list, as always, must be the specter of intentional irrealism—the thesis that intentional properties aren't "real properties of things." But surely intentional irrealism would be a preposterous conclusion to draw from the fact that intentional properties don't supervene on current, internal, physical properties. For there are lots of properties of objects that don't supervene on their current, internal, physical properties—often, it would appear, for much the same reason that intentional properties do not. And it would be quite absurd to suggest that nonsupervenience entails irrealism in *all* these cases. To see the point, consider a few examples. There are lots of copies of Picasso paintings in the world. And some of them are astoundingly accurate. Let us imagine that someone produces a "perfect" copy—a canvas that is an atom-for-atom duplicate of the original. Of course, the perfect copy would still be a *copy*, it wouldn't be the original. For to be an original Picasso, a canvas must have the right *history*—it must actually have been painted by Picasso. Much the same point can be made about real $100 bills. A master counterfeiter might produce a bill that is an atom-for-atom replica of one produced by the Bureau of Engraving and Printing. But it would still not be a *real* $100 bill. Indeed, as Fodor has noted, not even *God* can make a real $100 bill. Only a branch of the U.S. Treasury can do that (1987, 45). It follows, then, that neither the property of being an original Picasso nor the property of being a genuine $100 bill supervenes on the current, internal, physical states of an object. So, if a property's failure to supervene on current, internal, physical states were sufficient to show that nothing has the property, then it would follow that there are no genuine Picassos or real $100 bills. But that, of course, is just silly. The idea that intentional irrealism follows from failure to supervene on current, internal, physical states is equally silly.

Before pushing on, it will be useful to mention a rather different sort of example. Both genuine Picassos and real $100 bills are artifacts. And it might be thought that natural properties or categories are not linked to history in this way. But this is almost certainly a mistake. To see the point, consider the classification of organisms into species. Regardless of how similar a pair of organisms are, it is plausible to suppose that they will not count as members of the same species unless they also share the appropriate sort of evolutionary history. If there are creatures in Australia that evolved from birds, then they do not count as members of the same species as Stich's cat, Eggplant, no matter how similar their current, internal, physical states and Eggplant's current, internal, physical states may be. And if scientific explorers on Mars should come upon a macromolecule that is an atom-for-atom replica of an HIV virus isolated on Earth, it would not be an HIV virus unless it shared a common evolutionary ancestry with HIV viruses found on Earth. If this is right, then the property of being a cat and the property of being an HIV virus do not supervene on the current, internal states of the entities that have those properties. But here again, it would be simply absurd to conclude that there are no such things as cats or HIV viruses.

What we have been arguing in the last two paragraphs is that intentional irrealism does not even begin to follow from the fact that intentional properties do not supervene on the current, internal, physical states or organisms. Let's now ask whether one of our other discomforting conclusions follows from the failure of the intentional to supervene on this sort of base. Does it, perhaps, follow that intentional states, though they exist, must be causally impotent—that believings can't cause sayings, that wantings can't cause scratchings—and thus that the end of the world is near? It seems clear that the answer is no. To see why, consider an analogy. Suppose some poor fellow, call him Henry, is crushed to death when an original Picasso sculpture falls on him. Being crushed by an original Picasso caused Henry to die. In some possible world in which Henry exists, we may suppose that he has a twin who is crushed to death by an atom-for-atom identical statue but one which was not made by Picasso. So, being crushed by an original Picasso does *not* cause Twin Henry to die. Nonetheless, it is "literally true" that being crushed by an original Picasso caused Henry to die. Consider now the case of intentional causation. Suppose that both Bush and Twin Bush say, "Gorbachev is bold." Only Bush believes that Gorbachev is bold, however; Twin Bush believes that Twin Gorbachev is bold. Does this difference somehow entail that it could not be "literally true" that Bush's belief caused his utterance? Since it appears that this case is entirely parallel to the previous one, it's hard to see why we should be skeptical about one causal claim and not about the other.

Another worry that one might have at this point focuses on the causal efficacy of *properties* rather than *states*. The concern might be put like this:

> Though it is true enough that Bush's belief state causes his utterance despite its failure to supervene on his current, internal, physical properties, it isn't true that this state causes his utterance *in virtue of being the belief that Gorbachev is bold*. What is worrisome about this sort of failure to "naturalize" the intentional is that it makes intentional properties causally irrelevant.[12]

Now, we are none too clear about how one goes about determining the causal efficacy of properties. But, for argument's sake, let us grant that if intentional properties do not supervene on the current, internal, physical properties of organisms, then intentional properties are not causally efficacious. Would this be a major catastrophe? So far as we can see, it would be no catastrophe at all. For, given any intentional property, it is easy to find a "narrow" surrogate of that property which *does* supervene on the current, internal, physical state of the organisms. Following Stich (1991b), we can take the property of believing that *[p]* to be the narrow surrogate of believing that *p*. The extension of the expression, "_____ believes that *[p]*" is just the class of all possible individuals who believe *that p* along with all of their current-internal-physical-property doppelgangers.[13] Similarly, we could construct a "narrow" surrogate for the property of being an HIV virus. The extension of this surrogate property would be the class of all possible entities that have the property of being an HIV virus, along with all their current-internal-physical-property doppelgangers. Here, again, the narrow surrogate *will* supervene on the current, internal, physical states of the entities in question. Thus, even if we grant that intentional properties (and properties like being an HIV virus) are not causally efficacious, there is no reason to fear that the end of the world is near. In both cases, the properties fail to be causally efficacious because they have historical or relational components "built in." But it is easy enough to characterize narrow surrogates that factor out the historical or relational components. And we see no reason at all to suppose that these narrow surrogates are not causally efficacious. It's hard to think that even Fodor's Granny could ask for more.[14]

Let's turn to the worry about laws. Does the fact that intentional properties don't supervene on current, internal, physical states indicate that they cannot play a role in laws? There are, in the literature, a number of arguments aimed at establishing some sort of link between laws and properties that supervene on the current, internal, physical states of systems. But we don't propose to tackle these arguments head-on, for, if the truth be known, we are not at all sure we really understand them.[15] But we are sure that when one starts looking at cases, the proposed link seems very implausible. Consider the HIV virus. Though the details are still to be worked out, it is plausible to assume there is a law-like connection between infection by the HIV virus and the death of certain cells that play an important role in the immune system. Thus, something like the following might well turn out to be a law:

> For all x, if x is infected by the HIV virus (and certain further conditions are met), then most of x's T-cells will be destroyed.

But if the current worry were correct, then there could be no such law, because being infected by the HIV virus is not a property that supervenes on an organism's current, internal, physical state. For a rather different example, consider Greshem's law, which claims that bad money drives good money out of circulation. Plainly, neither the property of being money nor the properties of being good and bad money supervene on the current, internal, physical state of coins, banknotes, wampum, and the like. But this is no reason at all to suppose that Greshem's law is mistaken. Analogously, the fact that intentional properties do not supervene on the current, internal, physical states of organisms does not entail that intentional properties cannot play a role in laws. So, the reading of "naturalizing the intentional" which requires showing that the intentional supervenes on the current, internal, physical state of the organism fails to satisfy our first constraint. If the intentional can't be naturalized (in this sense), nothing on our list of unwelcome consequences will follow.

4.3.2   All Physical Properties

A second proposal for a supervenience base widens the base class by dropping the restriction to *current, internal* states. On this proposal, intentional properties will be naturalized if we can show that they supervene on *physical* properties of the organism. Though it is not entirely clear which properties to count as physical properties, a natural way to construe the current proposal is to take the physical properties to be those that might be invoked in physical laws. When the proposal is construed in this way, however, just about everything we said in the previous section can be repeated with minor modifications. More specifically:

> **1.** Intentional properties do not supervene on physical properties. The crucial difference between Bush and Twin Bush is that the former has had appropriate causal interactions with Gorbachev, while the latter has had completely parallel interactions with Twin Gorby. But having had appropriate causal interactions with Gorby

(rather than Twin Gorby) is not the sort of property that is likely to be invoked by a physical law.

2. Being a genuine Picasso or a real $100 bill doesn't supervene on physical properties either.

3. Thus, if the fact that a property, p, does not supervene on physical properties is sufficient to establish that nothing has p, then we would have to be irrealists about genuine Picassos and real $100 bills. And that's absurd.

4. So, the failure of the intentional to supervene on the physical will give no support at all to intentional irrealism.

5. The properties that differentiate people who are crushed by original Picassos from their twins who are crushed by perfect copies are not properties that will be invoked in physical laws. But it may still be literally true that Henry's death was caused by being crushed by an original Picasso. Analogously, the fact that Bush believes that Gorbachev is bold, while Twin Bush believes that Twin Gorbachev is bold, does not entail that Bush's utterance was not caused by his belief.

6. Finally, the properties that distinguish real HIV viruses from their atom-for-atom duplicates on Mars are not properties that physics is likely to invoke. Nonetheless, it may well turn out to be a law that if a person is infected by HIV, then most of his or her T-cells will die. So, the fact that a property does not supervene on physical properties does not preclude it from being invoked in a law. Thus, the failure of the intentional to supervene on the physical would not entail that intentional properties can't be invoked in laws.

We conclude that the second proposed base does no better than the first. If naturalizing the intentional means showing that the intentional supervenes on the physical, then if the intentional can't be naturalized, none of our catastrophic consequences will follow.

4.3.3 All Nonintentional Properties

The final proposal for a supervenience base that we will consider is the one that Fodor seems to be urging in the quotation with which we began this section. If semantic and intentional properties are real properties of things, he urges, they must be identical with or supervene on "properties that are themselves neither intentional nor semantic." So, let's ask whether our constraints are satisfied if we construe naturalizing the intentional to require that intentional properties weakly supervene on the class of all nonintentional and nonsemantic properties. The answer we would urge is no. But in this case, the problem is with the second constraint, not the first. For when naturalizing is understood in this way, the claim that the intentional can't be naturalized is extremely implausible—indeed it may be incoherent. To see the point, we need only remind ourselves of what has to be the case if one class of properties, S, does not supervene on another, B. For supervenience to fail, there must be a possible world in which there are B-doppelgangers that are not S-doppelgangers. That is, there must be objects, x and y, in some world that share all of their B properties but do not share all of their S properties. On the current proposal, the B properties are *all* nonintentional and nonsemantic properties. So the B-doppelgangers, x and y, must share their physical properties, their relational properties, their spatial location, their temporal location, and their history. But surely, if x and y share *all* of these properties, then x and y are *identical*. And if x and y are identical, then they share all their properties, including their intentional properties.

On the current reading of what naturalizing comes to, it would indeed be a catastrophe if the intentional could not be naturalized. For if this happened, then in some possible world there would be a single object which both did and did not have a certain property, and logic itself would crumble.[16] Fortunately, there is not the slightest reason to take this prospect seriously.

4.4   *Global Supervenience*

Before bringing this chapter to a close, we propose to take a brief look at a third strategy for spelling out the idea of one class of properties supervening on another, the one that goes by the label 'global supervenience.' In defining both weak and strong supervenience, the notion of *objects* that were B- or S-doppelgangers of one another played a central role. But, as the name suggests, in global supervenience the central notion is that of *worlds* that are doppelgangers of one another. A pair of possible worlds are doppelgangers of one another with respect to a given property if and only if the total distribution of the property in one of those worlds is the same as the total distribution of the property in the other. So, for example, a possible world which is exactly like our world except for the fact that Stich's cat, Eggplant, has a black nose rather than a pink one would be a shape- and size-doppelganger of the actual world. But that world would not be a color-doppelganger of the actual world. With this notion in hand, we can define global supervenience as follows: A class of properties, S, globally supervenes on a class of properties, B, if and only if all possible worlds that are B-doppelgangers are also S-doppelgangers. So if S globally supervenes on B, then if a pair of worlds are indistinguishable with respect to the properties in B, they will also be indistinguishable with respect to the properties in S.

In the previous section, we considered three proposals for the base class on which it might be thought that intentional properties should supervene. The first of these, the class of current, internal, physical properties of an object, has no obvious application when global supervenience is at issue. But the other two, the class of physical properties and the class of all nonintentional properties, might both be proposed as a global supervenience base for the class of intentional properties. Let's consider each of them in turn.

Recall that, as we proposed to unpack the notion, a physical property is one that might be invoked in a physical law. Do intentional properties globally supervene on physical properties, when physical properties are construed in this way? The answer, we think, is clearly no. For it seems extremely plausible to suppose that there is a possible World, W_1, that is a physical doppelganger of the actual world as it exists right now but which has no history at all. W_1 is one of those worlds that Russell often worried about. It was created just a few seconds ago, fully stocked with phony fossils and light waves racing toward earth just as they would be if they had been emitted by stars millions of years ago. But if W_1 has no history, then, according to many philosophers, the distribution of intentional properties in W_1 must be very different from the distribution of intentional properties in our world. For in our world, Laurence has lots of beliefs about Julius Caesar; he is connected to Caesar in just the right way to have these beliefs, whatever that way is. But in W_1, Laurence has no beliefs about Caesar. There was no Caesar to have beliefs about in W_1, so Laurence couldn't be connected to him in the right way.

Very well, then, intentional properties do not globally supervene on physical properties. What follows? Nothing terribly troublesome, so far as we can see. The arguments here are pretty much the same as those in 4.3.2. There are *lots* of properties that do not globally supervene on physical properties—the property of being a genuine Picasso, for example (there are no genuine Picassos in W_1), and the property of being a real $100 bill. But from the fact that these properties do not globally supervene on the physical, it surely does not follow that there are no real Picassos and $100 bills in our world. Analogously, from the fact that the intentional doesn't globally supervene on the physical, it does not follow that intentional properties are not instantiated in our world. The property of being an HIV virus doesn't globally supervene on the physical, either. But from this we cannot conclude that this property can't be invoked in laws, nor, alas, can we conclude that being infected by HIV doesn't cause people to die. And here, again, the situation for intentional properties looks to be exactly the same.

What about the broader base, the class of all nonintentional properties? Do intentional properties globally supervene on this base? Once again, so far as we can see, the answer is no. For it certainly seems to be logically possible for there to be a world W_2, that is a nonintentional doppelganger of the actual world but in which trees or cars or dead people have beliefs or desires or some other intentional states. And it also seems logically possible for there to be a world, W_3, that is a nonintentional doppelganger of the actual world but in which Dan Quayle has no thoughts at all—he's just a mindless organic robot. The sorts of worlds we are imagining are, near enough, the sorts that some property dualists suppose the actual world might be. And whatever problems one might think this sort of property dualism confronts, it certainly does not seem to be a logically incoherent view. If it is not logically incoherent, if worlds like W_2 and W_3 really are possible, then intentional properties do not globally supervene on nonintentional properties. But it is hard to see why anyone would think that catastrophic consequences follow. Surely the logical possibility of a world like W_2 or W_3 does not entail that intentional properties are not instantiated in the actual world. Nor, so far as we can see, does it even begin to entail that *in our world* intentional states are causally impotent or that they cannot be invoked in laws of nature.

At this point, we fear, a resolute opponent might begin fiddling with the notion of possibility that is embedded in the definition of global supervenience. Such an opponent might suspect that problems will arise if there are pairs of *nomologically possible* worlds or *metaphysically possible* worlds that are nonintentional doppelgangers but not intentional doppelgangers. The path on which our imagined opponent has embarked is not one we're tempted to follow, for we suspect that it leads directly to a metaphysical swamp. Moreover, even if unwelcome consequences really do follow in these cases—and we see no clear reason to suppose that they do—we are inclined to think that both of them violate our second constraint. It is certainly not intuitively plausible that there are pairs of nomologically or metaphysically possible words that *are* nonintentional doppelgangers but *are not* intentional doppelgangers. Most people, including many who seem to have exquisitely subtle metaphysical intuition, have no intuitions at all about matters like this. So, until someone presents a plausible argument that such world pairs are nomologically or metaphysically possible, we see no reason to take the prospect seriously.

5 *Conclusion*

It's time to sum up. We began with Fodor's observation that "the deepest motivation for intentional irrealism derives . . . from a certain ontological intuition: . . . that the intentional can't be *naturalized*." But we have had no success at all in making sense of this motivation. If the motivation is to stand up to scrutiny, there must be some account of what naturalizing the intentional comes to which satisfies a pair of constraints. First, the account must sustain an argument from the premise that the intentional can't be naturalized to the conclusion that nothing satisfies intentional properties (or perhaps to the conclusion that intentional states are causally impotent, or to the conclusion that there can be no intentional laws). Second, the claim that the intentional can't be naturalized must not turn out to be utterly implausible. None of the accounts we have been considering satisfy both of these constraints. Of course, it is always possible that there is some other account that will satisfy the constraints. But at this point we think the ball is in the other guy's court. Until some account of naturalizing is given that satisfies both constraints, the most plausible view is that the motivation that Fodor recounts is simply confused. There may be good reasons to take the prospect of intentional irrealism seriously, but the worry that the intentional can't be naturalized is not one of them.

Notes

We are grateful to Brian McLaughlin for many hours of helpful discussion. Versions of this essay have been presented at CUNY Graduate Center, Notre Dame University, the University of North Carolina–Greensboro, the Australian National University, and the University of Virginia. Comments and criticisms from those audiences are acknowledged with thanks. After completing work on this essay, early in 1992, we were delighted to discover that Michael Tye (1992 & 1994) had independently arrived at a very similar view.

1. See, for example, Block (1986), Devitt (1990), Dretske (1981; 1988), Field (1978), Fodor (1984; 1987; 1990b; 1990c), Loar (1981), Lycan (1988a), Millikan (1984), Papineau (1987), Schiffer (1982), Stalnaker (1984).

2. Schiffer provides a characteristically forthright illustration of this attitude. On his view, the question of how the semantic and the psychological are related to the physical is "an urgent question" since "we should not be prepared to maintain that there *are* semantical or psychological facts unless we are prepared to maintain that such facts are completely determined by, are nothing over and above, physical facts" (1982, 119).

On Fodor's view, the urgency of the issue reaches to the very core of contemporary academic life. For if the intentional can't be naturalized, then lots of people who work in cognitive science should no longer get government-sponsored research grants: "If it turns out that the physicalization—naturalization—of intentional science . . . is impossible, . . . then it seems to me that what you ought to do is do your science in some other way. . . . If you really can't give an account of the role of the intentional in the physical world . . . [then] by Christ . . . we should stop spending the taxpayer's money" (1990b, 202–3).

3. See also Dretske (1988, 80) and Dretske (1990, 6).

4. For a useful discussion of the classical view, see Smith and Medin (1981, chap. 3).

5. In the passage from Fodor (1984) quoted at the beginning of this section, he insists that "what we want at a minimum is something of the form 'R *represents S' is true iff C*. . . .'" But in later papers Fodor is prepared to accept a lot less. In the following passage, for example, he no longer insists on necessary and sufficient conditions. Rather, he tells us, merely sufficient conditions will do: "I want a *naturalized* theory of meaning; a theory that articulates, in nonsemantic and nonintentional terms, sufficient conditions for one bit of the world

to be *about* (to express, represent, or be true of) another bit." (1987, 98; see also Fodor, 1990c, 51–52). As noted by Jones et al. (1991), if we read him literally, this is just too easy. Here are two sufficient conditions that seem to meet Fodor's requirement:

> If R is Fodor's most recent utterance of "meaning holism is a *crazy* doctrine" (or the thought that underlies it), then R is *about* meaning holism, and R is true iff meaning holism is a crazy doctrine.

> If R is Laurence's most recent utterance of "Madonna is daring" (or the thought that underlies it), then R is about Madonna and expresses the proposition that Madonna is daring.

Obviously, it would be an easy task to produce indefinitely many more. But perhaps this reading is uncharitably literal. Perhaps what Fodor requires in a naturalized theory of meaning are sufficient conditions which follow from the meaning of the terms involved. It is easy enough to provide intuitively plausible sufficient conditions of this sort for many nonintentional terms. Here's one: "For all x, if x is a sow, then x is a pig." But, of course, examples like this are cheating. In the spirit of Fodor's requirement that sufficient conditions for representation or aboutness be stated in *nonsemantic* and *nonintentional* terms, we should require that the sufficient conditions for being a pig be stated in *nonporcine* terms. Once *this* requirement is imposed, however, providing meaning-based sufficient conditions for being a pig looks to be just about as intractable as providing a full-blown definition. If it is impossible to provide such sufficient conditions, that will be an interesting result in lexical semantics. But it will *not* entail that there are no pigs. Similarly, if it turns out that meaning-based sufficient conditions cannot be given for intentional locutions, it will not follow that meaning is a myth.

  6. See, for example, Millikan (1989, 290–91).

  7. Canfield (1983), Donnellan (1983), Leplin (1979;1988), Shapere (1982).

  8. See, for example, Devitt and Sterelny (1987, secs. 4.2 and 5.2).

  9. For some elaboration on the argument set out in the last two paragraphs, see Stich (1991a).

  10. Haugeland (1982), Horgan (1982), Kim (1978; 1982; 1984; 1987), Lewis (1983), Petrie (1987), Teller (1984).

  11. This idea, or something like it, is suggested in Stich (1978a; 1983) and in Fodor (1980; 1987; 1991). For the original account of Putnamian doppelgangers, see Putnam (1975).

  12. For a vivid illustration of this worry, see Dretske (1988, 79–80).

  13. Alternatively, if the reference to possible individuals is problematic, we can take the extension of "_____ believes that *[p]*" in a given possible world to be the class of all individuals in that world who believe that *p*, and all their current-internal-physical-property doppelgangers in that world, and all individuals in that world who are current-internal-physical-property doppelgangers of individuals in other possible worlds who believe that *p*. (The account in Stich 1991b neglects this last conjunct.)

  14. For more on Fodor's Granny and her views, see Fodor (1987, passim) and Loewer and Rey (1991, ii).

  15. One of these arguments is found in Fodor (1987, chap. 2). Another is

in Fodor (1991). Fodor himself no longer claims to understand the first of these. For a critique of the second, see Christensen (1992).

16. This argument will not work if naturalizing is unpacked in terms of strong supervenience, since in that case the B-doppelgangers might be in different possible worlds. Our view about the account of naturalizing that requires strong supervenience on all nonintentional properties is much the same as our view—set out at the end of 4.4—about the account that requires global supervenience on those properties.

CHAPTER 6

Naturalism, Positivism, and Pluralism

Epistemological considerations . . . led . . . [Russell and Carnap and Quine] at various times and in various ways, to various forms of operationalism, verificationism, behaviorism, conventionalism, and reductionism. Each of these was an expression of an underlying "philosophical puritanism" [the term is Davidson's] which held that anything incapable of being "logically constructed" out of certainties . . . was suspicious.

Rorty (1979, 259)

In this final chapter, I want to elaborate a bit on the strategy of the arguments that Laurence and I offered in "Intentionality and Naturalism" and to be more explicit about the pluralistic view of science and inquiry that underlies that chapter. It will, I think, be useful to begin by sketching some quite striking parallels between the current debate over the naturalistic acceptability of intentional properties and the debate that raged a half century ago about the "empirical meaningfulness" of various claims, including psychological claims.

1   Logical Positivism and the Tradition of Philosophical Puritanism

For many of the most important figures in the history of modern philosophy, a central goal of philosophy is to separate the good from the bad in matters intellectual by formulating criteria that the good stuff must satisfy. In Descartes and Hume, the criteria were stated in epistemic terms. And, notoriously, Hume recommends some rather draconian measures for dealing with doctrines that don't measure up:

> When we run over the libraries, persuaded of these principles, what havoc must we make? If we take in hand any volume . . . let us ask, *Does it contain any abstract reasoning concerning quantity and number?* No. *Does it contain any experimental reasoning concerning matters of fact and existence?* No. Commit it then to the flames for it can contain nothing but sophistry and illusion. ([1777] 1902, 165)

In the middle decades of the twentieth century, as language came to loom increasingly large in the thinking of many philosophers, the project of separating the good stuff from the bad stuff took a linguistic turn. The logical positivists sought to formulate criteria of meaningfulness (or "cognitive meaningfulness" or "empirical meaningfulness"), and sentences that failed to live up to the standard were condemned as "meaningless" or "nonsense." These projects usually began by specifying a privileged class of sentences whose empirical meaningfulness was beyond question, though there was more than a little dispute about which sentences were to be accorded this honor. For the most abstemious, only sentences reporting sense data were allowed. More permissive theorists included "physical object observation sentences" as well. Having specified this privileged class, the second stage of the project was to explain how additional sentences are allowed into the class of meaningful sentences. Typically, this was done by specifying a legitimating relation in which sentences must stand to the privileged sentences. But this proved to be no easy task. Some of the proposed relations were quickly shown to be too permissive—they allowed in all declarative sentences, including the most blatant nonsense. Other relations were shown to be too restrictive, since they excluded substantial parts of our best and most respected scientific theories. These proposals threw out the baby with the bath water. Ultimately, the positivists' project suffered the death of a thousand failures. Philosophers gradually became convinced that there is no way of separating sense from nonsense by finding a special relation, R, such that a sentence, S, is empirically meaningful if and only if S is R-related to physical-object sentences.[1]

The effort to draw a boundary between empirically meaningful and empirically meaningless sentences was not a purely theoretical project. Many of the philosophers who wanted to construct a definition of empirical meaningfulness also wanted to use it. For the logical positivists, as for Descartes and Hume before them, the intellectual world was in a sorry state. Nonsensical theories, both old and new, were as common as flowers in spring. Once a clear criterion of meaningfulness had been formulated and defended, there would be no need to develop detailed critiques of theism or Marxism or Heideggerian existentialism. We could simply show that the sentences in these theories failed to meet the criterion of meaningfulness, and thus they could be neither true nor false. There would be no need to enter into a debate over the plausibility of the arguments offered in favor of these theories. Nor was it necessary to wait for a final formulation of the criterion. Part of what made positivism so exciting and so controversial was the outpouring of polemical essays using various rough-and-ready versions of the criterion to argue that some venerable doctrine or trendy theory was meaningless nonsense.

These critiques did not go unanswered, of course. Some of the replies rejected the whole idea of testing sentences against a standard of empirical meaningfulness. But in other cases, the defenders accepted the challenge and sought to show that one or another category of sentence really could pass the test. However, it was often hard to judge whether these efforts had succeeded or failed since there was no agreement on the proper formulation of the criterion of empirical meaningfulness. One category of sentences often discussed in this literature were those that invoked the "mentalistic" vocabulary of commonsense psychology. Though several prominent behaviorist psychologists had suggested that mentalistic discourse was of a piece with magic and voodoo,[2] few positivists were prepared to see all of our mentalistic discourse dismissed as meaningless. So, a great deal of effort was devoted to defining commonsense psychological terms in ways that were approved by the evolving positivist standard.[3]

It was reasonable enough to pursue these polemical disputes about the implications of the positivist criterion of meaningfulness while the criterion itself was still evolving and imperfect. One needn't perfect one's tools before one begins to use them. But once philosophers became convinced that there just was no acceptable criterion to be found, the polemics could no longer be sustained, and debates about the empirical meaningfulness of psychological or theological or metaphysical sentences gradually disappeared from the literature.

This might be the appropriate place to interject a personal note. Ever since my undergraduate years, I have retained a deep admiration for many of the philosophers who played central roles in the logical positivist movement. While I no longer have any sympathy with their philosophical goals, I think their clarity and intellectual honesty was exemplary. To their enduring credit, they were not prepared to rest content with vague sketches of the alleged boundary between the meaningful and the meaningless. Nor were they willing to stop with the assertion that there must be *some* relation that all meaningful sentences bear to physical-object sentences. They actually tried to specify the relation. And once a candidate relation was proposed, they were their own most acute and most persistent critics. Without this sustained effort to articulate the boundary between meaningful and meaningless sentences as explicitly as possible, it would surely have taken much longer to realize that the entire project was misconceived.

2   *Naturalism and Positivism*

It is my contention that there are important similarities between the recent literature on naturalism—particularly that part of the literature that worries about "naturalizing the intentional"—and the earlier positivist literature sketched in the preceding section. Both fall squarely within the tradition of philosophical puritanism disparaged by Davidson and Rorty, the tradition that views philosophy as in the business of articulating standards that other disciplines must live up to if they are to be regarded as respectable. But I think the similarities go much deeper than that. The positivists' project and the naturalists' have much the same structure, and once this is recognized I think the shortcomings of the naturalists' project are easier to see. Here's a partial survey of the similarities between the two, along with a few dissimilarities worth noting.

1. The sort of puritanical naturalism that Laurence and I were criticizing in the previous chapter begins with a firm, though admittedly vague, conviction that at the most fundamental level our world is a physical world and that all the inhabitants of our world, all the things that really exist, are "nothing but" physical. If this is right, then our scientific ontology, indeed our total ontology, should be restricted to physical things. Theories whose ontological commitments go beyond the physical should be rejected. Though this initial formulation of naturalism is far from precise, it is generally agreed that gods and demons and supernatural forces are excluded by the criterion, and good riddance to them. Right-thinking people don't want them in their ontology. Analogously, positivism begins with the firm conviction that if a sentence is to be empirically meaningful, it must be verifiable by experience, though it is far from clear how the notion of "verifiable by experience" is to be understood. Despite the vagueness, however, it was generally agreed that certain particularly egregious bits of nonsense fall on the wrong side of the boundary and that we are well rid of them. Who could doubt that the notorious "Nothing noths" is unverifiable nonsense?

2. It is my impression that neither those who want to use the naturalist criterion to banish intentional entities from our ontology nor those who want to defend the naturalistic credentials of the intentional are as diligent as the positivists were about clarifying the criterion they are using. If that's right, then it is a disanalogy between the two projects, and by my lights an unfortunate one. But in any event, those who do attempt to say in more detail what the naturalist criterion requires typically suggest a story with two parts. First, some basic set of physical properties (or predicates) must be specified, though here, too, there can be considerable dispute about which these are. Second, some account must be given of the sense in which planets and pigs and presidential elections are "nothing but" physical. Most often, this is done by trying

to specify a legitimating relation, R, such that a property (or predicate) is naturalistically acceptable (it applies to "nothing over and above" the physical) if and only if the property in question is R-related to the basic physical properties. Here the similarity to the postivist project is obvious.

3. Even without a clear and convincing specification of the distinction between those properties that are naturalistically acceptable and those that are not, some theorists are anxious to put the distinction to polemical use. And, as was the case with the positivist criterion, the status of commonsense psychology is one major focus of debate. Some philosophers have tried to used naturalism (or "physicalism," as it is sometimes called) to cast aspersions on theories whose ontology includes intentional states. Many other philosophers have taken the threat seriously and sought to respond by showing that intentional properties are indeed naturalistically respectable. But, since there is no clear or widely accepted account of what is required for a property to pass naturalistic muster, it is no easy matter to judge how successful they have been.

3 Puritanical Naturalism versus Open-Ended Pluralism

Much of the chapter that Laurence and I wrote was devoted to proposing possible interpretations of the naturalist criterion and arguing that on those interpretations the criterion would not do the polemical work required of it. In most cases, the objection was that the proposal was too restrictive; lots of babies were being thrown out with the bath water. In setting out and arguing against these various interpretations of the naturalist criterion, we were trying to do for naturalism what the positivists were so admirably scrupulous about doing for themselves: We were trying to say as clearly as possible what the naturalist criterion comes to. Without a reasonably sharp and explicit specification of the standard that the naturalist is setting, it is inevitable that debates about the naturalizability of the intentional will remain as ill focused and inconclusive as the earlier debates over the empirical meaningfulness of mentalistic sentences.

It has been gratifying that a number of philosophers who responded to our paper have conceded that our efforts were at least partly successful. As always, Kim Sterelny is quite candid: "I have been half-aware of the vagueness of the notion of naturalising . . . ; this paper made me see that it is even vaguer than I thought" (1993, 133). I welcome this reaction, of course, and I encourage Sterelny and others to try their hand at remedying the situation by proposing clearer and more satisfactory accounts of what it takes to pass muster in a naturalist ontology. But, as you have probably already guessed, there is a hidden agenda lurking here. While I encourage Sterelny and other naturalists to set out a clear and plausible account of the naturalist criterion, I don't really expect them to succeed. For it is my contention that there is *no* defensible naturalist criterion, just as there is no defensible criterion of empirical meaningfulness. Unfortunately, I doubt there is any way of proving this claim, any more than there was a way of proving that there is no defensible criterion of empirical meaningfulness. But that's where Sterelny and company fit into my plans. For if they can be provoked into proposing and criticizing criteria with the same energy that the positivists displayed, then it's my bet that puritanical naturalism will ultimately suffer the same fate as positivism did: It will die the death of a thousand failures.

It is my experience that when I suggest there may be no defensible version of the naturalist criterion, many philosophers react with puzzlement. They agree that a defensible criterion may be hard to formulate. But they are also firmly convinced that our world is a physical world and that there are no facts "over and above physical facts."[4] So how could it possibly be the case that there is no criterion? This puzzlement is not an argument, of course. Rather, I think, it is the expression of a certain vague though widely shared conception or "picture" of the way in which the sciences and the predicates or properties they invoke must be related to one another. The only way I know to diminish the puzzlement is to sketch another picture—equally vague though, I think, considerably more plausible. On the open-ended pluralistic picture I would urge, we should not expect that we could find the sort of criterion that the naturalist seeks.

My starting point is the observation that the ontology embraced by the best of our physical and biological sciences—the range of things they talk about—is astoundingly diverse. There are quarks and predators and buckminsterfullerenes, strange attractors and curved regions of space-time, species, cheating genes, LISP-compilers, chaotic systems, and mass spectrometers. And that, obviously, is just the tip of the ontological iceberg. Moreover, if we throw in the ontology of the social sciences, the list seems even more heterogeneous. There are wars and phonemes, plagues, nouns, rituals, and periods of hyper-inflation. Now, according to the naturalist all of these (or at least all that are really respectable) must stand in some special relation to the properties of physics. This strikes me as a singularly implausible proposal.

My point is not that some of the things in the ontology of contemporary science (or the predicates or properties that pick them out) stand in *no* relation to physical properties. Relations are cheap; everything is related to everything else in endlessly many ways. Rather, what I am claiming is that there is no *single, special relation* that all and only the properties invoked in respectable sciences bear to physical properties. There are, no doubt, lots of interesting relations between physical properties and properties like being a buckminsterfullerene; some but not all of these also obtain between physical properties and the property of being a cheating gene; and some but not all of these obtain between physical properties and the property of being a strange attractor. Naturalists of the puritan persuasion would, of course, agree that there are lots of interesting relations in all these cases. But they would also insist that there is at least one crucial legitimating relation that obtains in each case, and that fails to obtain in the case of all properties that should be banished from respectable science. I have already conceded that I know of no way to prove them wrong. My point here is only that they *might* be wrong. There is nothing weird or mystical about a more pluralistic picture of the sciences in which the properties invoked in different sciences are related to physical properties in lots of different ways. Indeed, since naturalists are making a very strong and (by my lights) very implausible claim, I am inclined to think that the burden of argument is on them. Until they tell us what the relation is, or provide a serious argument for the claim that there must be one, I think the most plausible view is not merely that they might be wrong, but that they are.

Now, at this point a naturalist might well protest that I am construing naturalism very uncharitably. Perhaps there is no *single* relation in which all naturalistically kosher properties must stand to the physical. Perhaps there are two, or three, or a dozen. That will make it a bit harder for naturalists to specify the class of naturalistically acceptable properties. But this is not really a major challenge to the naturalists' picture. For once they have spelled out the full list of ways in which naturalistically acceptable properties can be related to physical properties, they can simply disjoin them to produce the naturalist criterion of acceptability: A property is naturalistically acceptable if and only if it is related to physical properties by relation R_1, or by relation R_2, . . . or by relation R_n. My response here is that I think the naturalist is once again misunderstanding the way that science works. It is not only the case that different sciences invoke properties that are related to physical properties in different ways, it is also the case that as science progresses, *new* properties are found to be useful, and some of these are related to physical properties in important *new* ways. Thus, for example, it's my guess that the property of being a mutation that enhances inclusive fitness is related to physical properties in important ways that have no precedent in science prior to Hamilton. Much the same could be said for the property of being a LISP-compiler and science before Babbage, or the property of being a strange attractor and science before Smale. If this is right, then cobbling together a long disjunction of legitimating relations will not provide naturalists with the relation they need. For on my picture, new properties with interestingly new relations to the physical are added as science progresses. There is no way of specifying the relations in advance, nor is there any reason to suppose that the list might not grow indefinitely.

Making a serious case for this picture of scientific progress would require lots of detailed work in the history of science. I don't pretend for a moment that I can deliver the goods. But, of course, I don't have to defend my picture in detail in order to make the point that the naturalists' project might well turn out to be impossible. For my picture is at least a possible one, and by my lights considerably more plausible than the one the naturalist presupposes. There is no more reason to suppose that there *must* be some fixed relation in which all scientifically legitimate properties stand to the physical than there is to suppose that there must be a fixed relation in which all empirically meaningful sentences stand to physical-object sentences or sense-data reports.

On the picture I am sketching, the naturalist has gotten things exactly backward. What "legitimates" certain properties (or predicates, if you prefer) and makes others scientifically suspect is that the former, but not the latter, are invoked in successful scientific theories. The problem with "spirits, telepathy, astrology and so on"[5] is not that they fail to stand in some suitable relation to physical properties and thus can't be "naturalized;" rather, the problem is that they play no role in any successful scientific theory. I don't claim to have an account of what it takes to be a successful scientific theory. Indeed, I suspect that that, too, is a pluralistic, open-ended, and evolving notion. But on the picture I am urging, being invoked in a successful science is all that it takes to render a property scientifically legitimate. On my view, the jury is still out on the question of whether successful science can be constructed using intentional categories. But it is working scientists constructing theories and gathering data who will resolve this question, not philosophers of the puritan persuasion. If there is good science to be made out of intentional categories, that's all the legitimation they need. And if an account of "naturalizing" rules against intentional properties (or any other sort of property) invoked in successful science, then it is the account that is defective, not the intentional properties.

Notes

This chapter is a revised version of "Puritanical Naturalism," which appeared in Neander and Ravenscroft (1993).

1. For two excellent surveys of this literature, see Hempel (1965) and Scheffler (1963, pt. 2).
2. See the references in chapter 1, n. 1.
3. See, for example, Carnap (1932/1959) and Hempel (1935/1980).
4. The quotation is from Schiffer (1982). See chap. 5 in this volume, n. 2.
5. The list is borrowed from Bigelow (1993).

References

Anderson, J. (1976). *Language, Memory, and Thought.* Hillsdale, N.J.: Lawrence Erlbaum.

Anderson, J. (1980). *Cognitive Psychology and Its Implications.* San Francisco: W. H. Freeman.

Anderson, J. (1983). *The Architecture of Cognition.* Cambridge, Mass.: Harvard University Press.

Anderson, J., and G. Bower (1973). *Human Associative Memory.* Washington, D.C.: Winston.

Astington, J., P. Harris, and D. Olson (eds.) (1988). *Developing Theories of Mind.* Cambridge: Cambridge University Press.

Baker, L. (1987). *Saving Belief.* Princeton, N.J.: Princeton University Press.

Baron-Cohen, S. (1995). *Mindblindness.* Cambridge, Mass.: MIT Press.

Baron-Cohen, S., A. Leslie, and U. Frith (1985). "Does the Autistic Child Have a 'Theory of Mind'?" *Cognition,* 21, 37–46.

Bickle, J. (1992). "Multiple Realizability and Psychophysical Reduction," *Behavior and Philosophy,* 20, 47–58.

Bigelow, J. (1993). "On Defining Naturalism," in Neander and Ravenscroft (1993), 111–14.

Block, N. (ed.) (1980). *Readings in Philosophy of Psychology,* Vol. 1. Cambridge, Mass.: Harvard University Press.

Block, N. (ed.) (1981). *Readings in Philosophy of Psychology,* Vol. 2. Cambridge, Mass.: Harvard University Press.

Block, N. (1986). "Advertisement for a Semantics for Psychology," in P. French et al. (eds.), *Midwest Studies in Philosophy: Studies in the Philosophy of Mind,* Vol. 10. Minneapolis: University of Minnesota Press, 615–78.

Block, N. (1991). "What Narrow Content Is Not," in Loewer and Rey (1991), 33–64.

Brandom, R. (1984). "Reference Explained Away," *Journal of Philosophy,* 81, 469–92.

Brandt, R., and J. Kim (1963). "Wants as Explanations of Behavior," *Journal of Philosophy,* 60, 425–35.

Broadbent, D. (1985). "A Question of Levels: Comments on McClelland and Rumelhart," *Journal of Experimental Psychology: General*, 114, 189–92.

Burge, T. (1986). "Individualism and Psychology," *Philosophical Review*, 95, 3–45.

Canfield, J. (1983). "Discovering Essence," in C. Ginet and S. Shoemaker (eds.), *Knowledge and Mind*. Oxford: Oxford University Press, 105–29.

Carnap, R. (1932/1959). "Psychology in Physical Language," in A. J. Ayer (ed.), *Logical Positivism*. Glencoe, Ill.: Free Press, 165–98.

Carnap, R. (1950). "Empiricism, Semantics and Ontology," *Revue International de Philosophie*, 4, 20–40. Reprinted in Carnap (1956), 205–21. Page references are to Carnap (1956).

Carnap. R. (1952). "Meaning Postulates," *Philosophical Studies*, 3, 65–73. Reprinted in Carnap (1956), 222–29.

Carnap, R. (1955). "Meaning and Synonymy in Natural Languages," *Philosophical Studies*, 7, 33–47. Reprinted in Carnap (1956), 233–47.

Carnap, R. (1956). *Meaning and Necessity*. Chicago: University of Chicago Press.

Cherniak, C. (1986). *Minimal Rationality*. Cambridge, Mass.: Bradford Books/MIT Press.

Chomsky, N. (1965). *Aspects of the Theory of Syntax*. Cambridge, Mass.: MIT Press.

Chomsky, N. (1975). *Reflections of Language*. New York: Pantheon.

Chomsky, N. (1992). "A Minimalist Program for Linguistic Theory," *MIT Occasional Papers in Linguistics*, No. 1. Distributed by MIT Working Papers in Linguistics.

Chomsky, N., and J. Katz (1974). "What the Linguist Is Talking About," *Journal of Philosophy*, 71, 347–67.

Christensen, D. (1992). "Causal Powers and Conceptual Connections," *Analysis*, 52, 163–68.

Christensen, S., and D. Turner (eds.) (1993). *Folk Psychology and the Philosophy of Mind*. Hillsdale, N.J.: Lawrence Erlbaum.

Churchland, P. M. (1970). "The Logical Character of Action Explanations," *Philosophical Review*, 79, 214–36.

Churchland, P. M. (1979). *Scientific Realism and the Plasticity of Mind*. Cambridge: Cambridge University Press.

Churchland, P. M. (1981). "Eliminative Materialism and the Propositional Attitudes," *Journal of Philosophy*, 78, 67–90.

Churchland, P. M. (1984). *Matter and Consciousness*. Cambridge, Mass.: Bradford Books/MIT Press.

Churchland, P. M. (1986). "Some Reductive Strategies in Cognitive Neurobiology," *Mind*, 95, 279–309.

Churchland, P. M. (1989). "Folk Psychology and the Explanation of Human Behavior," in *A Neurocomputational Perspective*. Cambridge, Mass.: MIT Press, 111–27.

Churchland, P. S. (1980). "Language, Thought, and Information Processing," *Nous*, 14, 147–70.

Churchland, P. S. (1986). *Neurophilosophy*. Cambridge, Mass.: Bradford Books/MIT Press.

Clark, A. (1989). *Microcognition*. Cambridge, Mass.: Bradford Books/MIT Press.

Clark, A. (1989/90). "Connectionist Minds," *Proceedings of the Aristotelian Society*, 90, 83–102. Reprinted in Macdonald and Macdonald (1995), 339–56.

Clark, A. (1991). "Radical Ascent," *Proceedings of the Aristotelian Society*, 65 (Supp.), 211–27.

Clark, A. (1993). *Associative Engines*. Cambridge, Mass.: Bradford Books/MIT Press.

Clement, J. (1983). "A Conceptual Model Discussed by Galileo and Used Intuitively by Physics Students," in D. Gentner and A. Stevens (eds.), *Mental Models*. Hillsdale, N.J.: Lawrence Erlbaum, 325–39.

Cohen, J. (1981). "Can Human Irrationality Be Experimentally Demonstrated?" *Behavioral and Brain Sciences*, 4, 317–70.

Collins, A., and M. Quillian (1972). "Experiments on Semantic Memory and Language Comprehension," in L. Gregg (ed.), *Cognition in Learning and Memory*. New York: Wiley.

Cummins, R. (1983). *The Nature of Psychological Explanation*. Cambridge, Mass.: Bradford Books/MIT Press.

Cummins, R. (1989). *Meaning and Mental Representation*. Cambridge, Mass.: Bradford Books/MIT Press.

Currie, G. (1995a). "Imagination and Simulation: Aesthetics Meets Cognitive Science," in M. Davies and T. Stone (eds.), *Mental Simulation: Evaluations and Applications*. Oxford: Blackwell, 151–69.

Currie, G. (1995b). "Mental Imagery as the Simulation of Vision," *Mind and Language*, 10, 25–44.

D'Andrade, R. (1987). "A Folk Model of the Mind," in D. Holland and M. Quinn (eds.), *Cultural Models in Language and Thought*. Cambridge: Cambridge University Press.

Daniels, N. (1979). "Wide Reflective Equilibrium and Theory Acceptance in Ethics," *Journal of Philosophy*, 76, 256–82.

Daniels, N. (1980). "On Some Methods of Ethics and Linguistics," *Philosophical Studies*, 37, 21–36.

Davidson, D. (1963). "Actions, Reasons, and Causes," *Journal of Philosophy*, 60, 685–700.

Davies, M. (1990). "Thinking Persons and Cognitive Science," *AI and Society*, 4, 39–50.

Davies, M. (1991). "Concepts, Connectionism, and the Language of Thought," in Ramsey et al. (1991), 229–57.

Dennett, D. (1969). *Content and Consciousness*. London: Routledge and Kegan Paul.

Dennett, D. (1978a). "Artificial Intelligence as Philosophy and Psychology," in Dennett (1978b), 109–26.

Dennett, D. (1978b). *Brainstorms*. Cambridge, Mass.: Bradford Books/MIT Press.

Dennett, D. (1978c). "Two Approaches to Mental Images," in Dennett (1978b), 174–89.

Devitt, M. (1990). "A Narrow Representational Theory of the Mind," in Lycan (1990), 371–98.

Devitt, M. (1994). "The Methodology of Naturalistic Semantics," *Journal of Philosophy*, 91, 545–72.

Devitt, M. (forthcoming). *Coming to Our Senses: A Naturalistic Program for Semantic Localism*. Cambridge: Cambridge University Press.

Devitt, M., and K. Sterelny, (1987). *Language and Reality*. Cambridge, Mass.: Bradford Books/MIT Press.

Donnellan, K. (1983). "Kripke and Putnam on Natural Kind Terms," in C. Ginet and S. Shoemaker (eds.), *Knowledge and Mind*. Oxford: Oxford University Press, 84–104.

Donovan, A., L. Laudan, and R. Laudan (eds.) (1988). *Scrutinizing Science: Empirical Studies of Scientific Change*. Dordrecht, The Netherlands: Kluwer Academic.

Doppelt, G. (1990). "The Naturalist Conception of Methodological Standards in Science: A Critique," *Philosophy of Science*, 57, 1–19.

Dretske, F. (1981). *Knowledge and the Flow of Information*. Cambridge, Mass.: Bradford Books/MIT Press.

Dretske, F. (1988). *Explaining Behavior*. Cambridge, Mass.: Bradford Books/ MIT Press.

Dretske, F. (1989). "Reasons and Causes," *Philosophical Perspectives*, 3, 1–15.

Dretske, F. (1990). "Does Meaning Matter?" in E. Villanueva (ed.), *Information, Semantics and Epistemology*. Oxford: Blackwell.

Dunbar, K. (1989). "Scientific Reasoning Strategies in a Simulated Molecular Genetics Environment," *Proceedings of the Eleventh Annual Meeting of the Cognitive Science Society*. Ann Arbor, Mich.: Lawrence Erlbaum.

Egan, F. (1995). "Folk Psychology and Cognitive Architecture," *Philosophy of Science*, 62, 179–96.

Eich, J. (1982). "A Composite Holographic Recall Memory," *Psychological Review*, 89, 627.

Enc, B. (1976). "Reference of Theoretical Terms," *Nous*, 10, 261–82.

Evans, G. (1981). "Semantic Theory and Tacit Knowledge," in S. Holtzman and C. Leich (eds.), *Wittgenstein: To Follow a Rule*. London: Routledge and Kegan Paul.

Feyerabend, P. (1981). *Philosophical Papers*, Vol. 1: *Realism, Rationalism and Scientific Method: Philosophical Papers Vol. 1*. Cambridge: Cambridge University Press.

Field, H. (1978). "Mental Representation," *Erkenntnis*, 13, 9–61. Reprinted in Stich and Warfield (1994), 34–77.

Field, H. (1986). "The Deflationary Concept of Truth," in G. MacDonald and C. Wright (eds.), *Fact, Science, and Value*. Oxford: Blackwell, 55–117.

Field, H. (1994). "Deflationist Views of Meaning and Content," *Mind*, 103, 249–85.

Fine, A. (1975). "How to Compare Theories: Reference and Change," *Nous*, 9, 17–32.

Fodor, J. (1968). "The Appeal to Tacit Knowledge in Psychological Explanation," *Journal of Philosophy*, 65, 627–40. Reprinted in Fodor (1981b), 63–78. Page references are to Fodor (1981b).

Fodor, J. (1975). *The Language of Thought*. New York: Thomas Y. Crowell.

Fodor, J. (1978). "Tom Swift and His Procedural Grandmother," *Cognition*, 6. Reprinted in Fodor (1981b), 204–24. Page reference is to Fodor (1981b).

Fodor, J. (1980). "Methodological Solipsism Considered as a Research Strategy in Cognitive Psychology," *Behavioral and Brain Sciences*, 3, 63–109.

Fodor, J. (1981a). "The Present Status of the Innateness Controversy," in Fodor (1981b), 257–316.

Fodor, J. (1981b). *Representations*. Cambridge, Mass.: Bradford Books/MIT Press.

Fodor, J. (1981c). "Some Notes of What Linguistics Is About," in Block (1981), 197–207.

Fodor, J. (1983). *The Modularity of Mind*. Cambridge, Mass.: Bradford Books/ MIT Press.

Fodor, J. (1984). "Semantics, Wisconsin Style," *Synthese*, 59, 231–50. Reprinted in Fodor (1990b), 31–49. Page references are to Fodor (1990b).

Fodor, J. (1985). "Fodor's Guide to Mental Representation," *Mind*, 94, 76–100. Reprinted in Stich and Warfield (1994), 9–33. Page references are to Stich and Warfield.

Fodor, J. (1987). *Psychosemantics*. Cambridge, Mass.: Bradford Books/MIT Press.

Fodor, J. (1989). "Making Mind Matter More," *Philosophical Topics*, 17, 59–80.

Fodor, J. (1990a). "Psychosemantics, or: Where Do Truth Conditions Come From?" in Lycan (1990), 312–37.

Fodor, J. (1990b). "Roundtable Discussion," in P. Hanson (ed.), *Information, Language, and Cognition*. Vancouver: University of British Columbia Press.

Fodor, J. (1990c). *A Theory of Content and Other Essays*. Cambridge, Mass.: Bradford Books/MIT Press.

Fodor, J. (1991). "A Modal Argument for Narrow Content," *Journal of Philosophy*, 88, 5–26.

Fodor, J., T. Bever, and M. Garrett (1974). *The Psychology of Language: An Introduction to Psycholinguistics and Generative Grammar*. New York: McGraw-Hill.

Fodor, J., and Z. Pylyshyn (1988). "Connectionism and Cognitive Architecture: A Critical Analysis," *Cognition*, 28, 3–71.

Giere, R. (1985). "Philosophy of Science Naturalized," *Philosophy of Science*, 52, 331–56.

Gillispie, C. (1960). *The Edge of Objectivity: An Essay in the History of Scientific Ideas*. Princeton, N.J.: Princeton University Press.

Godfrey-Smith, P. (1986). "Why Semantic Properties Won't Earn Their Keep," *Philosophical Studies*, 50, 223–36.

Goldman, A. (1989). "Interpretation Psychologized," *Mind and Language*, 4, 161–85.

Goldman, A. (1992). "In Defense of the Simulation Theory," *Mind and Language*, 7, 104–19.

Goldman, A. (1993). *Philosophical Applications of Cognitive Science*. Boulder, Colo.: Westview.

Goodman, N. (1949). "On Likeness of Meaning," *Analysis*, 10, 1–7. Reprinted in L. Linsky (ed.), *Semantics and the Philosophy of Language*. Urbana: University of Illinois Press, 1952, 67–74.

Goodman, N. (1965). *Fact, Fiction, and Forecast*. Indianapolis: Bobbs-Merrill.

Gopnik, A. (1993). "How We Know Our Own Minds: The Illusion of First Person Knowledge of Intentionality," *Behavioral and Brain Sciences*, 16, 1–14.

Gopnik, A., and H. Wellman (1992). "Why the Child's Theory of Mind Really Is a Theory," *Mind and Language*, 7, 145–71.

Gordon, R. (1986). "Folk Psychology as Simulation," *Mind and Language*, 1, 158–71.

Gordon, R. (1990). "Fodor's Intentional Realism and the Simulation Theory." Unpublished manuscript.

Gordon, R. (1991). "Simulation and the Theory-Theory." Paper presented at Pacific Division, American Philosophical Association.

Gordon, R. (1992). Replies to Stich and Nichols and Perner and Howes, *Mind and Language*, 7, 87–97.

Greeno, J. (1983). "Conceptual Entities," in D. Gentner and A. Stevens (eds.), *Mental Models*. Hillsdale, N.J.: Lawrence Erlbaum, 227–52.

Gregory, R. (1970). *The Intelligent Eye*. New York: McGraw-Hill.

Hacking, I. (1982). "Wittgenstein the Psychologist," *New York Review of Books*, 29, 5.

Hacking, I. (1995). *Rewriting the Soul: Multiple Personality and the Sciences of Memory*. Princeton: Princeton University Press.

Harman, G. (1967). "Quine on Meaning and Existence," Part 1, *Review of Metaphysics*, 21, 124–51.

Harman, G. (1973). *Thought*. Princeton: Princeton University Press.

Harré, R. (1986). *The Social Construction of Emotions*. Oxford: Blackwell.

Harris, P. (1992). "From Simulation to Folk Psychology: The Case for Development," *Mind and Language*, 7, 120–44.

Haugeland, J. (1982). "Weak Supervenience," *American Philosophical Quarterly*, 19, 93–103.

Hayes, P. (1985). "The Second Naive Physics Manifesto," in J. Hobbs and R. Moore (eds.), *Formal Theories of the Commonsense World*. Norwood, N.J.: Ablex, 1–36.

Heal, J. (1986). "Replication and Functionalism," in J. Butterfield (ed.), *Language, Mind, and Logic*. Cambridge: Cambridge University Press, 135–50.

Heil, J., and A. Mele (eds.). (1993). *Mental Causation*. Oxford: Oxford University Press.

Hempel, C. (1935/1980). "The Logical Analysis of Psychology," in Block (1980), 14–23.

Hempel, C. (1965). "The Empiricist Criteria of Cognitive Significance: Problems and Changes," in C. Hempel, *Aspects of Scientific Explanation*. New York: Free Press, 101–22.

Hinton, G., J. McClelland, and D. Rumelhart (1986). "Distributed Representation," in D. Rumelhart, J. McClelland, and the PDP Research Group (eds.), *Parallel Distributed Processing*, vol. 1. Cambridge, Mass.: MIT Press, 77–109.

Holland, J., K. Holyoak, R. Nisbett and P. Thagard (1986). *Induction: Processes of Inference, Learning, and Discovery*. Cambridge, Mass.: Bradford Books/ MIT Press.

Hooker, C. (1975). "Systematic Philosophy and Metaphilosophy of Science: Empiricism, Popperianism, and Realism," *Synthese*, 32, 177–231.

Hooker, C. (1981). "Towards a General Theory of Reduction," Parts 1, 2 and 3, *Dialogue*, 20, 38–59, 201–36, 496–529.

Horgan, T. (1982). "Supervenience and Microphysics," *Pacific Philosophical Quarterly*, 63, 29–43.

Horgan, T. (1989). "Mental Quausation," *Philosophical Perspectives*, 3, 47–76.

Horgan, T. (1993). "From Supervenience to Superdupervenience: Meeting the Demands of a Material World," *Mind*, 102, 555–86.

Horgan, T., and G. Graham (1990). "In Defense of Southern Fundamentalism," *Philosophical Studies*, 62, 107–34. Reprinted in Christensen and Turner (1993), 288–311.

Horgan, T. and J. Woodward, (1985). "Folk Psychology Is Here to Stay," *Philosophical Review*, 94, 197–226. Reprinted in Christensen and Turner (1993), 144–66.

Horwich, P. (1990). *Truth*. Oxford: Blackwell.

Hume, D. (1777/1902). *Inquiry Concerning Human Understanding*. Ed. L. Selby-Bigge. Oxford: Clarendon.

Jackson, F., and P. Pettit (1988). "Functionalism and Broad Content," *Mind*, 97, 381–400.

Jackson, F., and P. Pettit (1990). "In Defense of Folk Psychology," *Philosophical Studies*, 59, 31–54.

Jackson, F., and P. Pettit (forthcoming). "Causation in the Philosophy of Mind," in P. Millican and A. Clark (eds.), *Proceedings of the 1990 Turing Colloquium*. Oxford: Oxford University Press.

Johnson-Laird, P. (1983). *Mental Models: Towards a Cognitive Science of Language, Inference, and Consciousness*. Cambridge, Mass.: Harvard University Press.

Jones, T., E. Mullaire, and S. Stich (1991). "Staving off Catastrophe: A Critical Notice of Jerry Fodor's *Psychosemantics*," *Mind and Language*, 6, 58–82.

Kahneman, D., and A. Tversky (1982). "The Simulation Heuristic," in D. Kahneman, P. Slovic, and A. Tversky (eds.), *Judgment under Uncertainty*. Cambridge: Cambridge University Press, 201–8.

Kahneman, D., J. Knetsch, and R. Thaler (1990). "Experimental Tests of the Endowment Effect and the Coase Theorem," *Journal of Political Economy*, 98, 1325–48.

Kim, J. (1978). "Supervenience and Nomological Incommensurables," *American Philosophical Quarterly*, 15, 149–56.

Kim, J. (1982). "Psychophysical Supervenience," *Philosophical Studies*, 41, 51–70.

Kim, J. (1984). "Concepts of Supervenience," *Philosophy and Phenomenological Research*, 45, 153–76.

Kim, J. (1987). " 'Strong' and 'Global' Supervenience Revisited," *Philosophy and Phenomenological Research*, 48, 315–26.

Kim, J. (1989a). "Mechanism, Purpose, and Explanatory Exclusion," *Philosophical Perspectives*, 3, 77–108.

Kim, J. (1989b). "The Myth of Nonreductive Materialism," *Proceedings and Addresses of the American Philosophical Association*, 63, 31–47.

Kim, J. (1993). "Multiple Realization and the Metaphysics of Reduction," *Philosophy and Phenomenological Research*, 70, 1–26.

Kintsch, W. (1974). *The Representation of Meaning in Memory*. Hillsdale, N.J.: Lawrence Erlbaum.

Kitcher, Patricia (1984). "In Defense of Intentional Psychology," *Journal of Philosophy*, 81, 89–106.

Kitcher, Philip (1978). "Theories, Theorists, and Theoretical Change," *Philosophical Review*, 87, 519–47.

Kitcher, Philip (1982). "Genes," *British Journal for the Philosophy of Science*, 33, 337–59.

Kitcher, Philip (1983). "Implications of Incommensurability," in P. Asquith and T. Nickles (eds.), *PSA 1982*. Proceedings of the 1982 Biennial Meeting of the Philosophy of Science Association, Vol. 2. East Lansing, Mich.: Philosophy of Science Association, 689–703.

Kitcher, Philip (1984). "1953 and All That: A Tale of Two Sciences," *Philosophical Review*, 93, 335–73.

Kitcher, Philip (1992). "The Naturalists Return," *Philosophical Review*, 101, 53–114.

Kosslyn, S. (1981). "The Medium and the Message in Mental Imagery: A Theory," in N. Block (ed.), *Imagery*. Cambridge, Mass.: MIT Press, 207–44.

Kosslyn, S. (1994). *Image and Brain*. Cambridge, Mass.: Bradford Books/MIT Press.

Kripke, S. (1972). "Naming and Necessity," in D. Davidson and G. Harman (eds.), *Semantics of Natural Language*. Dordrecht, The Netherlands: Reidel, 253–355.

Kuhn, T. (1962). *The Structure of Scientific Revolutions*. Chicago: University of Chicago Press.

Kuhn, T. (1983). "Commensurability, Comparability, Communicability," in P. Asquith and T. Nickles (eds.), *PSA 1982*. Proceedings of the 1982 Biennial Meeting of the Philosophy of Science Association, Vol. 2. East Lansing, Mich.: Philosophy of Science Association, 669–88.

Langer, E. (1975). "The Illusion of Control," *Journal of Personality and Social Psychology*, 32, 311–28.

Langley, P., H. Simon, G. Bradshaw, and J. Zytkow (1987). *Scientific Discovery: Computational Explorations of the Creative Processes*. Cambridge, Mass.: MIT Press.

Laudan, L. (1987). "Progress or Rationality? The Prospects for Normative Naturalism," *American Philosophical Quarterly*, 24, 19–31.

Laudan, L. (1990). "Normative Naturalism," *Philosophy of Science*, 57, 44–59.

Laudan, L., A. Donovan, R. Laudan, P. Barker, H. Brown, J. Leplin, P. Thagard, and S. Wykstra (1986). "Scientific Change: Philosophical Models and Historical Research," *Synthese*, 69, 141–223.

Laudan, R., L. Laudan, and A. Donovan (1988). "Testing Theories of Scientific Change," in Donovan et al. (1988), 3–44.

Laurence, S. (1993). "Naturalism and Language: A Study of the Nature of Linguistic Kinds and Mental Representation." Ph.D. dissertation, Rutgers University.

Leplin, J. (1979). "Reference and Scientific Realism," *Studies in History and Philosophy of Science*, 10, 265–85.

Leplin, J. (1988). "Is Essentialism Unscientific?" *Philosophy of Science*, 55, 493–510.

LePore, E., and B. Loewer (1987). "Mind Matters," *Journal of Philosophy*, 84, 630–42.

Leslie, A. (1987). "Pretense and Representation: The Origins of 'Theory of Mind'," *Psychological Review*, 94, 412–26.

Leslie, A. (1988). "Some Implications of Pretense for Mechanisms Underlying the Child's Theory of Mind," in Astington et al. (eds.) (1988), 19–46.

Lewis, D. (1966). "An Argument for the Identity Theory," *Journal of Philosophy*, 17–25. Reprinted with additional material in David Lewis, *Philosophical Papers*. Oxford: Oxford University Press (1983).

Lewis, D. (1970). "How to Define Theoretical Terms," *Journal of Philosophy*, 67, 427–46. Reprinted in David Lewis, *Philosophical Papers*. Oxford: Oxford University Press, (1983), 78–95. Page references are to *Philosophical Papers*.

Lewis, D. (1972). "Psychophysical and Theoretical Identifications," *Australasian Journal of Philosophy,* 50, 249–58. Reprinted in Block (1980), 207–15. Page references are to Block (1980).

Lewis, D. (1983). "New Work for a Theory of Universals," *Australasian Journal of Philosophy,* 61, 343–77.

Loar, B. (1981). *Mind and Meaning.* Cambridge: Cambridge University Press.

Loar, B. (1983). "Must Beliefs Be Sentences?" in P. Asquith and T. Nickles (eds.), *PSA 1982.* Proceedings of the 1982 Biennial Meeting of the Philosophy of Science Association, Vol. 2. East Lansing, Mich.: Philosophy of Science Association, 627–43.

Loewer, B., and G. Rey (eds.) (1991). *Meaning in Mind: Fodor and His Critics.* Oxford: Blackwell.

Lowenstein, G., and D. Adler (forthcoming). "A Bias in the Prediction of Tastes," to appear in *Economic Journal.*

Luhrmann, T. (1989). *Persuasions of the Witch's Craft.* Cambridge, Mass.: Harvard University Press.

Lycan, W. (1981). "Form, Function, and Feel," *Journal of Philosophy,* 78, 24–50.

Lycan, W. (1988a). *Judgement and Justification.* Cambridge: Cambridge University Press.

Lycan, W. (1988b). "Toward a Homuncular Theory of Believing," in Lycan (1988a), 3–24.

Lycan, W. (ed.) (1990). *Mind and Cognition.* Oxford: Blackwell.

Macdonald, C. (1995). "Introduction: Connectionism and Eliminativism," in Macdonald and Macdonald (1995), 293–310.

Macdonald, C., and G. Macdonald (eds.) (1995). *Connectionism: Debates on Psychological Explanation.* Oxford: Blackwell.

Madell, G. (1986). "Neurophilosophy: A Principled Skeptic's Response," *Inquiry,* 29, 135–68.

Marr, D. (1982). *Vision.* San Francisco: W.H. Freeman.

McCarthy, J. (1968). "Programs with Common Sense," in M. Minsky (ed.), *Semantic Information Processing,* Cambridge, Mass.: MIT Press, 403–18.

McCarthy, J. (1980). "Circumscription: A Form of Non-Monotonic Reasoning," *Artificial Intelligence,* 13, 27–40.

McCarthy, J. (1986). "Applications of Circumscription to Formalizing Common-Sense Knowledge," *Artificial Intelligence,* 28, 89–116.

McCarthy, L., and J. Gerring (1994). "Revising Psychiatry's Charter Document DSM-IV," *Written Communication,* 11, 147–92.

McCauley, R. (1986). "Intertheoretic Relations and the Future of Psychology," *Philosophy of Science,* 53, 179–98. Reprinted in Christensen and Turner (1993), 63–81. Page references are to Christensen and Turner.

McCloskey, M. (1983a). "Intuitive Physics," *Scientific American,* 248, 4, 122–29.

McCloskey, M. (1983b). "Naive Theories of Motion," in D. Gentner and A. Stevens (eds.), *Mental Models.* Hillsdale, N.J.: Lawrence Erlbaum, 299–324.

McGinn, C. (1978). "Mental States, Natural Kinds and Psychophysical Laws," *Proceedings of the Aristotelian Society,* Supplementary Volume. Reprinted in McGinn (1991), 126–52. Page references are to McGinn (1991).

McGinn, C. (1989). *Mental Content.* Oxford: Blackwell.

McGinn, C. (1991). *The Problem of Consciousness.* Oxford: Blackwell.

Metcalf, J. (1989). "Composite Holographic Associative Recall Model (CHARM) and Blended Memories in Eyewitness Testimony," *Proceedings of the 11th Annual Conference of the Cognitive Science Society*, 307–14.

Milgram, S. (1963). "Behavioral Study of Obedience," *Journal of Abnormal and Social Psychology*, 67, 371–78.

Millikan, R. (1984). *Language, Thought, and Other Biological Categories*. Cambridge, Mass.: Bradford Books/MIT Press.

Millikan, R. (1989). "In Defense of Proper Function," *Philosophy of Science*, 56, 288–302.

Montgomery, R. (1987). "Psychologism, Folk Psychology, and One's Own Case," *Journal for the Theory of Social Behavior*, 17, 195–218.

Murdock, G. (1980). *Theories of Illness*. Pittsburgh: University of Pittsburgh Press.

Nagel, E. (1961). *The Structure of Science*. New York: Harcourt, Brace.

Neander, K., and I. Ravenscroft (eds.) (1993). *Prospects for Intentionality*, Working Papers in Philosophy, 2. Canberra: Research School for Social Science, Australian National University.

Needham, R. (1972). *Belief, Language, and Experience*. Chicago: University of Chicago Press.

Newell, A. (1973). "Production Systems: Models of Control Structures," in W. Chase (ed.), *Visual Information Processing*. New York: Academic Press.

Newell, A. (1980). "Physical Symbol Systems," *Cognitive Science*, 4, 135–83.

Newell, A., and H. Simon (1972). *Human Problem Solving*. Englewood Cliffs, N.J.: Prentice Hall.

Nichols, S., S. Stich, A. Leslie, and D. Klein (1996). "Varieties of Off-Line Simulation," in P. Smith and P. Carruthers (eds.), *Theories of Theories of Mind*. Cambridge: Cambridge University Press, 39–74.

Nickles, T. (1986). "Remarks on the Use of History as Evidence," *Synthese*, 69, 253–66.

O'Brien, G. (1991). "Is Connectionism Common Sense?" *Philosophical Psychology*, 4, 165–78.

O'Brien, G. (1993). "A Conflation of Folk Psychologies," in Neander and Ravenscroft (1993), 42–51.

O'Leary-Hawthorne, J. (1994). "On the Threat of Elimination," *Philosophical Studies*, 74, 325–46.

Olson, D., J. Astington, and P. Harris (1988). "Introduction," in Astington et al. (eds.) (1988), 1–15.

Papineau, D. (1987). *Reality and Representation*. Oxford: Blackwell.

Papineau, D. (forthcoming). "Theory-Dependent Terms," to appear in *Philosophy of Science*.

Perner, J. (1991). *Understanding the Representational Mind*. Cambridge, Mass.: MIT Press.

Petrie, B. (1987). "Global Supervenience and Reduction," *Philosophy and Phenomenological Research*, 48, 119–30.

Pinker, S. (1989). *Learnability and Cognition*. Cambridge, Mass.: MIT Press.

Putnam, H. (1975). "The Meaning of 'Meaning'," in K. Gunderson (ed.), *Language, Mind, and Knowledge: Minnesota Studies in the Philosophy of Science* Vol. 7. Minneapolis: University of Minnesota Press, 131–93.

Pylyshyn, Z. (1981). "The Imagery Debate: Analog Media versus Tacit Knowledge," in N. Block (ed.), *Imagery*. Cambridge, Mass.: MIT Press, 151–206.

Pylyshyn, Z. (1984). *Computation and Cognition.* Cambridge, Mass.: MIT Press.

Qin, Y, and H. Simon (1990). "Laboratory Replication of Scientific Discovery Processes," *Cognitive Science,* 14, 281–312.

Quillian, M. (1966). *Semantic Memory.* Cambridge, Mass.: Bolt, Branak, and Newman.

Quine, W. V. (1936). "Truth by Convention," in O. Lee (ed.), *Philosophical Essays for A. N. Whitehead.* New York: 1936. Reprinted in Quine (1966), 70–99.

Quine, W. V. (1951). "On Carnap's Views on Ontology," *Philosophical Studies,* 2, 65–72. Reprinted in Quine (1966), 126–35. Page references are to Quine (1966).

Quine, W. V. (1953a). "The Problem of Meaning in Linguistics," in *From a Logical Point of View.* Cambridge, Mass.: Harvard University Press, 47–64.

Quine, W. V. (1953b). "Two Dogmas of Empiricism," in *From a Logical Point of View.* Cambridge, Mass.: Harvard University Press, 20–46.

Quine, W. V. (1960). *Word and Object.* Cambridge, Mass.: MIT Press.

Quine, W. V. (1963). "Carnap and Logical Truth," in P. Schilpp (ed.), *The Philosophy of Rudolf Carnap.* La Salle, Ill: Open Court, 385–406. Reprinted in Quine (1966), 100–25.

Quine, W. V. (1966). *The Ways of Paradox and Other Essays.* New York: Random House.

Ramsey, W. (1989). "Parallelism and Functionalism," *Cognitive Science,* 13, 139–44.

Ramsey, W., S. Stich, and J. Garon (1990). "Connectionism, Eliminativism, and the Future of Folk Psychology." *Philosophical Perspectives,* 4, 499–533. Reprinted as chapter 2 in this volume.

Ramsey, W., S. Stich, and D. Rumelhart (1991). *Philosophy and Connectionist Theory.* Hillsdale, N.J.: Lawrence Erlbaum.

Rawls, J. (1971). *A Theory of Justice.* Cambridge, Mass.: Harvard University Press.

Rey, G. (1991). "An Explanatory Budget for Connectionism and Eliminativism," in T. Horgan and J. Tienson (eds.), *Connectionism and the Philosophy of Mind.* Dordrecht, The Netherlands: Kluwer Academic, 219–40.

Ripstein, A. (1987). "Explanation and Empathy," *Review of Metaphysics,* 40, 465–82.

Rock, I. (1983). *The Logic of Perception.* Cambridge, Mass.: MIT Press.

Rorty, R. (1979). *Philosophy and the Mirror of Nature.* Princeton, N.J.: Princeton University Press.

Rosenberg, A. (1990). "Normative Naturalism and the Role of Philosophy," *Philosophy of Science,* 57, 34–43.

Rumelhart, D., P. Lindsay, and D. Norman (1972). "A Process Model for Long Term Memory," in E. Tulving and W. Donaldson (eds.), *Organization of Memory.* New York: Academic Press.

Rumelhart, D., and J. McClelland (1985). "Level's Indeed! A Response to Broadbent," *Journal of Experimental Psychology: General,* 114, 193–97.

Rumelhart, D., J. McClelland, and the PDP Research Group (1986). *Parallel Distributed Processing,* Vols. 1 and 2, Cambridge, Mass.: Bradford Books/ MIT Press.

Rumelhart, D., P. Smolensky, J. McClelland, and G. Hinton (1986). "Schemata and Sequential Thought Processes in PDP Models," in Rumelhart, McClelland and the PDP Research Group (1986), Vol. 2, 7–57.

Schaffner, K. (1967). "Approaches to Reduction," *Philosophy of Science*, 34, 137–47.

Scheffler, I. (1963). *The Anatomy of Inquiry*. New York: Knopf.

Schiffer, S. (1982). "Intention Based Semantics," *Notre Dame Journal of Formal Logic*, 23, 119–56.

Sellars, W. (1956). "Empiricism and the Philosophy of Mind," in H. Feigl and M. Scriven (eds.), *The Foundations of Science and the Concepts of Psychology and Psychoanalysis: Minnesota Studies in the Philosophy of Science*, Vol. 1. Minneapolis: University of Minnesota Press, 253–329.

Shapere, D. (1982). "Reason, Reference, and the Quest for Knowledge," *Philosophy of Science*, 49, 1–24.

Sharpe, R. (1987). "The Very Idea of a Folk Psychology," *Inquiry*, 30, 381–93.

Simon, H. (1966). "Scientific Discovery and the Psychology of Problem Solving," in R. Colodny (ed.), *Mind and Cosmos: Essays in Contemporary Science and Philosophy*. Pittsburgh: University of Pittsburgh Press, 22–40.

Simon, H. (1973). "Does Scientific Discovery Have a Logic?" *Philosophy of Science*, 40, 471–80.

Skinner, B. (1974). *About Behaviorism*. New York: Random House.

Sklar, L. (1974). *Space, Time, and Space-time*. Berkeley: University of California Press.

Smith, E., and D. Medin (1981). *Categories and Concepts*. Cambridge, Mass.: Harvard University Press.

Smolensky, P. (1988). "On the Proper Treatment of Connectionism," *Behavioral and Brain Sciences*, 11, 1–74.

Soames, S. (1984). "Linguistics and Psychology," *Linguistics and Philosophy*, 7, 155–79.

Sober, E. (1984). *The Nature of Selection*. Cambridge, Mass.: Bradford Books/ MIT Press.

Stalnaker, R. (1984). *Inquiry*. Cambridge, Mass.: Bradford Books/MIT Press.

Stein, E. (1992a). "The Essentials of Constructionism and the Construction of Essentialism," in Stein (1992b), 325–53.

Stein, E. (1992b). *Forms of Desire*. New York: Routledge.

Stein, E. (forthcoming). *Without Good Reason*. Oxford: Oxford University Press.

Sterelny, K. (1990). *The Representational Theory of Mind*. Oxford: Blackwell.

Sterelny, K. (1993). "Why Naturalise Representation?" in Neander and Ravenscroft (1993), 133–40.

Stich, S. (1972). "Grammar, Psychology, and Indeterminacy," *Journal of Philosophy*, 59, 799–818.

Stich, S. (1975). "Competence and Indeterminacy," in J. Wirth and D. Cohen (eds.), *The Testing of Linguistic Hypotheses*. Washington, D.C.: J. Wiley, 93–109.

Stich, S. (1978a). "Autonomous Psychology and the Belief-Desire Thesis," *Monist*, 61, 573–91.

Stich, S. (1978b). "Beliefs and Subdoxastic States," *Philosophy of Science*, 45, 499–518.

Stich, S. (1982). "On the Ascription of Content," in A. Woodfield (ed.), *Thought and Object*. Oxford: Oxford University Press, 153–206.

Stich, S. (1983). *From Folk Psychology to Cognitive Science*. Cambridge, Mass.: Bradford Books/MIT Press.

Stich, S. (1988). "Reflective Equilibrium, Analytic Epistemology, and the Problem of Cognitive Diversity," *Synthese*, 74, 391–413.

Stich, S. (1990). *The Fragmentation of Reason*. Cambridge, Mass.: Bradford Books/MIT Press.

Stich, S. (1991a). "Do True Believers Exist?" *Aristotelian Society*, 65, Suppl. Vol., 229–44.

Stich, S. (1991b). "Narrow Content Meets Fat Syntax," in Loewer and Rey (1991), 239–54.

Stich, S. (1992). "What Is a Theory of Mental Representation?" *Mind*, 101, 243–61.

Stich, S. (1993a). "Concepts, Meaning, Reference, and Ontology," in Neander and Ravenscroft (1993), 61–77.

Stich, S. (1993b). "Naturalizing Epistemology: Quine, Simon, and the Prospects for Pragmatism," in C. Hookway and D. Peterson (eds.), *Philosophy and Cognitive Science*, Royal Institute of Philosophy, Suppl. 34. Cambridge: Cambridge University Press, 1–17.

Stich, S., and S. Nichols (1992). "Folk Psychology: Simulation or Tacit Theory?" *Mind and Language*, 7, 35–71.

Stich, S., and S. Nichols (1995). "Second Thoughts on Simulation," in M. Davies and T. Stone (eds.), *Mental Simulation: Evaluations and Applications*. Oxford: Blackwell, 87–108.

Stich, S., and T. Warfield (eds.) (1994). *Mental Representation*. Oxford: Blackwell.

Stich, S., and T. Warfield (1995). "Do Connectionist Minds Have Beliefs?: A Reply to Clark and Smolensky," in Macdonald and Macdonald (1995), 395–411.

Taylor, K. (1993). "Simulation and Eliminativism," *Proceedings of the 16th International Wittgenstein Symposium*, 16, 519–24.

Teller, P. (1984). "A Poor Man's Guide to Supervenience and Determination," *Southern Journal of Philosophy*, 22, Suppl. 137–62.

Thagard, P. (1988). *Computational Philosophy of Science*. Cambridge, Mass.: Bradford Books/MIT Press.

Thagard, P. (1992). *Conceptual Revolutions*. Princeton, N.J. Princeton: University Press.

Thaler, R. (1980). "Toward a Positive Theory of Consumer Choice," *Journal of Economic Behavior and Organization*, 1, 39–60.

Tye, M. (1992). "Naturalism and the Mental," *Mind*, 101, 421–41.

Tye, M. (1994). "Naturalism and the Problem of Intentionality," *Midwest Studies in Philosophy*, vol. 19: *Philosophical Naturalism*. Notre Dame, Ind.: University of Notre Dame Press, 122–42.

Van Gelder, T. (1991). "What is the 'D' in 'PDP'? A Survey of the Concept of Distribution," in Ramsey et al. (1991), 33–59.

Van Gulick, R. (1989). "Metaphysical Arguments for Internalism and Why They Don't Work," in S. Silvers (ed.), *Representations: Readings in the Philosophy of Mental Representation*. Dordrecht, The Netherlands: Kluwer Academic, 151–59.

Van Gulick, R. (1993). "Who's in Charge Here? And Who's Doing All the Work?" in Heil and Mele (1993), 233–56.

Von Eckardt, B. (1993). *What Is Cognitive Science?* Cambridge, Mass.: Bradford Books/MIT Press.

Waters, C. (1994). "Genes Made Molecular," *Philosophy of Science,* 61, 163–85.

Watson, J. (1930). *Behaviorism.* Chicago: University of Chicago Press.

Wellman, H. (1990). *The Child's Theory of Mind.* Cambridge, Mass.: MIT Press.

White, M. (1950). "The Analytic and the Synthetic: An Untenable Dualism," in S. Hook (ed.), *John Dewey: Philosopher of Science and Freedom.* New York: Dial Press. 316–30. Reprinted in L. Linsky (ed.), *Semantics and the Philosophy of Language.* Urbana, IL: University of Illinois Press, 1952, 272–86.

Wilkes, K. (1978). *Physicalism.* London: Routledge and Kegan Paul.

Wilkes, K. (1981). "Functionalism, Psychology, and the Philosophy of Mind," *Philosophical Topics,* 12, 147–68.

Wilkes, K. (1984). "Pragmatics in Science and Theory in Common Sense," *Inquiry,* 27, 339–61.

Wilkes, K. (1991). "The Relationship between Scientific Psychology and Common Sense Psychology," *Synthese,* 89, 15–39.

Wilson, T. (1985). "Strangers to Ourselves: The Origins and Accuracy of Beliefs about One's Own Mental States," in J. Harvey and G. Weary (eds.), *Attribution in Contemporary Psychology.* New York: Academic Press, 1–35.

Wimsatt, W. (1976a). "Reductionism, Levels of Organization, and the Mind-Body Problem," in G. Globus, G. Maxwell, and I. Savodnik (eds.), *Consciousness and the Brain.* New York: Plenum.

Wimsatt, W. (1976b). "Reductive Explanation: A Functional Account," in R. Cohen, C. Hooker, A. Nicholas, and J. van Evra (eds.), *PSA 1974: Proceedings of the Philosophy of Science Association.* Dordrecht, The Netherlands: Reidel.

Index

Adler, D., 164, 167 n. 11
aether, 68, 70, 93
analytic/synthetic distinction, 62, 79–82, 88 n. 54
Anderson, J., 113 nn. 9 & 11
argument from the heterogeneity of content taxonomy, 26–27
argument from neuroscience, 19–20
atoms, 72, 78
autism. *See* simulation theory and autism

back propagation, 103
Baron-Cohen, S., 137, 166 n. 10
Bickle, J., 27
big bang, 7, 51
big bang eliminativism, 51–52, 53
Bigelow, J., 199 n. 5
binge eating disorder, 90 n. 67
black hole eliminativism, 52
black holes, 7, 51
Block, N., 83 n. 17, 112, 114 n. 18, 189 n. 1
Bower, G., 113 nn. 9 & 11
Brandom, R., 79, 86 n. 45
Brandt, R., 16
Burge, T., 83 n. 15

caloric fluid, 3, 63, 70, 93, 94, 102, 112, 133
and oxygen, 89 n. 64
Papineau on, 76–77
Canfield, J., 190 n. 7
Carnap, R., 192
on the analyticity of the principle of semantic ascent, 86 n. 45
on defining commonsense psychological terms, 199 n. 3
and the description theory of reference for theoretical terms, 30, 34, 35, 74, 75
on the material mode and the formal mode, 55
versus Quine on analyticity and ontology, 80–82, 90 n. 74
causal holism, 21
Cherniak, C., 113 n. 8
Chomsky, N., 136
on the goals of grammatical theory, 128
on grammar as a tacit theory, 14, 127, 137
on the nature of grammatical properties, 41–42, 86 n. 36
Christensen, D., 191 n. 15

Churchland, P. M., 65, 84 n. 28, 112
 n. 1, 113 n. 6, 117, 134 n. 2,
 137, 146
Churchland, P. S., 19, 71, 83 n. 8, 84
 n. 28, 134 n. 2
Clark, A., 61, 62, 82 n. 6, 83 n. 10,
 88 nn. 50, 51, 52 & 54
Clement, J., 13
Clouseau, Inspector, 97, 111
Cohen, J., 88 n. 56
Collins, A., 97
competence-performance distinction,
 40
computational models of cognition,
 24–25, 102
concepts, 173–174
 classical view of, 173–174
 exemplar theory of, 173
 prototype theory of, 173
conceptual analysis. *See* naturalizing
 and conceptual analysis
conceptual modularity, 21, 83 n. 10
conceptually necessary properties, 8,
 60–63, 88 n. 55
connectionism
 connectionist accounts of folk
 psychology, 130, 131, 146, 147,
 148
 connectionist models of memory, 5,
 21, 91–92, 103–109
 connectionist representation, 14, 21
 and eliminativism, 91–114
constitutive properties. *See*
 conceptually necessary properties
content, 15, 22–23, 28–29
Copernicus, 93
Cottrell, G., 112, 114 n. 16
Cummins, R., 86 n. 40, 136
Currie, G., 137, 166 n. 2
Cussins, A., 112, 114 n. 16

D'Andrade, R., 137
da Vinci, L., 13
Daniels, N., 88 n. 56
Davidson, D., 16, 144, 192, 195

Davies, M., 21, 83 n. 10, 88 nn. 49 &
 54
declarative representation, 15
deconstructionism, 9
 and eliminativism, 9, 35, 60, 63
 and tacit assumptions, 9, 34
Dennett, D., 114 n. 15, 137, 154
Descartes, R., 193
Devitt, M., 35, 83 n. 17, 86 n. 38, 87
 n. 48, 189 n. 1, 190 n. 8
discrete encoding, 109–111
dispositions to produce activation
 patterns, 110–111
distributed representation, 99, 101,
 103, 105, 106, 112
don't care cases, 67–68
Donnellan, K., 190 n. 7
Doppelt, G., 89 n. 62
Dow, W., 90 n. 70
Dretske, F., 88 n. 51, 189 nn. 1 & 3,
 190 n. 12

Egan, F., 88 n. 51
Eggplant, 182, 186
electrons, 67, 70, 77, 78
eliminative materialism. *See*
 eliminativism
ELIMINATIVISM*, 51
eliminativism, 3, 92–94
 about beliefs versus about believers,
 84 n. 21
 arguments for, 4, 116
 arguments for, based on semantic
 commitments of folk psychology,
 17, 22–29
 arguments for, based on structural
 or nomological commitments of
 folk psychology, 17–22
 conclusions of the argument for, 4
 conclusions not interesting, 7, 48,
 50–52
 First Premise in the argument for,
 4, 8, 9–16, 20, 28, 33
 indeterminacy of, 32, 48, 52–53,
 72, 74, 80, 84 n. 25

the link between premises and
conclusions in arguments for, 4,
5, 29–34, 35–37, 45, 60, 62, 63,
84
nonontological interpretations of,
83 n. 21
Second Premise in the argument
for, 4, 16–29, 65, 88 n. 55
troubling consequences, 3, 115–
116
Enç, B., 89 nn. 61 & 64
endowment effect, 164–165
Evans, G., 88 n. 49
explanatory levels, 101–102, 112

Feyerabend, P., 3, 112 nn. 3 & 5
Field, H., vii, 58–59, 79, 86 nn. 35 &
45, 87 n. 47, 189 n. 1
Fine, A., 67, 89
Fodor, J.
on the appeal to tacit knowledge in
psychological explanation, 121–
123, 126, 130, 137
on computational models of
cognition, 24, 159
on conceptual analysis, 172, 173
critique of connectionism, 92, 100–
101, 113 nn. 12 & 14
on grammar and grammaticality,
86 n. 39, 128, 136
on Granny, 183, 190 n.14
on the language of thought, 19, 20,
82 n. 4, 146
on the link between belief and
rationality, 88 n. 50
on meaning holism, 83 nn. 16 & 18
on mental imagery, 154
on naturalizing intentional
properties, 28, 168, 171, 175,
178, 188, 189 nn. 1 & 5
on the requirement that
propositional attitudes have
causal powers, 88 n. 51, 169
on supervenience, 83 n. 15, 190
nn. 11 & 15

on the theory-theory, 113 nn. 6,
137, 146
on the virtues of folk psychology,
134 n. 2
on why eliminativism would be a
catastrophe, 115–116, 169, 189
n. 2
folk physics, 10–14, 40–43, 153
acquisition of, 151
folk psychological capacities, 10, 124–
126, 131, 137
folk psychological laws, 147–148
folk psychology, 4, 10–16, 91–92,
94–97, 115–135
acquisition of, 150–151, 154–158
austere accounts of, 16
connectionist accounts of, 130, 131,
146, 147, 148
internal versus external accounts,
85 n. 34, 128–129, 130–131,
132, 134
opulent accounts of, 16, 28
platitudes of, 33, 85, 125–126, 127
futurology, 17, 20

Galileo, 13, 82 n. 2, 93
Garon, J., 5, 6, 21, 34, 83 n 10
Gauker, S., 7, 51–54
genes, 67, 76, 93, 94
Gerring, J., 90 n. 67
Giere, R., 89 n. 62
Gillespie, C., 68
Godfrey-Smith, P., 86 n. 42
Goldman, A., 133, 134, 135 n. 10,
136–167
Goodman, N., 64, 88 nn. 54 & 56,
113 n. 10
Gopnik, A., 137, 146
Gordon, R., 133, 134, 135 n. 10,
136–167
Graham, G., 16, 83 n. 6
grammar, 14, 39–40, 41–43
acquisition of, 150
grammatical properties, 41–43

grammar (*continued*)
  internal versus external accounts,
    128–129
grants, 71
Greeno, J., 136
Gregory, R., 136

Hacking, I., 90 n. 67, 134 n. 4
Harman, G., 82 n. 4, 83 n. 17, 88 n.
  54
Harris, P., 133, 137, 161, 166 n. 2
Haugeland, J., 92, 190 n. 10
Hayes, P., 136
Heal, J., 137
Heil, J., 88 n. 51, 112
Hempel, C., 199 nn. 1 & 3
hidden node activation patterns,
  110–111
Hinton, G., 82 n. 5
holographic representation, 14
homosexuality, 70
Hooker, C., 19, 112 n. 4
Horgan, T., 16, 83 nn. 6 & 11, 88 n.
  51, 134 n. 2, 190 n. 10
Horwich, P., 79, 86 n. 45
Hume, D., 193
Hunt, I., 135 n. 11

impetus (in folk physics), 11
implicit agreement about essential
  properties, 68
infra-linguistic catastrophe, 18–19
intentional properties and states, 15–
  16, 168
  causal impotence of, 28, 170, 174,
    177, 182–183, 185
  invoked in laws, 170, 174, 177,
    183–184, 185
  nonreducibility of, 27, 28
  realism and irrealism about, 28,
    168–169, 174, 176, 178, 181–
    182, 185, 188
intuitions, 38–41, 44–45, 46–51, 61–
  62, 85–86 n. 35

Jackson, F., 7, 83 n. 6, 88 n. 52, 112,
  114 n. 18, 134 n. 2
  on the appeal to intuitions to settle
    ontological questions, 52–54, 86
    n. 44
Johnson-Laird, P., 82 n. 5, 130, 146
Jones, T., 83 n. 17, 190 n. 5

Kahneman, D., 148, 164
Katz, J., 128
Keller, H., 26
Kim, J., 16, 27, 83 n. 20, 190 n. 10
kinetic theory of heat, 93, 94, 102
Kirsh, D., 112
Kitcher, Patricia, 112, 134 n. 2
Kitcher, Philip, 89 nn. 57, 58, 62 &
  63, 90 n. 66, 112 nn. 3 & 4
Knetsch, J., 164
Kosslyn, S., 82 n. 5, 154
Kripke, S., 22, 35, 39, 83 n. 12, 85 n.
  31, 87 n. 47
Kuhn, T., 91, 112 nn. 3 & 5

Langer, E., 161, 162, 163
language of thought, 14, 19, 20, 130,
  159, 160
Laudan, L., 66, 88 n. 57, 89 nn. 59 &
  62, 90 n. 72
Laurence, S., 29, 86 nn. 36 & 39,
  192, 195, 196
Lavoisier, 68, 89 n. 64, 90 n. 71, 113
  n. 5
Leplin, J., 190 n. 7
LePore, E., 88 n. 51
Leslie, A., 137, 159, 160, 166–167
  nn. 9 & 10
Lewis, D.
  on folk psychological platitudes,
    127
  on the meaning and reference of
    theoretical terms, 29–34, 35, 36,
    49, 74, 75, 79, 84 nn. 23 & 24,
    85 n. 29
  on mistaken theories, 31–32
  on supervenience, 190 n. 10

on treating predicates as names, 84 n. 26
linguistic capacities, 14
linguistic frameworks, 81
linguistic and quasi-linguistic representation, 14–15, 20, 146
Loar, B., 20, 189 n. 1
localist representation, 99, 101
Loewer, B., 88 n. 51
logical positivism, 192–195
Lowenstein, G., 164, 167 n. 11
Luhrmann, T., 69, 90 n. 66
Lycan., 5, 6, 34–37, 49, 112–113 n. 5, 114 n. 17, 137, 189 n. 1

Macdonald, C., 89 n. 61
Madell, G., 113 n. 6
Marr, D., 135
McCarthy, L., 90 n. 67
McCauley, R., 65
McClelland, J., 82 n. 5, 113
McCloskey, M., 11–13, 82 n. 2, 136
McGinn, C., 85 n. 28, 130
McLaughlin, B., 189
meaning holism, 23–26
meaning postulates, 81
meaningfulness, criterion of, 193–194
Medin, D., 189 n. 4
Mele, A., 88 n. 51
Mendel, G., 67
mental illness, 72
mental imagery, 154
mental models, 14, 130, 131, 146
mental simulation, 148–150
metarepresentation, 159
Milgram, S., 139, 166 n. 4
Millikan, R., 189 n. 1, 190 n. 6
mimicry, 166 n. 6
Montgomery, R., 137
Mrs. T., 24–25
Mullaire, E., 83 n. 17, 190 n. 5
multiple personality disorder, 90 n. 67
Murdock, G., 86 n. 37

myth of Jones, 18, 33, 118–121, 124
See also Sellars, W.
myth of the given, 118

Nagel, E., 112 n. 4
narrow properties, 183
natural kinds, 99, 107–108, 135 n. 5, 174–178
naturalizing, 28–29, 168–191, 196–197
and conceptual analysis, 171–174
and essential properties, 174–178
and natural kind terms, 174–178
and supervenience, 178–188
See also supervenience
Needham, R., 134 n. 4
Newell, A., 113 n. 9, 159
Nichols, S., 133–134, 161, 162, 163, 164, 165, 166 n. 2, 167 n. 12
Nickles, T., 89 n. 63
nihilism, 73–74
normative naturalism, 63–72, 73, 80, 88 n. 57

O'Brien, C., 135 n. 8
O'Brien, G., 21, 135 n. 11
O'Leary-Hawthorne, J., 84 n. 21
ontological inference, rational principles governing. *See* rational ontological inference
ontologically conservative theory change, 94, 102
ontologically radical theory change, 94, 102, 112, 112–113 n. 5
oxygen, 68, 89 n. 64, 94

Papineau, D., 74–82, 83 n. 17, 86 n. 44, 90 n. 65, 189 n. 1
Peirce, C., 72
Perner, J., 137, 158, 159, 166 n. 10
personality and psychological factors, role in resolving ontological disputes, 67, 70, 72, 73, 77, 78, 80, 82
Petrie, B., 190 n. 10

Pettit, P., 83 n. 6, 88 n. 52, 134 n. 2
philosophical puritanism, 192–195
phlogiston, 3, 29, 63, 70, 72, 73, 78, 93, 133
  and ontologically radical theory change, 94, 112, 113 n. 5
  and oxygen, 36, 68, 89 n. 64, 113 n. 5
  and social negotiations, 90 n. 71
pictorial (and quasi-pictorial) representation, 14
Pinker, S., 136
pluralism, 196–199
political and social factors, role in resolving ontological disputes, 67, 68–69, 70, 71, 72, 73, 74, 77, 78, 80, 82
porcine irrealism, 174
pragmatism, 8, 80, 82
pretend beliefs and desires, 133, 140, 156, 165
principle of autonomy, 23, 83
problem of error, 35–6, 38, 175, 178
projectable predicates, 96, 99, 106–107
propositional attitudes
  causally active in some cognitive episodes and causally inert in others, 96–97
  individuation of, 15, 22–23, 28
propositional modularity, 21, 95–99, 106, 111, 112
Putnam, H., 22, 35, 74, 79, 83 n. 12, 175, 181, 190 n. 11
Pylyshyn, Z., 92, 100–101, 113 n. 12, 154

Quillian, M., 97
Quine, W., 144, 192
  on the analytic/synthetic distinction, 62, 75, 79–80, 88 n. 54
  versus Carnap on analyticity and ontology, 80–82, 90 n. 74
  and eliminativism, 3
  on grammar, 85 n. 32

and pragmatism, 8, 72
and semantic ascent, 55

Ramsey, F., 30, 49, 74, 75, 78
Ramsey, W., vii, 5, 6, 21, 34, 83 n. 10, 113 n. 13, 134 n. 2
rational ontological inference, principles of, 8, 63–72, 73
Ravenscroft, I., 10, 135 n. 11
REFERENCE*, 49–51, 52, 57
reference, idiosyncrasy of, 6, 7, 48–52, 86 n. 42
reference, indeterminacy of, 6, 48, 52–53, 75–78, 79, 80
reference relation used in the sciences, 43–45
reference, theories of
  causal-historical theories, 5, 6, 34–37, 39, 49, 74, 79, 85 n. 29, 87 n. 47, 174, 178
  deflationary theories, 55, 56–59, 79, 87 n. 47
  description theories, 5, 6, 34–37, 39, 45, 60, 74, 84 n. 28, 85 n. 29, 87 n. 47
  folk semantics accounts, 6, 7, 38–41, 45–51, 58, 87 n. 47
  grounding the reference relation, 49, 57, 174
  nondeflationary theories, 55, 56–59
  proto-science accounts, 6, 7, 41–45, 46, 53, 58, 87 n. 47
  reference preserving transmissions, 49, 57, 174
  what facts must they capture? 6, 37–45
reflective equilibrium, 64
Rey, G., 61, 88 n. 49
Ripstein, A., 137, 166 nn. 3 & 7
Rock, I., 136
Rorty, R., 3, 8, 72, 86 n. 35, 87 n. 47, 192, 195
Rosch, E., 173

Rosenberg, A., 89 n. 62
Rumelhart, D., 82 n. 5, 113 nn. 9 &
    12, 149
Russell, B., 192

satisfaction conditions, 15
Schaffner, K., 112 n. 4
Scheffler, I., 199 n. 1
Schiffer, S., vii, 189 nn. 1 & 2, 199
    n. 4
science fiction, 17, 21, 24
scientific revolutions, 91
Searle, J., 7, 51–54
Sellars, W., 18, 19, 20, 113 n. 6, 118–
    121, 123, 124, 137
semantic ascent, 7, 55–59, 60
semantic network models, 97–99,
    102, 104
semantic properties
    nature of, 42–44
    generalizations stated in terms of,
        95–97
    See also intentional properties
Shapere, D., 190 n. 7
Sharpe, R., 113 n. 6, 134 n. 3
Simon, H., 64, 89 n. 60, 113 n. 9
simulation theory, 8, 133–134, 136–
    167
    and the acquisition of folk
        psychological capacities, 154–158
    and autism, 158–160
    and explanation of behavior, 138,
        142–144
    and imagination, 153–154
    and intentional description, 138,
        144
    and the meaning of intentional
        terms, 138, 144–145
    off-line simulation, 140, 145, 149,
        150
    and prediction of behavior, 138–
        142
    and simplicity, 151–153
Skinner, B., 82 n.1

Sklar, L., 86 n. 39
Smith, E., 189 n. 4
Smolensky, P., 21, 99, 100, 101, 102,
    113 n. 12
Soames, S., 85 n. 32, 128
Sober, E., 68, 86 n. 39
social construction, 8, 72
Stalnaker, R., 20, 189 n. 1
Stein, E., 88 n. 56, 90 n. 67
Sterelny, K., 35, 68, 86 n. 38, 134 n.
    2, 190 n. 8, 196–197
Stich, S.
    on connectionism and
        eliminativism, 21, 83 nn. 9 & 10
    on the description theory of
        reference, 34, 84 n. 24
    on eliminativism about beliefs
        versus eliminativism about
        believers, 84 n. 21
    on folk psychology, 117
    on grammar, 85 n. 32, 128
    on meaning holism, 23–25, 83 nn.
        16 & 17
    on normative naturalism,
        rationality and reflective
        equilibrium, 66, 88 n. 56, 90 nn.
        68 & 72
    on the principle of psychological
        autonomy, 83 n. 14, 190 n. 11
    on simulation theory and its
        implications, 133–134, 135 n. 11,
        161
    on why eliminativism isn't
        troubling, 48–51, 86 n. 43
subdoxastic states, 137, 141
subsymbolic representation, 99, 101
supervenience, 23, 28, 83, 178–188
    on all nonintentional properties,
        185–186, 187–188
    on all physical properties, 184–185,
        187
    on current internal physical
        properties, 181–184
    global supervenience, 179, 186–
        188

supervenience (*continued*)
  strong and weak supervenience,
    179, 180
syntactic theory of the mind, 25

tacit theory, 14, 121–124, 127, 134,
    136, 139–140
Taylor, K., 135 n. 11
Teller, P., 190 n. 10
Thagard, P., 89 nn. 58, 60, 62 & 64
Thaler, R., 164
theoretical terms, 30–34, 77–78
  description theories of the meaning
    of, 30–34, 79
  eliminability of, 75, 78
  vagueness or imprecision, 74, 75–
    78
theory-theory, 136–167
  arguments for, 160–165
  and autism, 158–160
  and simplicity, 151–153
token physicalism, 27
Tversky, A., 148

Twin-Earth, 22–23
Tye, M., 189

Van Gelder, T., 19
Van Gulick, R., 27, 83 nn. 15 &
    20
Von Eckardt, B., 83 n. 15, 134 n. 2

Warfield, T., 82, 90 n. 69
Waters, K., 89 n. 63
Watson, J., 82 n. 1
Wellman, H., 137, 146
White, M., 88 n. 54
wide content, 22
Wilkes, K., 113 n. 6, 134 n. 3
Wilson, T., 22
Wimmer, H., 158, 159, 166 n. 10
Wimsatt, W., 65
witches, 3, 29, 36, 39, 63, 76, 78, 92,
    133
  contemporary, 68–69
Woodward, J., 83 n. 11, 134 n. 2